Japanese Prisoners of War in Revolt

The Outbreaks at Featherston and Cowra during World War II

Charlotte Carr-Gregg

ST. MARTIN'S PRESS
New York

All rights reserved. For information, write:
St. Martin's Press, Inc., 175 Fifth Avenue, New York, N.Y. 10010
Printed in Australia
Library of Congress Catalog Card Number 78-2103
ISBN 0-312-44060-X
First published in the United States of America in 1978

Contents

Illustrations   *vii*

Foreword   *ix*

Acknowledgments   *xv*

Introduction   *1*

1 The Status of Prisoners of War in Western and Japanese Society   *16*

2 Events at Featherston Camp and at Cowra   *38*

3 Cultural Continuity in a Changing Society   *85*

4 Japanese Personality and Value Orientation   *128*

5 External Influences and Possible Explanations   *169*

Postscript   *199*

Appendix A: Letter to the editor of the *Dominion*, Wellington   *206*

Appendix B: Message to Sergeant-Major Kanazawa   *207*

Bibliography   *211*

Official Documents   *217*

Index   *219*

Illustrations

Crown Prince Akihito at the Japanese War
  Cemetery, Cowra   14
Léon Bossard   18
Dr G. Morel   18
Featherston prisoner-of-war camp   20
Featherston military training camp   39
Layout of compounds at Featherston   40
Japanese officers at Featherston   43
Japanese prisoners of war boarding ship in
  Wellington   43
Japanese work party and New Zealand guard   45
Work party loading shingle and sand   46
Prisoner on hut-cleaning duty   47
Watchtower with guard at Featherston   49
No. 12 Prisoner of War Group, Cowra   57
Sketch plan of Cowra prisoner-of-war camp   58
Weapons found on prisoners after breakout   71
Blankets and articles of clothing on barbed-wire
  fences   72
Some of the burnt huts after the riot   75
Burial of Japanese prisoners of war killed in the
  Cowra outbreak   76
Shaving brushes used by Tamagawa and Suzuki   176
Toshio Adachi in 1975   200
Michiharu Shinya in 1973   200
Reunion of former prisoners of war at Featherston   202

Foreword

It has frequently been remarked that Australia emerged as a nation through wartime experiences—the Anglo-Boer war, Gallipoli, Tobruk, the war in and around the Pacific and, with less certainty, in Vietnam. Despite the ghastly events still celebrated annually on Anzac day it was the experiences associated with the Pacific war that still provoke the most controversy and raise the strongest emotions. That war was for the most against a baffling and inexplicable enemy. The cliched inscrutability of the Japanese in the eyes of Australians—and the rest of the "west"—is legendary. All the evidence is that that inscrutability was, and is, reciprocated by the Japanese. Rarely can any two people have so misunderstood each other as the Australians and the Japanese. There are many reasons to believe that these misunderstandings have hardly abated since 1945 though there are many reasons to work to end them.

The immediate value of Charlotte Carr-Gregg's work is that it interprets and explains Australian/New Zealand/and Japanese behaviour at its most inexplicable. The treatment of Australian and other "western" POWs by the Japanese was thought so exceptional as to have the Japanese denied their basic humanity. What happened to those unfortunates who fell into Japanese hands was seen as quite literally inhuman. It has frequently been portrayed and impressed on "western" consciousness—perhaps most notably by Alec Guiness' performance in *The Bridge Over the River Kwai*.

Few have bothered, until Mrs Carr-Gregg, to systematically examine that behaviour. No social scientist should be satisfied with a reference to inhumanity as an explanation of human behaviour. Indeed to leave things there is both a remarkable abdication of scholarly responsibility and essentially racist. What is little realized is that the treatment of those Japanese in "western" hands was at least as inexplicable to the Japanese. Why this was so demands explanation and we have had to wait until this book for it.

If most "westerners" find individual Japanese inscrutable then it must be pointed out that most non-Japanese social scientists have found Japanese social structure as impenetrable. Japanese culture and values are so strange to westerners as to, with some notable exceptions, defy analysis. The industrialization and modernization of Japan, it is frequently argued, took a form dramatically different from most of the "west". While there is much debate over whether the Japanese "organization-oriented" industrial system (as opposed to the "market-oriented" system of Britain, the USA, *and* Australia) is a manifestation of Japan's unique culture or a cultural-lag from some pre-industrial past no one underestimates the sheer difference of Japan from most other societies even today.

One explanation is that Japan took what Marx called the "second" or the "Prussian" road to capitalism. Barrington Moore's account of modernization in his *Social Origins of Dictatorship and Democracy* [Boston: Beacon Press, 1966] specifically puts Japan alongside Prussia. Both, he maintains, were states that imposed a bourgeois revolution from above through the metamorphosis of a traditional ruling class into a bourgeois one. And both ruling classes transformed themselves under external compulsion and internal ferment—defeat by Napoleon in the Prussian case and the threat of foreign invasion after Perry's expedition to Japan. Their responses were remarkably similar. The new regimes made extreme nationalistic appeals for discipline and for a rededication to the supposed solidarity of the traditional order. In both societies under and within a rhetoric of restoration and tradition a revolutionary transformation of the social structure took place. This rhetoric has not totally disappeared in Japan even today.

Japan is, as the historian Eugene Genovese says, "the success story of continuity in traditionalism". In pre-industrial Japan social relations between social classes such as nobles, samurai, peasants, and merchants were reminiscent of those of western-European feudalism. There was a system of vertical loyalties and reciprocal obligations. While there are many specialists who see the Meiji Restoration as a bourgeois revolution from above there are others who see it as roughly the same as the establishment of a centralized and modernized prebourgeois absolute monarchy. Both sides agree on the continuity of certain centralized patterns under the new regime.

Sociologists such as Ronald Dore have ably described the relationships between capital and labour which continue today to display many of the characteristics of patron and client—has survived the transition to a new economic system. to western bourgeois individualism and the Protestant ethic without disturbing the traditional system of deference. The greatest success of the Restoration was in maintaining social order during a period of rapid economic political change. This was in part due to the appearance of ideological continuity. That is to say the appeal for a restoration of "traditional" loyalty to the emperor and a reaffirmation of old values. To a quite extraordinary extent the older paternalism—the actual personal relationship of patron and client—has survived the transition to a new economic system.

The Meiji regime reinforced the ideology of reciprocal personal obligations but as *obligations to the state personified by the Imperial dynasty* rather than to specific nobles. The new regime managed to lead the masses through the great economic transformation of Japan in two ways: firstly, through what is essentially ideological continuity and, secondly, with great skill it ·fitted loyalty to the emperor as symbolic patron into the need for national cohesion to resist foreign domination. All classes came to see national unity as vital to their interests. The shattering defeat of the second World War and the consequent social and economic reforms probably fatally destroyed the traditional ideology. Yet as the activities of Mishima and his followers show this is far from certain. At the time about which Charlotte Carr-Gregg writes the tragic consequences of Japanese traditionalism, of ideology—or put simply of being Japanese—were all too clear. The very success of the imposition of loyalty to the emperor and the state leads directly to the awful events at Cowra and Featherston.

Well before 1945 American social scientists, including Talcott Parsons and most famously Ruth Benedict in *The Chrysanthemum and the Sword*[2] did set out to understand Japan. America's problem, during MacArthur's pro-consulship after the second World War, was how to demobilize the antagonistic elements within Japanese capitalism without undermining the entire system.

The problem would seem to have been solved successfully if Australian–Japanese trade relationships are any indicator. Since the mid-1960s Japan has been Australia's leading export market. Since the beginning of this decade Japan has been taking over 80 percent of Australia's exports of iron ore, nearly all of the coal exports, and well over half of all mineral exports. Australian mining and, since Britain joined the EEC, rural (both agricultural and forest) exports are now heavily dependent on Japan. "Co-prosperity" has been achieved by other means.

But in late 1977 New Zealand in a difficult economic situation was the first country to try approaching Japan, not on the basis of anti-communism, free trade, the Free World, or other cloudy—by highly bankable from the Japanese point of view—abstractions but rather on the more concrete ground of mutual self-interest, long-term and freely negotiated. The Japanese were not interested immediately to establish an economic relationship on this new basis.

Just how far things have changed since the second World
War and the racist anti-Japanese policies that immediately
followed that time is perhaps most typified by the fact that
in 1969 Australia was the first "western" nation to take part
in joint naval manoeuvres with Japan. That governmental
relationships have perforce changed is unarguable. That the
understanding of most individual Australians and New
Zealanders of Japan has changed hardly at all would seem
also unarguable. We can begin here in this book to
understand, through a tragic occurrence in the past, the
present which will help us prepare for an uncertain future.

By focussing so clearly on these narrow events—the
revolts at Cowra and Featherston, Charlotte Carr-Gregg is
able to illuminate the stark contrast between the culture
and values of Australia and New Zealand on the one hand,
and Japan on the other. Her work has thrown light on a
dark corner of history. These events are nearly forgotten
—one could almost say repressed in our collective history.
They are like guilty secrets and like any guilty secret tell
us a great deal about the values and cultures of those it
shames. There could well be other dark corners and human
catastrophies albeit less tragic and unpleasant in many
nations' history that, if handled with the care, imagination,
and scrupulousness displayed here, would give us a new
understanding of both culture and history.

Charlotte Carr-Gregg has gone on since her research
reported here to a wider consideration of the treatment of
POWs. She has discovered in their treatment a sensitive and
keen indicator of culture and social structure. The comparative study of such things as the alimentation and
communication rights and the manipulation of welfare
conditions of POWs is far from mundane. By comparing,
for example, what happened to POWs in the American
Civil War with those in the Franco-Prussian War we learn
a great deal about "civilization". And again, to compare
what happened after the battle of Adowa (a rare occurrence
when "Europeans", in this case Italians, were captured in
large numbers by "Africans", in this case Abbysinians)

allows us an understanding of social change that has turned out to be both perceptive and deep. Such a genuinely comparative sociology is now an extremely rare activity, but without it social science is impoverished. In the light of her later work, which I hope will also be published, this book will be even more significant.

By our treatment of prisoners, of all sorts, we come to know ourselves. That what we find out is unpleasant is in itself an important lesson that we should be extremely grateful to have been taught.

Colin Bell
Professor of Sociology
University of New South Wales
November 1977

Acknowledgments

Looking back to the time when I wrote this book I recall with pleasure the many people who smoothed the way for me and assisted in my research. My thanks must first go to Professor Peter Lawrence of Sydney University, whose friendship and unfailing support have been invaluable; his seminal comments and almost encyclopedic knowledge proved to be a constant source of intellectual stimulation. Sincere appreciation must also be expressed to Professor Colin Bell of the University of New South Wales for kindly sponsoring this work for publication and writing the Foreword which places it so admirably in a contemporary context. My colleague, Dr David Boardman of Victoria University at Wellington, permitted me to draw on his extensive expertise in the field of Japanese studies while his wife, Motoko, made a significant contribution with her sensitive translations of my correspondence with some of the Japanese survivors of the Featherston incident.

I am greatly indebted to Mr Takeo Yamashita, currently chief of police in Osaka, for allowing me to publish extracts from poems found on Japanese prisoners killed in the Cowra outbreak, and to Miss Chris Naylor of Sydney University, who translated the poems together with some of the passages I have quoted from Mr Yamashita's volume of war memoirs, *Nihonjin Koko Ni Nemura*. In addition, my thanks are due to Mr E.H. Thompson of Auckland, for his characteristic generosity in permitting me to make use of his as yet unpublished translations of Michiharu Shinya's book, *Shi No Umi Yori Seidan*, and Seihachiro Saito's article, "Gimei Senshi No Haka". Important insights into conditions at Featherston Camp were provided by Mr Keith Robertson of Mount Maunganui, the late Mr Russell Orr of Hastings, and Mrs G. Bossard of Auckland. The rare objectivity and frankness with which Mr T. Adachi, the Reverend Michiharu Shinya and a number of other former Japanese prisoners of war replied to the queries I submitted to them will always be deeply appreciated.

Alderman Oliver, the former mayor of Cowra, New South Wales, and Mrs George Freudenstein of Young, New South Wales, were at all times ready with assistance, as were the staff of the Australian Archives Office, Canberra, particularly the Senior Archivist, Mr J.L. Cleland, and Mrs K.M. Kinsella. Next I should like to mention the warm hospitality of Mr and Mrs L. Bevan of the British High Commission, who provided me with a home away from home in Canberra, and the reference librarians and archivists of the Australian War Memorial and the Australian National Library for helping me in the search for vital documents and publications.

No list of acknowledgments would be complete without referring to the co-operation I received from M.P. Vibert, Chef de Documentations et Publications, International Committee of the Red Cross, Geneva, and from the staff of the New Zealand National Archives and the Alexander Turnbull Library. Last but not least I owe a debt of gratitude to my husband for his unflagging encouragement and to our son Michael, who acted as a most efficient and tireless research assistant.

Introduction

It is not always possible for an author to recall with certainty the precise moment when he or she began to be intrigued by a particular subject; however, I can vividly remember the moment when this happened in my own case. I had accompanied my husband, who is a member of the British Diplomatic Service and was then stationed in Sydney, on a routine visit to Cowra, a country town in north-western New South Wales, to attend the opening of the new Civic Centre by the premier of the state. It was November 1968, and we had driven through the Blue Mountains and the historic city of Bathurst in fine Australian spring weather. Cowra looked like a properous middle-sized country town, surrounded by a pleasant, lush-green countryside.

The first item on a busy programme was a formal luncheon at the Returned Service League (RSL) Club, and it was during the welcoming speech of the mayor, Alderman Oliver, that I had the first indication that Cowra might after all be of greater significance than just an attractive country town of purely local importance. For after extending the customary greetings to the assembled guests—which, in addition to the premier, included diplomats from Canberra and Sydney, as well as a host of federal, state, and local officials—the mayor singled out the Japanese ambassador for a particularly warm welcome and referred to the "special relationship" which existed between Japan and Cowra.

I was puzzled by the reference to a close link between Cowra and Japan, and speculated all through the lunch what kind of special relationship the mayor could have had in mind. Curiosity finally overcame my reluctance to ask an embarrassing question, and I turned to my neighbour, a jovial MP from Canberra, for enlightenment. He seemed slightly surprised that I was unaware of the fact that there had been a prisoner-of-war camp at Cowra during World War II, where Japanese captives had been held. My informant then told me that in 1944 these men had made an escape attempt, which had ended tragically when a number of Japanese and Australian servicemen had lost their lives in the incident. The prisoners were buried in a Japanese cemetery, just outside of Cowra, together with other Japanese who had died in different locations in Australia during World War II; in recent years many delegations from Japan had visited the cemetery. I later realized that while most Australians, certainly those in the over-forty age bracket, had at least heard of this event, the incident, although the most massive escape attempt in British military history, is largely unknown in Europe and the United States.

After lunch the deputy mayor and his wife, Alderman and Mrs Capps, took us and another diplomatic couple on a sightseeing tour of Cowra and its environs. I expressed a desire to see the Japanese War Cemetery, where I had heard the victims of the escape attempt had been buried. The Cappses talked quite freely about the outbreak, which had taken place in the early hours of 5 August 1944, and showed us the cemetery, which was surrounded by a low stone wall and green trees, surmounted by an *ishidoro*, or stone lantern, typical of those seen in front of shrines or temples all over Japan. Apparently former prisoners of war who had returned to Japan had subscribed money for purchase of plants and trees, as a fitting memorial "to comfort the souls of their former comrades in arms". Once inside the cemetery we saw 530 identical flat gravestones set out on well-tended lawns; 234 of them bore the same inscriptions: "died on 5 August 1944". The Australian servicemen who died in the same incident are buried in a plot near by. I was deeply moved by the serene and peaceful setting of the cemetery, which contrasted so sharply with the desperation and violence that must have characterized such a large-scale outbreak. Later the Cappses showed us a memorial further out of town, erected on the site of the former camp, now overlooking green fields. The deputy mayor, realizing that I was interested to know more about the Cowra outbreak, offered to lend me a book on the subject, and indicated that according to local opinion the escape attempt was regarded as a bid by the captives to commit mass suicide.

As promised, the Cappses brought me the book, Hugh Clarke's *Break-Out*, the next morning, before we left for Canberra. I read the book with great interest, but being steeped in Western cultural traditions, I found it very difficult to accept the conclusion that the Japanese prisoners of war had indeed sought death and therefore embarked on this near hopeless escape attempt. The circumstances surrounding the outbreak began even further to arouse my interest as a social anthropologist when I discovered that a similar incident had taken place in February 1943 at Featherston Camp in New Zealand. I then resolved to examine these two incidents more closely and, by comparing the two events, try to establish a characteristic, peculiarly Japanese pattern to account for the behaviour of the prisoners.

Western society is only too familiar with the ignominious treatment accorded Allied servicemen in Japanese prisoner-of-war camps during World War II. I wondered whether there might be a connection between this aspect and the different conception of the status of prisoner of war which, according to Clarke and his co-author Takeo Yamashita, had motivated the Japanese "mass suicide attempt" at Cowra and possibly the riot earlier at Featherston camp. The shocking conditions at Changi, the Japanese detention prison at Singapore, have been described by a number of reputable eyewitnesses at the War Crimes Trials in 1946, as well as in numerous autobiographical accounts; the prisoner-of-war camps along the notorious Burma Railway, as well as the detention centres in Indonesia and in Japan, were labelled "death camps", since many Allied servicemen and women lost their lives through deliberate mistreatment, starvation, and brutal victimization. The film *The Bridge over the River Kwai*, for instance, dramatized these happenings, contrasting British stubborn determination not to give in, even under the most demeaning and debilitating circumstances, with Japanese cruelty and needlessly brutal treatment. But there have been few accounts by Japanese captives held by the Allies. When I began to examine this aspect more closely, I realized firstly that there had been relatively few Japanese prisoners of war and, secondly, that those who had surrendered to the enemy were clearly unwilling to publicize this fact and did not wish to share their experiences with their countrymen.

There are, of course, always exceptions; it would be unfair to assume that all Japanese prisoner-of-war camps were administered by cruel and sadistic men; indeed during the Singapore War Crimes Trials some Australians, for instance, had testified that several of the Japanese commanders in Malayan camps had behaved in a manner that was both humane and correct. I also discovered that there were some Japanese who had recorded their experiences in Allied prisoner-of-war camps, such as Yuji Aida, who was captive of the British in Burma, and Teruhiko Asada, who wrote about the experiences of one of his friends at Cowra in *The Night of a Thousand Suicides*. However, there are no heroic escape accounts in the vein of those by Paul Brickhill or Eric Williams, and it is significant that the fate of the Japanese prisoner of war in World War II is seldom, if ever, discussed in post-war Japanese literature. Takeo Yamashita's moving account, *Nihonjin Koko Ni Nemuru* (*Here Lie the Japanese*), which throws fresh insight on the events at Cowra—and which the author was good enough to send me—was privately printed.

When I decided to probe more deeply into the events

at Cowra and Featherston I was surprised to encounter many different attitudes towards my project. These varied from astonishment as to why I thought it necessary to find out whether a typically Japanese conception of prisoners of war existed, to rank hostility from friends and casual acquaintances whose loved ones had either died in Japanese prisoner-of-war camps or returned with physical or mental scars, and who implied that it was a sheer waste of my time to try to understand such "sub-human" people. Nor was it easy, once I embarked on my research programme, to gain the assistance and co-operation of the relevant authorities. Many delays and difficulties were encountered before I was granted access to Cowra files in the Australian Archives and the War Memorial Museum. However, once the authorities realized that my inquiries were motivated by purely scientific interest, their helpfulness and co-operation were readily forthcoming.

The New Zealand authorities were even more reluctant to let me scrutinize their official records, but I was eventually granted access to the *Proceedings of a Court of Inquiry on Mutiny at Prisoner of War Camp, 25 February, 1943*. I was then on the staff of the Victoria University of Wellington and vouched for by my departmental chairman, Professor J. Robb, who kindly requested that I should be permitted to see the relevant documents. But the problem of gaining access to archive material was not confined to the authorities in Australia and New Zealand; even supra-national organizations such as the International Committee of the Red Cross (ICRC) in Geneva were at first unwilling to release any information contained in their files.

The initial unwillingness of the ICRC to release documents even for scholarly research purposes can perhaps be understood, since the day-to-day operations of that organization depend entirely upon maintaining the co-operation and good will of the national Red Cross societies throughout the world. There are no provisions under the Geneva Convention of 1929, which regulated the conditions under which prisoners were held during World War II, stipulating that the reports of delegates designated by the ICRC to inspect camps should be made public. This is in sharp contrast with the reports of visits to POW camps during World War I, which were published by the ICRC as they became available; but then these agreements for the mutual inspection of detention camps had been based on *ad hoc* agreements concluded between the belligerents during the war and had not been codified in an international convention.

The importance of the reports of the delegates of the ICRC to the researcher should, however, not be underrated; for these men, usually locally appointed Swiss citizens, not only proved to be perceptive observers, but provided factual evidence I was unable to find in other sources. I was fortunate to obtain the complete reports of Dr G. Morel, the Australian ICRC delegate, from the National Archives in Canberra. It was more difficult to gain access to the reports of Dr Léon Bossard, the delegate of the ICRC in New Zealand; the New Zealand authorities seemed unable to provide me with their copies of Dr Bossard's reports, despite the fact that Bossard has visited Featherston camp regularly. Nevertheless, after a personal interview with the Chef de Documentation et Publications of the ICRC in Geneva, M. Vibert, I was able to obtain a summary of Bossard's reports, which Mme Gisèle Douvernoz of the ICRC staff was good enough to extract from their archives. This summary proved invaluable in my research, and while I should still add an eloquent plea for granting selective access to the archives of the ICRC to *bona fide* researchers, I wish to record here my gratitude to the Chef de Documentation and his staff for the courtesy with which they responded to my inquiries.

It must be said at once that the reluctance of the authorities to make the relevant source material available could not have been motivated by any desire to conceal evidence in order to cover up unpleasant aspects which might be considered damaging to national prestige. More than thirty years have passed since the incidents occurred, and the individuals involved are either old men or have died, while the names of the Japanese who acted as informers and drew attention to the potential dangers of the situation are largely meaningless since most of these men used fictitious names.

Why then should it have been necessary to overcome so many obstacles and to reassure the authorities concerned that this was an objective inquiry, designed to unravel some of the many strands in a complex and often perplexing skein of events? One of the reasons may have been the natural propensity of the armed forces to safeguard the anonymity of those who were in positions of command at the time of the two incidents. This is also understandable, for it would indeed be presumptuous to level criticism based on hindsight at the decisions made by such men in a crisis. I accept, as the two duly constituted courts of enquiry did, that the camp commanders and their men acted in the best interests of the camp populations as well as of the civilian communities in the immediate vicinity of the camps. Both the Australian and New Zealand guards reacted promptly and in the expected fashion to the challenge presented to them by the Japanese prisoners. Who could blame them? It is not the task of the social anthropologist to question whether the guards at Cowra and Featherston should have been ordered to shoot more often above the heads of the rioting prisoners; whether a more adequate security system, involving smaller camp areas, might have been devised; or whether more intensive forms of indoctrination should have been introduced to explain to the Japanese the legal and moral status of a prisoner of war as defined in the Geneva Convention.

Although apparently there was neither the need nor the disposition to suppress facts which might have proved damaging, the suspicion nevertheless remains that official reluctance to release the documentation about the two incidents may reflect an almost universally shared sense of guilt about the frequently unnecessary sufferings endured by prisoners of war, irrespective of their nationality. The

record of ill-treatment inflicted upon prisoners of war from
the notorious Andersonville stockade during the American
Civil War to the tortures and brainwashings of Korea, is
a sad commentary on man's inhumanity to man which
many would like to forget. Despite a plethora of international agreements and conventions regulating the treatment
of men captured during hostilities—including many
bilateral treaties such as that signed between the United
States and Prussia in 1785, as well as international agreements, from the Brussels Conference of 1876 to the present
revision of the 1949 Geneva Convention—improvements in
the status and treatment of prisoners of war invariably
lagged behind efforts to ameliorate the plight of these
innocent victims of warfare.

Thus, at the outbreak of World War I, while the
treatment of prisoners of war had been discussed and
codified at the Hague Conferences of 1899 and 1907, no
formal arrangements had been devised for the inspection
of prisoner-of-war camps, either by representatives of the
protecting powers or by delegates of the International
Committee of the Red Cross. The role of the protecting
power dates back to the sixteenth century, according to Jean
Pictet, who suggests in his study *Humanitarian Law and
the Protection of War Victims* that since only the larger
states maintained embassies at that time, the smaller
countries requested such great nations to represent their
interests during times of armed conflict. Later, neutral
countries tended to assume reponsibility for the protection
of enemy nationals, mainly on the commercial level.
However, during World War I, when rumours of the
deliberate mistreatment and victimization of prisoners of
war brought a spate of retaliatory actions from both sides,
it became necessary to make *ad hoc* arrangements for visits
by delegates from the protecting powers to inspect prisoner-
of-war camps.

The United States ambassador in Germany, James
Gerard, accordingly undertook to draft a protocol which
permitted members of his staff to visit prisoners held in

German camps, and for American officials to be granted access to German prisoners held in British camps, not only to reassure themselves of the prisoners' well-being but also to hear any complaints out of earshot of camp officials. This proposal was accepted eventually by both the belligerents and led to considerable improvements in the conditions prevailing at POW camps. However, these provisions were not internationally recognized until they were incorporated in the Geneva Convention of 1929, which was drafted eleven years after the end of World War I. Although the convention was theoretically in force during World War II, Japan was among a number of powers that had failed to ratify it.

In this context it is important to stress that even international agreements, such as the Geneva Convention of 1929, failed to take into account many aspects of POW welfare. A notable omission was the absence of safeguards to ensure that prisoners of war would be provided with food which was acceptable to their respective national requirements. Article 11 of the Geneva Convention stated:

> The food ration of prisoners of war shall be equivalent in quantity and quality to that of depot troops.
> Prisoners shall also be afforded the means of preparing for themselves such additional articles of food as they may possess. Sufficient drinking water shall be supplied to them. The use of tobacco shall be authorised. Prisoners may be employed in the kitchens.
> All collective disciplinary measures affecting food are prohibited.

Although these carefully worded provisions would appear to cover all possible eventualities, they are based on the assumption that standards of alimentation in one belligerent nation will always be acceptable to the nationals of another country which is a party to the conflict. This fallacy was exposed during World War I, when many complaints were made about the food provided by Germany to their French and British prisoners, and vice versa, particularly in respect of bread. The provisions of article 11 of the convention proved even more inadequate during World War II when Asian and European prisoners with radically different traditional diets were held captive for long periods; thus, while Japanese soldiers could apparently subsist in good health on dried fish and rice as J.V.Dillon put it, European servicemen could not. Similarly, Japanese prisoners tended to find a European diet unpalatable, as their request for rice and suitable cooking implements in the Cowra camp indicates.

It was only after World War II that national standards determining the supply and quality of food were discarded. Article 26 of the 1949 convention set out to rectify an omission which had caused much suffering and deprivation among World War II prisoners, by providing absolute standards in repects of the alimentation of prisoners of war. It stated:

> The basic daily food ration shall be sufficient in quantity, quality and variety to keep prisoners of war in good health and to prevent loss of weight or the development of nutritional deficiencies. Account shall also be taken of the habitual diet of the prisoners.
>
> The Detaining Power shall supply prisoners of war who work with such additional rations as are necessary for the labour on which they are employed.
>
> Sufficient drinking water shall be supplied to prisoners of war. The use of tobacco shall be permitted.
>
> Prisoners of war shall, as far as possible, be associated with the preparation of their meals; they may be employed for that purpose in the kitchens. Furthermore, they shall be given the means of preparing, themselves, the additional food in their possession.
>
> Adequate premises shall be provided for messing.
>
> Collective disciplinary measures affecting food are prohibited.

Thus, the alimentation of prisoners has now been safeguarded, at least in theory, by the convention's insistence on more adequate standards. But will these regulations be implemented? If a country such as Germany during World War I lacked sufficient food supplies to meet the requirements of its civilian population or indeed of its own front-line troops (who fared little better than the civilians after 1916, according to Erich Maria Remarque's novel *All Quiet on the Western Front*, for example), how can one expect its prisoners of war to be supplied with adequate rations? It is true that in similar emergencies which may arise in the future, the International Committee of the Red Cross would be expected to come to the assistance of the prisoners of war, as it has in the past, by providing them with additional food supplied by their national Red Cross societies. But during periods of acute food shortages Red Cross parcels tend to be pilfered, and during World War I frequent complaints were heard of supplies that failed to arrive at the camps or were delayed for long periods owing to breakdowns in the transportation system. Despite attempts by the 1929 Geneva Convention to ensure that sufficient food should be provided for prisoners of war, there was little real improvement during World War II, when many thousands of prisoners suffered from malnutrition and other illnesses caused by inadequate or incorrect diet.

The experience of prisoners of war captured in the "limited" conflicts that have occurred since World War II, such as Korea and Vietnam, has been far from reassuring; in these wars the problems of ensuring proper alimentation of prisoners grew to alarming proportions, and the Geneva Convention's prohibition concerning collective disciplinary measures involving withholding food supplies was flouted on numerous occasions. I do not wish to infer from this that the great efforts that have been made on the political, legal, and humanitarian level to frame more effective provisions safeguarding the welfare of prisoners of war have been in vain, but merely to demonstrate that one should not be too sanguine in expecting that well-intentioned international agreements can always be implemented. Warfare's chief characteristic is its unpredictability, and in the disruptions that follow in its wake circumstances may arise to prevent even the countries that have ratified the

Geneva Conventions from honouring the agreement.

At a time when countries that only a few decades ago were locked in mortal combat are jointly striving to achieve a *modus vivendi*, leading to peaceful co-existence, one should not despair. The wounds of modern war now seem to heal more rapidly, and old enmities tend to be forgotten within a generation. An example of this trend can be found in the Australian country town of Cowra, whose citizens have shed over time the feelings of bitterness experienced during World War II and have deliberately set out to build a bridge of reconciliation with their former enemies. It has been a gradual process, beginning with the extension of the care given by members of the RSL Club to the graves of the Australian soldiers who died in the Cowra outbreak to those of the German and Italian detainees, and finally to the graves of the Japanese prisoners of war. As Mayor Oliver put it, the decision to include the graves of the former enemies was discussed informally by the group of ex-servicemen, who decided to forget the horrors of war. In October 1963, with the approval of the commonwealth government, the Japanese government sent out a well-known architect, Shigeru Yura, to design a Japanese cemetery. The building of the cemetery was financed by the Japanese government, and some of the former prisoners who had returned safely to their homeland subscribed to buy plants, trees, and other features, such as the typical white pebbles and paving stones. The cemetery became not only a symbol of reconciliation; it also marked the beginning of a unique link between the people of Cowra and Japan.

After the opening of the new cemetery in 1964, Cowra began to receive the visits of many Japanese, including parliamentarians, government officials, trade delegations, union leaders, and perhaps most importantly, youth goodwill missions. Quoting again from a personal communication from the mayor, whose contribution to the existing spirit of conciliation should not be underestimated, the young Japanese and the Cowra senior students who met informally at these gatherings seemed "to communicate immediately, even in broken English," and began to establish friendships. These observations led Mayor Oliver to suggest the establishment of a private exchange of students between Cowra and Japan; the headmaster of the local high school and the New South Wales Minister for education gave their support to the project, and when Mayor Oliver and his wife visited Japan in 1969, the Japanese government, who had invited the Olivers to be their official guests for a week, arranged for the mayor to visit several schools in the Tokyo area. He selected the Seikei Upper Secondary School, in Musashino, and made appropriate arrangements for a private student exchange programme.

Eight Australian students and nine Japanese have so far benefited from the programme. The families of the Seikei students who have participated in the exchange scheme have formed a Cowra students association and meet regularly. The former headmaster of the Seikei Upper Secondary School has paid a visit to Cowra. Furthermore, members of the Cowra Rotary Club who visited Tokyo in 1975 were not only invited to a luncheon by the Student Council of the Seikei Upper Secondary School, but also taken on a two-day sightseeing tour. The friendships established between students and host families have been perpetuated; Jenny Billington, for instance, the first exchange student from Cowra, returned to her host family in 1976 for a holiday; after her stay as a student in Tokyo she had taken up the study of the Japanese language at the College of Advanced Education in Canberra, and went to work at the Japanese Embassy.

The student exchange programmes and the many visits from Japanese dignitaries, including Crown Prince Akihito and Princess Mishiko in 1973, have furthered the close ties between Cowra and Japan; the population of Cowra as a whole has consequently become not only much more aware of the nature of Japanese art and culture, but also of the importance of Japan as an important outlet for its primary

Japanese Crown Prince Akihito lays a wreath at the Japanese War Grave Cemetery, Cowra, in 1973. (Photo: John Fairfax & Sons Ltd)

products. The establishment in 1975 of a small Japanese wool-top-making industry, which employs eighty-five local employees, is regarded as an economic asset for the district.

The latest project to commemorate Cowra's special link with Japan is the establishment of a Japanese garden and cultural centre which is to be financed jointly by the Japanese government, the Australian government, the New South Wales government, and a loan from the Cowra Municipal Council. As Mrs Shibaoka, who designed the layout for the garden, put it: "The concept of the garden is a contact point for Japanese and Australian culture."[4] A four-hectare site on Bellevue Hill, overlooking the town, has been set aside for this development. The garden will feature trees that change colour with the season: cherry trees, which blossom in the spring, are being imported from Japan, and only those Australian trees which turn to golden hues in the autumn will be planted. Thus the traditional design of the garden will be a constant reminder of Japan's cultural traditions and festivals which are so closely intertwined with the seasons. The continuity of these cultural traditions is much more firmly rooted in Japanese than in Western societies, and when attempting to offer explanations for the behaviour of the Japanese prisoners during the outbreaks at Cowra and Featherston, this factor—the rootedness of traditions—must always be borne in mind.

Notes

1. Manley O. Hudson, ed., *International Legislation*, vol.5 (Washington, DC: Carnegie Endowment for International Peace, 1936), p.30.
2. J.V. Dillon, "The Genesis of the 1949 Convention Relative to the Treatment of Prisoners of War", in *University of Miami Law Quarterly* 40 (1950), p.44.
3. Ibid., p.45.
4. *Sydney Morning Herald*, 24 January 1976.

1

The status of Prisoners of War in Western and Japanese Society

During World War II Japanese prisoners of war were involved in two major disturbances at camps in New Zealand and Australia. Both incidents resulted in substantial casualties. At Featherston Camp in New Zealand, on 25 February 1943, several hundred prisoners armed themselves with stones, tools and other improvised weapons, and attacked the camp guards, who were forced to open fire, killing forty-eight Japanese and wounding many others. A year and a half later, at Cowra in New South Wales, in the early hours of 5 August 1944, over nine hundred Japanese stormed the barbed wire perimeter and attacked the camp gun positions. In this incident 234 Japanese died and 108 were wounded. Although there are some similarities between the two incidents, the circumstances surrounding them were very different. It is also significant that the Featherston casualties did not include any cases of suicide among the prisoners; at Cowra no less than "31 Japanese killed themselves and 12 were burnt to death in huts set on fire by Japanese. Sixteen of the wounded showed signs of attempted suicide."[1]

Mass confrontations and attempts by prisoners of war to escape were not, of course, confined to Japanese servicemen during World War II. Many such incidents involving Allied or Axis prisoners of war have been recorded. However, the majority of these attempts were conceived differently. Most of them were planned by individuals or small groups with the aim of regaining their freedom in order to rejoin the armed forces of their country or to be reunited with their families. The objective in the greatest mass escape staged by Allied prisoners of war—at Stalag Luft 3, near Sagan in Germany, in March 1944—was to outwit the German guards and to avoid engaging them in a hopeless confrontation. According to Paul Brickhill's account *The Great Escape*, the organizer of the project, Roger Bushell, had worked out that at the most 220 of the 600 prisoners who had dug a tunnel under the prison wall might be able to escape on the night of the break, which meant "no joy" for most of the men who had been engaged in digging out the tunnel. To enhance the chances of their escape attempt each prisoner had planned his own method of continuing his flight—sometimes alone, sometimes in a small group, and for that purpose had provided himself with forged papers and civilian clothes. The action of these men was clearly motivated by the desire to live and rejoin their own forces, rather than to seek death.

The events at Featherston and Cowra bear little similarity to the Western model escape attempt, for the purpose of the Japanese prisoners' action did not seem to be either to rejoin their own forces or to return to their homeland. It is quite possible that the Japanese prisoners, motivated by their cultural conditioning, endeavoured to create a situation which would permit them to achieve an "honourable" death, in order to atone for their violation of a military code which forbad surrender to the enemy.

One explanation of why these events occurred is that the escape attempt was the result of victimization of the prisoners by their captors; brutal, inhuman practices together with unbearable conditions in the camps, aggravated by starvation diets, insufficient or contaminated water, and lack of fundamental hygiene or medical care could have triggered off these incidents. Here one must be very careful; "victimization" of captives is interpreted differently in different cultural contexts. For example, Yuji Aida, now professor of history at Kyoto University, who was a prisoner

Dr. L. Bossard, delegate of the International Committee of the Red Cross in New Zealand during World War II. (Photo: Mrs. G. Bossard)

Dr G. Morel, Red Cross delegate in Australia during World War II. (Photo: I.C.R.C., Geneva)

of war during World War II, suggests that he would have preferred violence and anger to the cool indifference and mental cruelty he believed he suffered from the hands of the British. His translator, Professor Louis Allen, on the other hand asserts that the only answer one can give to someone who says he would really prefer savage beating and bayoneting to hard labour is: if you believe that you will believe anything.[2]

Whether isolated acts of physical brutality which are unlikely to be mentioned in official reports, or ongoing acts of mental cruelty—which may range from calling people names and humiliating them to cool disdain as practised by Aida's British captors—constitute victimization and may have influenced the decision of the prisoners to escape is not within the scope of this study. However, there seems little room for such speculations as far as the Featherston and the Cowra incidents are concerned. Both camps had been visited by neutral observers before the incidents occurred. The delegates of the International Committee of the Red Cross, Dr Bossard and Dr Morel, both reported that the conditions in the Featherston and Cowra camps as far as accommodation, food, hygiene, and medical care were concerned were completely satisfactory and the relationship between guards and prisoners courteous.

Bossard visited Featherston for the first time on 15 December 1942, and after that inspected the camp and interviewed prisoners there regularly every three months. He noted on the occasion of his first visit, the only one that took place before the riot, that the captives voiced appreciation of their food, accommodation, and general treatment and indicated that the relationship between guards and prisoners appeared to be very satisfactory. He gathered the same impression in his conversations conducted privately, out of earshot of the New Zealand authorities; he received no complaints, either about the treatment accorded to the captives or about the conditions prevailing in the camp. The Japanese only asked Bossard to intercede with the camp commandant on their behalf to obtain his permission to take

Featherston prisoner-of-war camp. (Photo: Russell Orr)

walks in groups outside the camp area and to go fishing. Bossard transmitted this request, but the camp commandant rejected it as involving too many risks.

New Zealand in late 1942 and early 1943 must be regarded as a "special" case. The mother country—Britain —had suffered a series of resounding defeats, particularly the sinking of the *Prince of Wales* and the *Repulse* as well as the fall of Singapore; the United States Navy and Air Force had been surprised by the Japanese attacks on Pearl Harbour and the Philippines and were only slowly recovering from the losses suffered in these actions. The majority of men of military age were serving with the British forces overseas, and New Zealand felt threatened by possible enemy attacks, isolated from the big powers' bases. The successful American actions in the Solomon Islands had served to reassure the New Zealanders, as did the ever-increasing American military presence, but they had not really been prepared to look after a relatively large number of enemy captives by 1942.

The location of the prisoner-of-war camp was dictated by the availability of the former training camp near Featherston, sixty-nine kilometres north-east of the capital, Wellington. Although the camp was separated from Wellington by a range of mountains, the fact that it was located in the vicinity of several thriving agricultural communities presented those responsible for guarding over eight hundred potentially dangerous enemy captives with a large number of security problems. Until a workable routine was established and the difficulties of supply overcome, tempers among the guards were possibly short. Issues that were settled swiftly and efficiently in later stages of the prisoners' internment took on added and sometimes dangerous dimensions at first. Individual confrontations between prisoners and guards, handicapped by the problems of linguistic communications, might easily have become distorted into contests of strength.

There were three interpreters among the New Zealand garrison, and a few Japanese had a knowledge of English.

But the basic misunderstandings were on the cultural level, and it is quite possible that in this critical initial stage the New Zealanders failed to comprehend that the Geneva Convention was virtually unknown to the Japanese prisoners and that their captives felt they had transgressed against military ethics by permitting themselves to be captured alive, while the Japanese probably did not understand at that stage that in the eyes of the New Zealander they held a status as prisoners of war which was internationally recognized and regulated by internationally agreed rules. Whatever personal feelings each individual guard may have had towards his captives, on the whole they felt bound to adhere as closely as possible to the terms of the Geneva Convention and issued orders strictly in keeping with their interpretation of the relevant clauses of the convention. The French say *c'est le ton qui fait la musique*—and the tone and manner in which the guards issued their instructions may well have sounded harsh to the oversensitive, guilt-ridden Japanese. But then one cannot in a situation of this kind expect psychological finesse from camp guards, who surely did not relish their task. Nonetheless, the many misunderstandings that must have occurred cannot be interpreted as deliberate acts of victimization.

Since the Japanese prisoners did not receive any parcels from their national Red Cross society (as had Allied prisoners of war, as well as German and Italian captives), they approached Dr Bossard and asked whether the International Committee of the Red Cross could supply them with books and games to improve the quality of their leisure hours. Bossard noted that there were not only signs of tension between the prisoners at the beginning of their captivity, but also some difficulties between the captives and the administration: "Certains frottements entre eux, et, au début de la captivité entre eux et l'administration, purent être supprimés grâce à l'intervention de notre délegué."[3] The use of the term *frottements* would indicate that Bossard did not think that these difficulties touched on very serious or fundamental issues.

According to the evidence available (which includes the testimony of a number of Japanese prisoners at the court of inquiry), victimization or organized brutality can be rejected as a motive for the outbreak at Featherston. As far as conditions at Cowra before the outbreak were concerned, Dr Morel, who had visited the camp on several occasions, notes on the occasion of his last visit before the outbreak that he found the relations between garrison and prisoners satisfactory and the conditions of the camp excellent, and added that the camp spokesmen stressed the co-operative attitudes of the various camp commandants.[4]

However, judging from studies of prisoner-of-war camps in various wars, one could generalize that whenever an unexpected, relatively large influx of captives occurs, a certain (perhaps inevitable) amount of disorganization and unpreparedness on the part of the captor, rather than deliberate victimization, tends to cause physical hardship and tensions. Usually the accommodation for the prisoners is inadequate and makeshift; disused training camps or factories are often quickly pressed into service to house men who are often mentally and physically exhausted and therefore less able to cope with strange surroundings and have difficulty in coming to terms with their own changed status. Under such circumstances all the difficulties tend to be magnified, orders from the enemy take on an ominous tinge, and the general uncertainty puts captor as well as captive on edge.

While the events at Featherston occurred in the initial phases of the prisoners' confinement, and at a time when the military strength of New Zealand and the Allies was at a low ebb, the outbreak in Cowra took place after the captives had been held at the camp for a considerable period. If one divides captivity into several phases such as surrender, transport to a camp, initial adjustment, accommodation, and repatriation, the "crisis points" would generally arise in the initial phases. In the Western model of escape attempts, the next crisis would be likely to arise either during the accommodation period or when provoked

by victimization and other external factors. In the incident
at Cowra a crisis had arisen owing to several factors during
the accommodation period: firstly, the arrival of a large
number of prisoners from the Pacific theatre of war who
could not easily be housed in a camp such as Cowra, which
had not been established to cater for such an influx of
potentially dangerous captives; and secondly, that the war
was going badly for Japan. Since the prisoners could not
look forward to a happy homecoming at the end of the
war, the cumulative effects of these two factors was bound
to have a depressing effect on them.

At the time of the 1943 incident at Featherston Camp,
the outcome of the war hung very much in the balance,
and the New Zealanders had good reasons to regard the
presence of eight hundred enemy prisoners as a potential
security risk. In August 1944, however, the situation looked
very different. Australia was not isolated and bereft of
manpower as New Zealand had been in 1942–43, and while
the presence of over a thousand Japanese captives at the
Cowra camp was fraught with certain dangers, it did not
represent the same type of threatening situation as did the
presence of the Japanese captives at Featherston. The
security precautions, which had been rather easy-going, had
been tightened up since reports of a planned outbreak had
reached the authorities in June of 1944. According to *Dead
Men Rising*, a novel by Kenneth Mackenzie based on the
Cowra outbreak, and Asada's *The Night of a Thousand
Suicides*, the guards, while aware of the potentially dangerous nature of their captives, tended to be indifferent rather
than hostile towards the Japanese. As in Featherston,
however, the cultural dimension, the fact that the Japanese
captives regarded themselves as violators of their traditional
ethical code—who were dead as far as their nation and
families were concerned—had not been completely realized
by the military authorities. Some of the men among the
captives were convinced that only an honourable death
could restore their good name, and fear of an uncertain
future tended to increase their influence on their fellow
captives, who might have not initially held such views.

"Ideal Type" Behaviour in Wartime

In every cultural tradition certain generally accepted rules exist governing behaviour in warfare. Among Western nations, which largely share a single cultural tradition, there are, as Ruth Benedict puts it in *The Chrysanthemum and The Sword*, "certain clarion calls to all-out war effort, certain forms of reassurance in case of local defeats, certain regularities in the proportion of fatalities to surrenders, and certain rules of behavior for prisoners of war".[5] Members of any Western army who have fought courageously and done their best but nevertheless find themselves facing overwhelming and hopeless odds are likely to surrender to the enemy. Individual soldiers are not disgraced, neither as citizens nor as fighting men nor in their own families. Their treatment and conditions of internment by the enemy are regulated by an international agreement, the Geneva Convention of 1929.

The Japanese defined the situation quite differently—the honour of a soldier is bound up with fighting unto death. The Japanese Military Field Code, also known as the Field Service Code or the Battlefield Commandments, states under the heading "Regard for Reputation" (chapter 2): "Those who know shame are strong. Have regard for the honour of your family first and endeavour to satisfy the wishes of the family group. Never live to experience shame as a prisoner. Never die in disgrace."[6] Another translation of the same passage, in *The Night of a Thousand Suicides*, reads: "He who knows shame is strong and should at all times endeavour to keep before him the honour of his homeland and live up to what it expects of him. Rather than live and bear the shame of imprisonment by the enemy, he should die and avoid leaving a dishonourable name."[7] Hideki Tojo, then minister of war, promulgated the Military Field Code on 8 January 1941, thus officially emphasizing the disgrace involved in surrendering to the enemy. The Japanese press turned to this theme over and over again, exhorting the virtue of accepting life-and-death risks and repudiating surrender as unworthy of the spirit of the Japanese forces.

The notion of the expendability of Japanese fighting men was further expressed in the official Japanese attitude with regard to the rescue of the wounded or care for the disabled and sick. As Ruth Benedict puts it: "Japanese valor repudiates such salvaging . . . precautions were unworthy . . . wounded and . . . malarial patients . . . were damaged goods and the medical services provided were utterly inadequate even for reasonable effectiveness of the fighting force."[8] Thus no adequate provisions existed for the care of the wounded under fire; rescue teams trained to administer first aid were virtually non-existent; where small field hospitals operated, no contingency plans had been formulated for the evacuation of patients in case of withdrawal. According to Benedict, "the medical officer in charge often shot the inmates of the hospital before he left or they killed themselves with hand grenades" rather than permit themselves to fall into the hands of the enemy.[9]

Capture by the enemy, even when wounded or unconscious and unable to move, was equated with irrevocable shame. Lord Russell of Liverpool, in *The Knights of Bushido*, suggests that rather than surrender to the enemy, the Japanese soldiers were directed by their Military Field Code to keep the last round of ammunition for themselves or charge the enemy in a suicidal assault. Were a member of the Japanese fighting forces to be captured, "he could never again hold up his head in Japan. He and his family would be disgraced forever."[10]

Consequently only on very rare occasions, particularly during the early stages of World War II, were Japanese taken prisoner. Even in the later phases, such as the campaign in Burma, "the proportion of the captured to the dead was 142 to 17,166",[11] a ratio of 1 man captured to 120 dead soldiers. The expected ratio of dead to wounded in Western armies is more like one soldier killed to four men captured. Another significant factor ought to be noted: among the 142 Japanese prisoners of war in camps in Burma, "all except a small minority were wounded or unconscious when taken; only a few had 'surrendered' singly or in groups of two or three".[12]

That the Japanese government dissociated itself completely from its prisoners of war is clearly illustrated by the account of Joseph C. Grew, the American ambassador in Japan from 1932 to 1941, who in the course of his routine diplomatic duties had occasion to transmit to the Japanese government a message from a Japanese prisoner of war, held in China during the "Manchurian Incident". The prisoner wished his family in Japan to know that he was alive and well; Grew transmitted the information to the Japanese government and received in due course a curt official reply to the effect that "the Japanese Government was not interested in receiving such information. So far as they, the Government, were concerned, and also so far as his own family was concerned, that man was officially dead. Were he to be recognized as a prisoner of war, shame would be brought upon not only his own family, but also his Government and his nation."[13]

Unlike Japanese prisoners of war, Allied prisoners were aware that neither their patriotism nor their loyalty to their country had been tarnished by having surrendered to the enemy when facing overwhelming odds or having run out of ammunition and food. Furthermore, they knew that under the terms of the Geneva Convention they were entitled to specified treatment by their captors: "They shall at all times be humanely treated and protected, particularly against acts of violence, from insults and from public curiosity . . . Prisoners of war are entitled to respect for their persons and honour."[14]

Elaborate provisions under the terms of the Geneva Convention ensure that belligerents inform each other of all captures of prisoners through the intermediary of the information bureaux, set up in accordance with article 77 of the convention. The belligerents are further required to inform each other of the addresses to which letters from the prisoners' families are to be forwarded. "As soon as possible every prisoner shall be enabled to correspond personally with his family."[15] The International Committee of the Red Cross was designated to look after the relief of prisoners of war, with the object of serving as an intermediary for charitable purposes such as transmitting food parcels, medical supplies, books and cigarettes, recreational equipment, and, of course, letters between prisoners and their families.

Neutral powers, charged with the protection of the interests of the belligerents—Switzerland, for example, acted in this capacity during World War II for Japan and the British Commonwealth countries—are authorized under the provisions of article 86 of the Geneva Convention "to proceed to any place, without exception, where prisoners of war are interned. They shall have access to all premises occupied by prisoners and may hold conversation with prisoners, as a general rule without witnesses, either personally or through the intermediary of interpreters."[16]

Prisoners of war also have the right, under article 42 of the convention, to bring to the notice of the military authorities in whose hands they are "their petitions concerning the conditions of captivity to which they are subjected. They shall also have the right to communicate with the representatives of the protecting Powers in order to draw their attention to the points on which they have complants to make."[17] Work by prisoners of war, transfers of the prisoners from one camp to another, discipline, and sanctions with respect to breaches of discipline are some of the aspects which are covered by the provisions of the Geneva Convention. At a later stage some of the effects of the provisions of the convention on the events in Featherston and Cowra will be discussed in greater detail.

The signatories of the Geneva Convention thus perceived the status and the rights of prisoners of war very differently from the Japanese government. Allied governments did not withdraw their support from members of their armed forces who were captured and subsequently interned by the enemy; nor did Allied governments expect members of their armed forces to take unreasonable risks or fight on against overwhelming odds until they were killed. Contrary to the stance adopted by the Japanese government, Allied governments maintained a continuous and keen interest in the

welfare of their prisoners, through the good offices of the
protecting power and the delegates of the International
Committee of the Red Cross.

The families of Allied prisoners did not feel disgraced,
nor did they turn their back upon them; on the contrary,
they endeavoured to keep in close touch with them by
correspondence. Thus, despite the often grim conditions of
prisoner-of-war camps, the morale of Allied prisoners was
sustained during captivity by the knowledge that their
surrender was not regarded as an irrevocable disgrace and
that their government and family were continuing to give
them every support.

The Japanese prisoner of war largely lacked the emotional supports provided for Allied prisoners of war.
Furthermore, since the Japanese government had not
ratified the 1929 Geneva Convention in 1934, Japanese
prisoners were unaware of the rights and obligations
inherent in their new status. Japan had initially signed the
Geneva Convention in 1929, and the failure to ratify it is
attributed by Lord Russell to the opposition of the Japanese
military establishment, which expressed concern that
ratification would necessitate a revision of the Japanese
Military and Naval Disciplinary Codes, which was considered "undesirable in the interests of discipline". [18]

On the other hand, the steadily heightened consciousness
of the uniqueness of the Japanese nation, its moral superiority in all spheres, promoted during the early 1930s by
kokutai no hongi, the national polity, according to Masao
Maruyama, author of *Thought and Behaviour in Modern
Japanese Politics*, left little "room for a concept of international law which [was] equally binding on all nations".[19]
The ultranationalism which gradually permeated all sectors
of Japanese society in the 1930s "recognized no ethical
restraints upon the nation's conduct", wrote Kotaro
Tanaka, Japan's chief justice in post-war years, "and
justified immoral policies of imperialistic aggression".[20]

During World War II, therefore, the Japanese government did not recognize the special status which the Geneva

Convention confers on "the armed forces of belligerents who are captured by the enemy" in the course of military, naval, and aerial operations.[21] The Japanese completely disregarded regulations governing the custody and treatment of prisoners of war throughout the campaigns in the Pacific. While the Japanese foreign minister, Togo, had given formal assurances that Japan, although not bound by the Convention "would apply it, *mutatis mutandis*, to all American, Australian, British, Canadian and New Zealand prisoners of war",[22] Tojo, Japan's prime minister at that period, gave instructions to commandants of prisoner-of-war camps which emphasized that "in Japan we have our own ideology concerning prisoners of war which should naturally make their treatment more or less different from that in Europe and America".[23] Furthermore, Tojo virtually gave his commandants *carte blanche* to impose rigid discipline upon prisoners: "in case a prisoner of war is guilty of an act of insubordination, he shall be subject to imprisonment or arrest, and any other measures deemed necessary for the purpose of discipline may be added."[24] Consequently ill-treatment of Allied prisoners of war, often resulting in their death, was more frequently reported from camps administered by the Japanese than from those in the European theatres of war. Russell notes that of "235,473 British and American prisoners of war . . . captured by the Germans and Italians . . . 9,348, or 4 per cent of the total, died in captivity. In the Pacific theatres of war the percentage was 27".[25]

As far as their own forces were concerned, the Japanese military authorities expected automatic compliance with the provisions of the Military Field Code, which ordered Japanese forces not to surrender to the enemy under any circumstances. According to Benedict, Japanese soldiers, sailors, and airmen had not been instructed how they ought to behave when captured. They did not know what to say, what to keep silent about; their responses "were strikingly unregimented".[26] The shame of having surrendered, however, "burned deeply into the consciousness of the

Japanese".[27] Japanese prisoners expected to be treated in
an arbitrary manner, even harshly, since they were largely
unfamiliar with the terms of the Geneva Convention, which
defined the status of prisoner of war and protected their
rights.

In the early stages of the war Japanese servicemen were
firmly convinced that "the enemy tortured and killed any
prisoners",[28] a notion that may have reinforced their
decision not to surrender and may have led to some of the
initial atrocities against Allied prisoners of war. Benedict
reports that many Japanese prisoners asked to be killed
upon capture; others were deeply distraught and remained
irreconcilable to their fate, attempting suicide at the earliest
opportunity. Yet others, however, became model prisoners:

> They were better than model prisoners. Old Army hands and
> long-time extreme nationalists located ammunition dumps,
> carefully explained the disposition of Japanese forces, wrote
> our propaganda and flew with our bombing pilots to guide
> them to military targets. It was as if they had turned over
> a new page; what was written on the new page was the
> opposite of what was written on the old, but they spoke the
> lines with the same faithfulness.[29]

Instances of co-operative behaviour by Japanese prisoners
of war are also confirmed by Professor G. Henderson, of
Tufts University, who served as an interpreter with the
United States Marines during World War II. He was
attached for a brief period to a prisoner-of-war stockade
on Saipan in 1945. He suggested, however, that as soon as
the military hierarchy was re-established in the stockade,
after the initial period of interrogations, co-operation in a
positive sense tended to disappear. The behaviour of
Japanese prisoners who surrendered to the Allies differed
in many respects from that expected of Allied prisoners,
who had been briefed during their training about the
information they were required to give when interrogated
by the enemy. Under the provisions of the Geneva Convention, a prisoner was obliged merely to volunteer his true
name and rank or regimental number. Allied prisoners

when conforming to these rules expected that this information would be transmitted through the appropriate channels, the protecting power or the International Committee of the Red Cross, to their own government, who would inform their family that they were alive but in captivity. The Japanese were, however, openly contemptuous to find that Allied prisoners of war requested that their names should be forwarded to their governments or that they wished to communicate with their family, for the Japanese found it difficult, if not impossible, to accept the fact that the Allied prisoners did not experience shame or feel dishonoured when captured.

The Japanese expected other military forces to conform to their own code of behaviour and fight until death rather than surrender. These notions were not purely based on ethnocentricity, but may have been fostered by their first confrontation with a Western army; Christopher Martin in his study *The Russo-Japanese War* notes that the Russian general Kondratenko told the troops defending Port Arthur that they were honour bound to fight to death for the honour of Russia. Upon internment the Japanese prisoners of war therefore found themselves in a totally unexpected situation for which their military training had not prepared them. Realizing that they had brought shame and dishonour upon themselves and that their government and their families would reject and abandon them, the Japanese prisoners' response to imprisonment was not unlike the reaction of mental patients upon first admittance to an asylum.

In his study *Asylums*, Erving Goffman analyses the standard sequence of changes which occur in the manner in which a patient conceives of his own "self" and the selves of others. By following a patient's "moral career", Goffman traces the effects of "total institutions", such as mental hospitals or prison camps, on the individual's self. The term *career* is not used by Goffman in this context in the more conventional sense of indicating, for example, the steps up the ladder in a profession, but in a broader sense as referring to any social strand of any person's course through life.[30]

Goffman marks the various turning points in the way the patient views his own self and the world, which begin already in the pre-patient phase of his career. "The disintegrative re-evaluation of himself"[31] which is brought about by the patient's feelings of having been abandoned by relatives and friends is exacerbated by the new almost equally pervasive circumstance of attempting to conceal from others what he takes to be the new fundamental facts about himself, and attempting to discover whether others, too, have discovered them.[32] The patient realizes in the first stages of the in-patient phase—whether justified or not— that he has been deserted by society, turned out by those closest to him, and he tends to experience feelings of bitterness and isolation.

Goffman conceptualizes the self as a ceremonial thing, a sacred object which must be treated with proper ritual care and in turn must be presented in proper light to others.[33] This self is established by the individual, who acts with proper demeanour when interacting with others and, in turn, expects to be treated by others with appropriate deference. Goffman suggests that demeanour and deference are institutionalized in wider society and enable an individual to present a viable self; normal social life thus seems to depend on a mutually beneficial conspiracy between the participants in social interactions.

Goffman postulates that the conventions governing everyday social interactions are violated in the setting of "total institutions"; not only do these institutions refuse to defer to the new inmate's presentation of self, but it seems that attacking the inmate's self-concept directly by not according him the deference his demeanour normally elicits outside the institution is part of their strategy. They deprive the patient of his "identity kit", which he recurs to "for the management of his personal front",[34] and provide institutional issue of clothes and shoes, which are often unbecoming and ill-fitting. Furthermore, his personal belongings, such as his watch, comb and brush, make-up, or photographs, are often put out of his immediate reach. The goal of the total institution is, therefore, to impress upon the patient by restricting his freedom of action and associations that he has failed in some over-all way and that here he is of little social weight, being hardly capable of acting like a fully fledged person.[35]

Thus on entering a mental hospital the patient may experience a strong desire not to be known to anyone as a person who could possibly be reduced to his present circumstances;[36] he may withdraw from the hospital community in an effort to preserve his devalued self. After a period it appears that most patients "give up this taxing effort at anonymity, at non-hereness"[37] and tend to present themselves for conventional social interaction to the hospital community. They tend to readjust to their circumstances, presenting a new self. Goffman suggests that this making of oneself available "marks a new stand openly taken and supported by the patient, and resembles the 'coming out' process that occurs in other groupings".[38] A similar process marks the transition from childhood to adulthood in some tribal societies, or among homosexual groups when an individual presents himself finally and frankly to a "gay" gathering as available.

The processes of self-annihilation and role dispossession, therefore, which the mental patients observed by Goffman underwent may be analogous to those experienced by the Japanese prisoners of war. The "total institution" had effectively annihilated their role and had also impressed upon them that the rules of behaviour and the values that had regulated their social interactions on the outside were no longer appropriate or applicable. The culturally appropriate demeanour of the Japanese soldier in prison did not elicit the deferential response he had learned to expect, either from his guardians or from his fellow inmates, who, like himself, endeavoured to conceal their sense of shame and failure.

The moral aspects of the Japanese prisoners' "career" were made worse by the fact that their government had abandoned them, and that their families had rejected them. The refusal of many Japanese prisoners to volunteer their true name and rank is another indication of their withdrawal from the community. Often the prisoners assumed the names of famous warriors or culture heroes to hide their real identity. It is also significant that the large majority of Japanese prisoners refused to avail themselves of the opportunity to communicate with their families, thus manifesting their belief that they were social failures and that their relatives would only have been deeply embarrassed to receive letters from them.

Inter Arma Caritas, the report issued by the International Committee of the Red Cross on its work during World War II, notes that most Japanese prisoners refused to make use of mail facilities, preferring to leave their relations in the belief that they had died in battle rather than "inflict upon them the shame of his captivity". The Japanese prisoner did not ask for any kind of attention; indeed, "he could not understand why he should be treated humanely, or why the Red Cross should take any interest in his fate".[39]

While the fact that Japan had not ratified the Geneva Convention of 1929 explains some of the difficulties the Red Cross experienced in carrying out its task in the Pacific theatre of war, the Japanese conception of prisoners of war made the situation far worse: "In the official bureaux at Tokyo, nominal rolls of Japanese prisoners and prisoner mail were left untouched . . . the information bureaux would have acted more cruelly had they sent next of kin news that would have brought them far more sorrow than relief."[40] The attitude of the prisoners' relatives, as reported by the Red Cross, correlates closely with the behaviour of the Japanese prisoners interned by the Allies. In the first stages of their imprisonment they tended to keep themselves very much to themselves, but even in the later stages of their internment, when they seemingly had come to terms with their new situation and "presented a new self", they refrained from disclosing their real names, discussing their families, or communicating with them.

Against this background of conflicting notions regarding the expected and culturally appropriate conduct of military personnel on active service, the following chapter briefly traces the sequence of events at Featherston Camp and Cowra, which lead to the incidents of 25 February 1943 and 5 August 1944.

1. Gavin Long, *The Final Campaigns* (Canberra: Australian War Memorial, 1963), p.624.
2. Yuji Aida, *Prisoner of the British*, trans. Louis Allen (London: Cresset, 1966), pp.201–202.
3. International Committee of the Red Cross, "Prisonniers de guerre, japonais en Nouvelle Zélande, 1942–1945; conditions générales de captivité—evasions—mésures disciplinaires", mimeographed (Geneva, 4/1/77 GD), p.5.
4. Commonwealth Archives Office, Canberra, CRS A989, item 44/925/1/140, p.2.
5. Ruth Benedict, *The Crysanthemum and the Sword* (London: Routledge, 1967), p.14.
6. Sankei Shimbun, Special Research Team, *The Last Japanese Soldier* (London: Stacey, 1972), p.94.
7. Teruhiko Asada, *The Night of a Thousand Suicides* (Sydney: Angus and Robertson, 1970), p.2.
8. Benedict, *The Crysanthemum and the Sword*, p.25.
9. Ibid., p.26.
10. Lord Russell of Liverpool, *The Knights of Bushido* (London: Cassell, 1958), p.56.
11. Benedict, *The Crysan'themum and the Sword*, pp.26–27.
12. Ibid.
13. Joseph Grew, *Report from Tokyo* (Sydney: Angus and Robertson, 1943), p.20.
14. Manley O. Hudson, ed., *International Legislation*, vol.5 (Washington, DC: Carnegie Endowment for International Peace, 1936), pp.26–27.
15. Ibid., p.29.
16. Ibid., p.55.
17. Ibid., p.40.
18. Russell, *The Knights of Bushido*, p.58.
19. Maseo Maruyama, *Thought and Behaviour in Modern Japanese Politics* (London: Oxford University Press, 1963), p.21.

20. Ryusaku Tsunoda, Wm. Theodore de Bary, and Donald Keene, comps., *Sources of Japanese Tradition* (New York: Columbia University Press, 1964), vol.2, p.374.
21. Hudson, *International Legislation*, p.26.
22. Russell, *The Knights of Bushido*, p.54.
23. Ibid., p.56.
24. Ibid., p.58.
25. Ibid., p.57.
26. Benedict, *The Crysanthemum and the Sword*, p.21.
27. Ibid., p.40.
28. Ibid., p.41.
29. Ibid.
30. Erving Goffman, *Asylums* (Harmondsworth, Mddx.: Penguin, 1970), p.117. A "total institution" is defined by Goffman as "a place of residence and work where a large number of like situated individuals, cut off from the wider society for an appreciable period of time, together lead an enclosed, formally administered round of life" (p.11).
31. Ibid., p.123.
32. Ibid.
33. Erving Goffman, "The Nature of Deference and Demeanour", *American Anthropologist* 59 (1956): 497.
34. Goffman, *Asylums*, p. 29. Goffman suggests that an individual's possessions have a special relation to the self. An individual expects normally to exert some control over the guise in which he appears before others. For this he needs clothing, cosmetics, and tools for applying them.
35. Ibid., p.141.
36. Ibid., p.136.
37. Ibid.
38. Ibid., p.137.
39. International Committee of the Red Cross, *Inter Arma Caritas* (Geneva, 1947), p.104.
40. Ibid.

2

Events at Featherston Camp and at Cowra

Sequence of Events at Featherston

The Japanese prisoner-of-war camp at Featherston was established on a site formerly occupied by a military training camp during World War I, "at the request of the American authorities in September 1942",[1] following the Allied actions at Guadalcanal. The camp area was divided into four rectangular compounds and covered some twenty-four hectares of the stony portion of the fertile and closely settled Wairarapa Plains.

At the time the official delegate of the International Committee of the Red Cross paid his first visit to Featherston Camp, on 15 December, 1942, 687 Japanese prisoners were held there; in the beginning of 1943 their number rose to 805.[2] There is a slight disparity in the reported number of captives held at Featherston between the figures reported by Dr Bossard, the Red Cross delegate, and those mentioned in the New Zealand reports. Bossard notes that there were more or less at all times 805 captives present in Featherston until the moment of repatriation, while the New Zealand sources refer always to 812 prisoners. Bossard notes the presence of eight officers; the New Zealanders maintain there were seven.

There were two distinctive groups among the captives. The first group consisted of some 500 members of the Imperial Work Force, who had been captured while building an extension to the Japanese airfield in Guadalcanal. Many among them had been recruited from

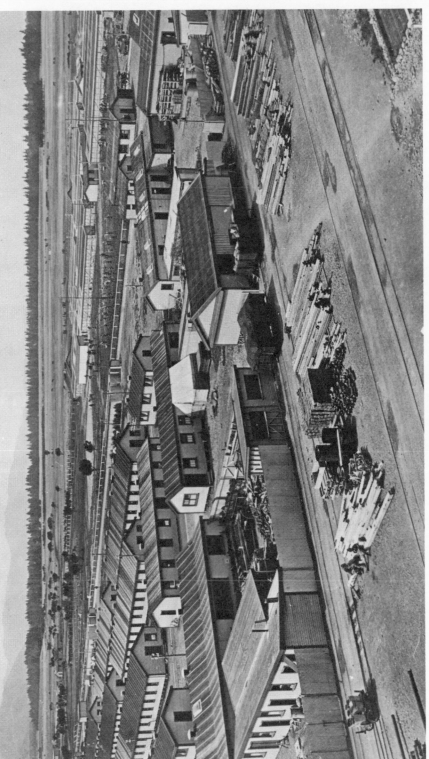

Featherston military training camp. (Photo: Alexander Turnbull Library, Wellington, NZ)

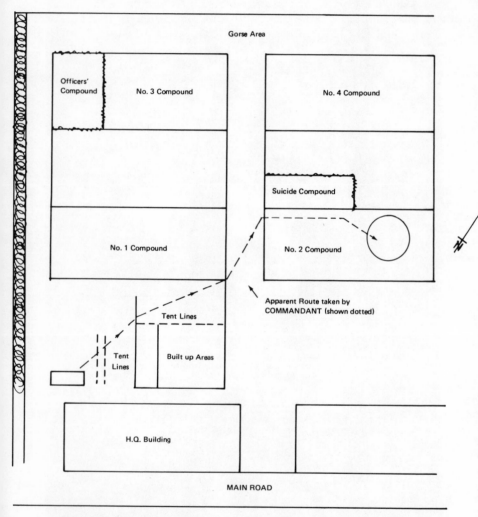

Layout of compounds at Featherston prisoner-of-war camp at the time of the riot.

minority groups, such as Japanese of Korean descent, and occupied a very low status in the Japanese military hierarchy. The second group of prisoners, which numbered 296 at the time the mutiny took place in February 1943, comprised 240 non-commissioned officers and other ranks who were members of naval units. The members of the first group seemed to adjust fairly quickly to their new circumstances and tended to follow the instructions of their guards scrupulously, presenting only isolated disciplinary problems. The second group, however, who were held in compound 2, from the very beginning of their captivity manifested in various ways their resentment at being given orders or instructions to muster fatigue parties to maintain the compound and perform tasks around the camp area. They had obstructed the camp staff on many occasions, and the camp commandant had found it necessary to explain to the senior NCOs, who were regarded as responsible for the uncooperative attitude of the captives, that under the provisions of the Geneva Convention of 1929 it was obligatory for prisoners to maintain their camp under the supervision of their own NCOs, who in turn had selected a representative—*un homme de confiance*—who would receive his instructions from the authorities of the detaining powers.

Both groups had seemingly absorbed the precepts of the Japanese Military Field Code and keenly felt the stigma attached to those Japanese servicemen who surrendered to the enemy. For neither group availed themselves of the opportunities provided by the New Zealand authorities to communicate with their families or friends in Japan. Léon Bossard, a perceptive, and sympathetic observer, describes in his reports the moral isolation in which these men found themselves, and suggests that this may well have been one of the reasons why they appeared to attach such importance to his regular visits. He gathered from his conversations with the captives that they felt no inclination whatsoever to write to their families since, as they had surrendered, they knew full well that they had dishonoured not only their own but their families' names, and they were convinced that any indication that they were alive, and in captivity, would create difficulties for their families and make a very unfavourable impression in Japan. Thus despite the fact that the International Committee of the Red Cross had forwarded a nominal list of the captives at the earliest opportunity to the Japanese government, Bossard reports that while the prisoners were permitted to write two letters a week and even send telegrams in case of urgency, the Featherston captives received not a single message or parcel during the whole period of their internment: this is from late 1942 until their repatriation in August 1945.[3]

While the different attitudes of the two groups and their level of indoctrination with the precepts of the Military Field Code manifested themselves in their relationship with their guards, the two groups appeared to be in complete agreement as far as their debased status as prisoners of war was concerned. They were certain that according to Japanese cultural tradition they were considered outcasts who had transgressed against the ethical principals of the Military Field Code. They continued to share their apprehension with the Red Cross delegate and when it came to their repatriation at the end of hostilities their anxieties with regard to their reception in Japan mounted. Bossard had inspected the ships chosen for their repatriation, and in view of the long journey—one month—demanded that improvement be made in the accommodation and hygienic conditions, which caused further delays in the departure of the ships. When it finally came to their embarkation, the captives, who continued to feel very uneasy about their return to Japan, made every effort to prevail on Bossard to accompany them. Bossard, however, assured them that there would be a delegate of the International Committee of the Red Cross present on their arrival in Japan. Until the very last moment, Bossard, who had gained the confidence of the captives, endeavoured to answer their queries, straighten out difficulties, and reassure them. It is

Japanese officers at Featherston Camp. *Back row, right*: Sub-Lieutenant T. Adachi; *front row, second from left:* Lieutenant M. Shinya. (Photo: Russell Orr)

Japanese prisoners of war boarding ship in Wellington for the journey back to Japan and repatriation at the end of the war. (Photo: Russell Orr)

relevant that Bossard never indicated in any way that the members of the Imperial Work Force, who held a lower social status, were less concerned than the naval ratings or the officers about their future. Both groups accepted the "non-status" given to Japanese servicemen who surrendered to the enemy, and one can thus surmise that this idea of the duty of any member of Japanese forces—to die rather than surrender—appears to have been deeply entrenched in the minds of the men.

However, the attitude of the second group of prisoners toward their guards was more militant and aggressive. The representative whom they had appointed in accordance with international practice constantly questioned the appropriateness of mustering the naval ratings not only to work outside the compound—to clear gorse, for instance —but also to perform tasks within the compound. He claimed frequently that there were not enough healthy prisoners available to perform the tasks that had been allocated to them.

Further symptoms of unrest, and even danger signals, may have been recognized from disclosures by prisoners of alleged plots. Early in December 1942 the authorities were warned that a working party returning with its tools from its task was planning to overpower its escort, rush the guards' tents while part of the guard was at lunch, and seize the arms to use them against the camp. Another prisoner of war disclosed a plan to set fire to the huts and overpower the guards while they were occupied in extinguishing the fire. The most serious indication of impending trouble, however, was the information about a mass suicide plot conveyed to Captain Ashton, the senior camp interpreter, by two naval officers who claimed that they were in imminent danger from an attempt on their lives.[4] Apparently some of the naval ratings had agreed among themselves that it was their duty as Japanese servicemen who had surrendered to commit suicide, and they insisted that it was the responsibility of the officers to give the lead by doing "the right thing". Since the officers apparently

Japanese work party and New Zealand guard at Featherston Camp. (Photo: Alexander Turnbull Library, Wellington, NZ)

A Japanese work party loading shingle and sand from a river bed in the Wairarapa region near Featherston. (Photo: Alexander Turnbull Library, Wellington, NZ)

A Japanese prisoner on hut-cleaning duty. (Photo: Russell Orr)

had refused to accept the viewpoint of these men, they felt
that their lives were now in jeopardy and appealed to the
authorities for protection.

The camp adjutant, Lieutenant Malcolm, took prompt
action and initiated measures to ensure the safety of the
officers and of those men who were not inclined to commit
suicide. After the officers had submitted a list of twenty-
six captives who had instigated the mass suicide plot, these
were removed from compound 2 and segregated in a closely
supervised suicide compound. One of the naval officers,
Sub-Lieutenant Adachi, volunteered to act as a general
supervisor of compound 2 and proposed to the camp
authorities that he be permitted to pay daily visits to the
compound, with the specific task to ensure the smooth
running of the compound and supervise the mustering of
fatigue parties. Since the naval ratings had displayed
"insubordinate behaviour"[5] and permitted their compound
to become untidy, the camp commandment accepted
Adachi's offer, and for a short period the compound
appeared to function in a satisfactory manner.[6]

However, a week before the actual incident, the NCOs
in no. 2 compound ordered a group of OR (other ranks)
prisoners engaged in work outside their compound to return
before they had finished their tasks. The NCOs responsible
for this breach of discipline were warned by the camp
authorities, who ordered them to see that work considered
necessary for the maintenance of the camp was duly carried
out. The NCOs who had adopted an insolent attitude, were
given three days to improve their own behaviour and re-
establish order in the compound.

On 25 February the NCOs in compound 2 again refused
to supply a work party, and the camp adjutant was called
upon to deal with the situation. Sub-Lieutenant Adachi was
present in the compound at this time, and the adjutant
addressed his orders to him. Not only did Adachi disregard
the adjutant's orders but, styling himself as the spokesman
of compound 2, he informed the adjutant that the prisoners
would not parade until they had an opportunity to submit

Sentry watchtower with guard at Featherston Camp. (Photo: Russell Orr)

their complaints to the camp commandant.

The adjutant then called for reinforcements, and forty guards armed with automatic weapons entered the compound and faced the prisoners. Four unarmed guards were detailed to arrest Adachi, who had refused to comply with the adjutant's order to leave the compound. Adachi, however, had retired to one of the huts in the compound and the other prisoners obstructed the entry of the guards to the hut. Subsequently, four armed guards undertook to arrest Adachi, but they too were unable to execute their mission. Next, Lieutenant Nishimura, another naval officer, whose presence in compound 2 was not authorized, emerged from the hut, apparently ready to negotiate on behalf of the prisoners. He was overpowered by the guards and removed from compound 2, protesting loudly.

The attitude of the prisoners became more menacing after the removal of Nishimura. Adachi now came out of the hut and, "picking up two large stones, . . . took up a position in the centre of the prisoners".[7] The adjutant, with the assistance of the interpreter, again ordered Adachi to leave the compound quietly and informed him of the consequences which were likely to ensue for the prisoners as well as himself if he continued to disobey orders. "Adachi hesitated, then, encouraged by the surrounding prisoners, definitely refused" to comply with the order to leave the compound.[8] Another unsuccessful effort to remove Adachi by force was then undertaken by the guards.

These negotiations had now lasted for well over an hour, and the adjutant "warned the guard that it might be necessary to use arms; if so, the first round must be fired high and there must be no wild or indiscriminate shooting".[9] In the meantime many of the prisoners had picked up large stones. The adjutant reacted to the threatening behaviour of the prisoners by openly borrowing a pistol "with the idea of intimidating" the prisoners,[10] for he had previously stood unarmed between the prisoners and the guards. "Adachi stood up, thumped his chest with both fists and called out something in a defiant manner",[11] inviting the adjutant to shoot him. The adjutant responded by firing a warning shot over Adachi's head, an action which immediately brought a shower of stones on the adjutant and the guards. The adjutant fired another shot, wounding Adachi in the shoulder.

The conflict now escalated rapidly: the prisoners, about 240 of them, made a concerted rush towards the adjutant and the guards.[12] The guards opened fire when the nearest prisoners were only about seven yards away, and the burst of fire, which lasted fifteen to twenty seconds, killed 48 prisoners and wounded 63, effectively putting an end to the rebellion.[13]

Although the prisoners' perception of the situation influenced as it was both by their cultural conditioning and value orientation, was a crucial factor determining these events, it would seem likely that the confrontation and its tragic sequel was the culmination of a series of mutual misunderstandings. The New Zealand authorities adhered strictly to the provisions of the Geneva Convention of 1929, which stipulates that tasks such as cleaning compound huts, mess halls, sanitary facilities, etc., were the responsibility of the OR prisoners, whose "fatigue duties" were to be supervised by their own NCOs. Under the provisions of the Geneva Convention, work connected with the maintenance of the camp is not remunerated. Article 34 states: "Prisoners of war shall not receive pay for work in connexion with the administration, internal arrangement and maintenance of camps. Prisoners employed on other work shall be entitled to a rate of pay, to be fixed by agreements between the belligerents."[14] Article 31 refers to "Prohibited Work", stipulating that "work done by prisoners of war shall have no direct connexion with the operations of the war",[15] and expressly prohibits employment of prisoners in the manufacture of arms and munitions or the transport of such material to combatant troops.

Under the terms of the Convention, officers are, however, not required to work, although they can "ask for suitable work"[16] and volunteer for duties for which they are

peculiarly qualified: thus doctors may apply to work in the
camp hospital and look after fellow prisoners who are ill.
Furthermore, officers are permitted to have batmen allotted
to them to maintain their compound, clean their huts, wash
their laundry, cook for them, and wait on them at the table.
This provision may well explain Lieutenant Nishimura's
presence in compound 2, for, as Lieutenant-Colonel
Donaldson, the camp commandant, put it—

> Nishimura had no right whatever to be in No. 2 compound
> on the morning of the 25th. Owing to the conditions obtaining
> in the officers' compound, there was, throughout the day,
> movement from No. 2 compound into the officers' compound.
> This was required by the carriage of meals, water, etc., and
> by the necessity for batmen and waiters moving between the
> two compounds.
>
>   Such movement was quite legitimate, and I imagine that
> Nishimura passed himself off to the sentries and escorts as one
> of the waiters or batmen.[17]

Nishimura later testified at the court of inquiry that he went
to no. 2 compound with the intention of preventing a
serious incident.

It would appear that the prisoners of Featherston Camp
were largely unfamiliar with the provisions of the Geneva
Convention of 1929[18] and that they chose to interpret the
orders of the camp authorities with regard to mustering
fatigue parties as merely compounding the shame and
disgrace inherent in their status as prisoners of war.
Undertaking camp maintenance work was equated by them
with working for the enemy.

Another feature which might have made the mustering
of fatigue parties an even more demeaning chore was the
fact that the naval ratings were expected to work side by
side with the members of the Imperial Work Force, who
held a much lower status in the Japanese military hierarchy,
and moreover had to perform identical tasks. As Adachi
expressed it in the testimony he volunteered to give the
court of inquiry: "I think it was a mistake by the officer
commanding to make men of the armed forces and

labourers go out to work together. Japanese people have
pride. . . . "[19]

A crucial factor, however, may have been the sense of
guilt felt by the ratings towards those of their comrades
who had given their lives at Guadalcanal. Adachi may have
accurately summarized the feelings of the prison community when he stated at the proceedings of the court of
inquiry: "Many of our comrades have died bravely in battle.
We have disgraced them by becoming prisoners of war and
for this reason many among us thought that, although we
were prisoners of war, it was totally against our Japanese
tradition to work for the enemy."[20]

Adachi raised several important points in his testimony.
First, he stressed that it would have been far more desirable
for a member of the Japanese armed forces to have been
killed in action rather than be captured by the enemy. To
follow the injunction of the Military Field Code would have
been the honourable way to die. Adachi clearly indicated
that he and the prisoners involved in the incident were
acutely aware of the stigma attached to those who surrendered to the enemy. Second, Adachi's objections to the
performance of fatigue duties indicates clearly that he was
unfamiliar with the provisions of the Geneva Convention
of 1929 regulating the tasks allotted to prisoners of war.
Adachi and his fellow prisoners apparently misconstrued the
orders of the camp authorities to supply fatigue parties as
deliberate attempts to humiliate and shame the prisoners,
largely because of their ignorance regarding the terms of
the convention.

The New Zealand authorities, on the other hand, may
not have been fully aware of the Japanese prisoners'
ignorance of the provisions of the Geneva Convention, and
that their captives did not realize that the status and the
treatment of prisoners of war had been regularized by a
generally recognized international agreement. The military
authorities at Featherston Camp may well have interpreted
the prisoners' refusal to adhere to their instructions and
orders, which were in keeping with the provisions of the

Geneva Convention, as obstructionist tactics. Such behaviour patterns were expected "strategies", employed by New Zealand and other Allied servicemen when they found themselves in internment camps (the television series "Hogan's Heroes", which shows the Germans as being constantly outsmarted by their Allied captives, is an example of this). Furthermore, it is doubtful whether the authorities as well as the members of the garrison at Featherston realized the extent of the difference between their own perception of the status of prisoners of war and that of the Japanese. The deeply rooted feelings of shame and dishonour held by the Japanese prisoners were, however, given due recognition by the court of inquiry, as mitigating circumstances.

The prisoners thus may have deliberately set out to create a state of affairs that would permit them to remove some of the stigma imposed upon them by having been captured. Such an event "might offer a chance of escape or other offensive action which would redound to the credit of the prisoners of war in their own country",[21] and as the court of inquiry put it, these fundamental divergencies of views had been further aggravated by the lack of common language and traditions between captor and captives. In the course of the inquiry the question whether the tragedy could have been avoided was thoroughly investigated; quite naturally the problem that concerned the New Zealand military authorities most deeply was whether their own military personnel had acted properly. Was it necessary to open fire, and after the action had begun, had the firing stopped at the earliest possible moment?

As in every situation where a small force armed with weapons is confronted by a much larger fanatical group with makeshift weapons at their disposal, it is difficult in military terms to set out what the "rational" action pattern should have been. From all accounts the patience and endurance of the New Zealand guards had been tested by the prisoners for a prolonged period of time, and several attempts had been made by various members of the

garrison to dampen down the dangerous situation. Finally
the matter of asserting their authority, of upholding order,
and the notion of self-preservation may have overridden
all other considerations.

The role played by Lieutenant Malcolm, who endeavoured to deal with Adachi as the "reasonable" and
responsible officer, which was the impression he had gained
in his earlier dealings with the naval officer, was particularly
difficult. For it appears that both Malcolm and Adachi were
the victims of circumstances which had slipped out of their
control; after Malcolm had made the decision to fire a
warning shot, i.e., resorted to force which had always been
available to him, there appeared to be no turning back as
far as the Japanese officer was concerned if he were not
to lose face with his subordinates.

In a letter to the editor of the Wellington newspaper the
Dominion of 31 March 1973 (see appendix A) Tony
Simpson interprets Lieutenant Malcolm's action differently.
He suggests that the officer fired two shots in succession,
forgetting that this would be interpreted as the signal for
opening fire by the other guards. The court of inquiry did
not express this view; on the contrary it suggested that "the
final decision was taken by the guards themselves and not
by their officers and was dictated primarily by the instinct
of self-preservation".[22]

The role of the guards was an important one, not only
during the confrontation but in the events leading up to
it. They are likely to have interpreted the prisoners'
intransigence and their disregard of orders within their own
frame of reference. By insisting on obedience to orders, and
unwilling as well as unable (through lack of facility in their
captives' language) to explain the rationale behind their
commands, they may have contributed to the feelings of
shame and dishonour experienced by their captives. Strains
and tensions tend to be heightened in a "total institution"
like an internment camp: weighed down by feelings of guilt
engendered by their "deviant behaviour"—having surrendered to the enemy rather than killed themselves as the

Military Field Code prescribed—the naval ratings needed
only one fatal spark to turn the resentment they harboured
into a conflagration of violence.

Events at Cowra

Apart from the primary-source material describing the
sequence of events at Cowra, there are three books which
provide further insight into how the Japanese prisoners
perceived the situation: Kenneth Mackenzie's prize-winning
novel *Dead Men Rising* (1951), Hugh Clarke's factual
appraisal *Break-Out!* (1965), and Teruhiko Asada's *The
Night of a Thousand Suicides*, which was first published
in English in 1970.

It may be helpful here to give some information about
these books and their authors. Kenneth ("Seaforth")
Mackenzie, a well-known Australian poet and novelist, was
stationed as a guard at the Cowra camp during World War
II, and the novel is largely based on his own experiences.
In a letter to George Ferguson, publishing director of Angus
and Robertson, on 29 January 1952, Mackenzie wrote that
all the characters in the novel were "real people"; it may
have been because of that admission that Angus and
Robertson, after seeking legal advice, refused to publish
Dead Men Rising in 1951, for fear of incurring libel suits.
Thereafter, Mackenzie denied the close connection between
fact and fiction, asserting that the characters in his novel
were "a combination of dozens of people" and himself.[23]
Dead Men Rising was consequently first published in
England by Cape and only reprinted by Angus and
Robertson in 1969, after the author's death.

Hugh Clarke, who together with Takeo Yamashita was
co-author of *Break-Out!*, was a prisoner of the Japanese
during World War II. After working on the notorious
Burma-Thailand railway, he was transported to the
Japanese island of Kyushu, where he laboured in the
dockyards and coal-mines until the end of the war. On a

No. 12 Prisoner of war group, Cowra, New South Wales. (Photo: Australian War Memorial, Canberra)

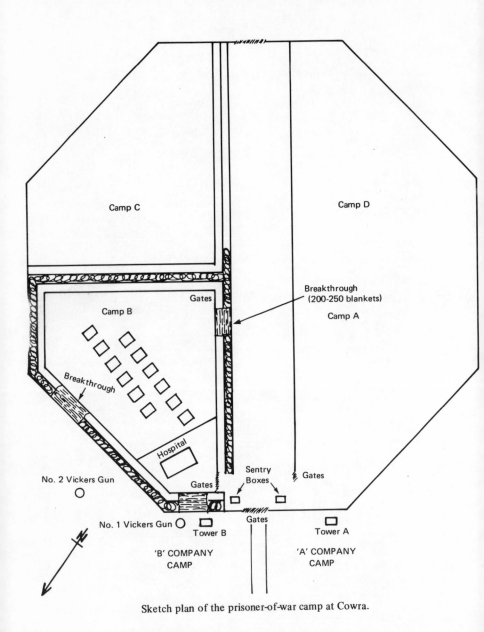

Camp C

Camp D

Breakthrough
(200-250 blankets)

Camp A

Gates

Camp B

Breakthrough

Hospital

No. 2 Vickers Gun

Sentry
Boxes

Gates

Gates

No. 1 Vickers Gun

Gates

Tower B

Tower A

'B' COMPANY
CAMP

'A' COMPANY
CAMP

Sketch plan of the prisoner-of-war camp at Cowra.

visit to Japan in 1964 in his capacity as chief of publications and exhibits in the Department of Territories he met Yamashita, then the deputy chief of police in Osaka; Yamashita had been a prisoner of the Australians in the Celebes Islands. Clarke and Yamashita's common bond of experiences "and their similar ideas on the futility of war"[24] led to their collaboration. Their account is based on information provided by two Japanese survivors of the Cowra incident, as well as on official Australian reports.

The author of *The Night of a Thousand Suicides*, Dr Teruhiko Asada, served as a medical officer with the Japanese Army during World War II. His novel is based on an account of the events at Cowra by one of the survivors, a medical officer, who was a fellow student of Asada before the outbreak of the war. While the author uses a pseudonym "Captain Kaji" for his protagonist, official records confirm that a Captain Nishio, also a medical officer, was held at Cowra during the relevant period. Captain Nishio's "career" at the prison camp was almost identical to that of "Captain Kaji".

Each one of the authors in his own way is well qualified to contribute to our understanding of the sequence of events at Cowra. None of them has departed very far from verifiable facts. While it is necessary to take the inevitable bias in the mind of individual observers into consideration, their perception of the development of the situation "from opposite sides of the wire" contributes greatly to the analysis.

No. 12 Prisoner of War Group, situated about three kilometres north-east of Cowra, was established by the Australian Army in 1941. The group "consisted of four separate 17-acre camps, each designed to hold 1,000 prisoners, enclosed within a twelve-sided, almost circular, perimeter";[25] a thoroughfare 46 metres wide and 685 metres long, known as Broadway, flanked on both sides by deep storm drains, separated B and C camps on the eastern side from A and D camps on the western side. Strips of land each 9 metres wide and over 300 metres long divided B camp from C camp and A camp from D camp. Each individual camp was surrounded by "three barbed wire fences, 30 feet apart".[26]

The entrances to all four camps were from Broadway, and the only way out of the camp was through guarded double gates at both ends of Broadway. Six nine-metre towers were erected at intervals around the camp perimeter, armed with "obsolete Lewis and Hotchkiss light automatic machine guns", which were later replaced— when it was realized that the Japanese prisoners might become dangerous—with "Brens and Vickers and Owens". The Australian novelist E.V. Timms, who was the commandant of C Camp at the time of the incident, suggests that the layout and security arrangement of the camp would have been different had the internment of Japanese prisoners been envisaged. The camp was in the first instance intended to accommodate Italians and Germans; in Timm's assessment it was suitable "for the holding of Italians who had 'given the war away' as far off as the Middle East, but was palpably dangerous and chancy for the caging of more than a thousand Japanese fanatics".[27]

The camp was guarded by the 22nd Australian Garrison Batallion, which had been raised solely for this purpose and specially trained to ensure the security of the Cowra camp. Australian Military Forces personnel on the night of 4 August 1944 comprised a total of 39 officers and 607 ORs including 1 officer and 49 ORs from 16 Australian Garrison Batallion, Hay, who were there for the purpose of escorting the Japanese to Hay on August 7. Most of the members of the batallion were older men, some veterans of World War I, but it also included some younger men who had returned to Australia from active combat duty and had been "medically downgraded"[29]. Mackenzie, who served with this batallion, describes the monotony of garrison duty, which lacked not only the excitement generated by active combat duty but also the spirit of comradeship which tends to develop among soldiers who share danger and hardship.

The attitude of the guards towards the German and Italian prisoners had at first been one of indifference, but after a while the cheerfulness and co-operation—particularly that of the Italians—provoked a more friendly response. However, the arrival of the first Japanese prisoners early in 1943 brought about "a subtle change in the atmosphere of tolerance and security" at Cowra.[30]

The Japanese prisoners were in a poor physical condition after prolonged periods of fighting and retreating in the malarial jungles of New Guinea. When captured they had been in a completely exhausted state, suffering from malaria and other tropical diseases, and ravaged by hunger and thirst. It may be relevant at this stage to refer to Asada's account of the ordeals suffered by Captain Kaji who, with his orderly, had tried unsuccessfully to rejoin his unit during the New Guinea campaign. At the end of his strength he was finally picked up, unconscious, by American troops.

Kaji's first reaction upon recovering consciousness in an unknown hospital tent is one of "unspeakable shame", for capture is "the most dishonourable thing that could befall a soldier".[31] There seems only one course of action open to a Japanese officer—to commit suicide, to remove the stain from his name; his repeated attempts to kill himself are, however, frustrated by the watchful Americans. As he recovers his health owing to excellent medical care and proper food, his natural desire to go on living is strengthened by his interaction with an American medical officer who treats him as an esteemed colleague.

He is surprised to find that the American officer considers himself as first and foremost a doctor, whose primary role is to minister to the sick, regardless of nationality. Kaji conceives his role in a different light; his duties as a soldier are more important than those of a medical officer because, as he puts it—

a Japanese medical officer was required to fight when confronted with the enemy. I had a sword and revolver and of course a bag of instruments and a stethoscope as well, and although I had cast away the bag during the tortures of the forced march, I kept my sword to the last. Of course one knew that a thing like a sword was actually quite useless in battle but it was looked to as a kind of crutch or prop for the soul of its possessor.[32]

Kaji is deeply impressed by the professional attitude of the American doctor who treats his wounds with the new wonder drug, penicillin; the rules which had hitherto regulated his behaviour no longer seem to apply in his new situation. In addition, he is half persuaded by the arguments of a nisei interpreter who endeavours to convince him of the futility of attempting to commit suicide:

"Far from being moved if you do suicide, we'll despise you. The Japanese notion that death solves all problems is sheer vainglory". . .
"Have you committed a crime that deserves death? Aren't you proud of the fact that you have fought to the utmost of your power? You're not a criminal but a victim, bound hand and foot by that outmoded morality called bushido."[33]

The interpreter finally succeeds in convincing Kaji that his own country may, after all, require his services again, and that his suicide will serve no useful purpose; and Kaji realizes that as a non-combatant officer he might after all not be compelled to set an example to others. However, he continues to be apprehensive about meeting other Japanese prisoners, particularly those with whom he had served previously.

Thus it is not surprising that Kaji's resolve to go on living is undermined when, on his way to prison camp in Australia, he encounters another Japanese prisoner, Aoyama, an enlisted man. Kaji is deeply embarrassed by the presence of the other, whose tongue appears to be badly lacerated, indicating that, like Kaji, the soldier had unsuccessfully attempted to kill himself. Kaji's feelings of overwhelming shame return; while the two Japanese do not exchange any words during the flight to Brisbane, they act spontaneously in unison when a guard leaves his pistol inadvertently unguarded for an instant. However, the pistol is not loaded, and although the attempt fails in the eyes of the other, Kaji has shown that he is still motivated by the true spirit of the Japanese fighting man.

Asada may well have dramatized the initial impact of capture, but Australian Intelligence reports tend to confirm that the majority of Japanese prisoners harboured the thought of committing suicide as soon after capture as possible. The Australian authorities were aware of this tendency and endeavoured to counteract it by issuing leaflets in Japanese to the prisoners upon their arrival at the Graythorne Transit Camp, near Brisbane. These leaflets detailed the prisoners' new status and their rights and duties, and encouraged them to regard it as their first responsibility to continue to live and to prepare to serve their country again.

Intelligence reports assessed the effects of the leaflets as quite satisfactory. The leaflets were handed out to the new arrivals, who were then left on their own to think matters over for a few days. Many of the prisoners appeared relieved and favourably impressed with the treatment they received at first contact from the Australian authorities. Yet, when joined by other prisoners, and particularly as the size of the groups increased, the effect of the leaflets tended to wear off. A measure of despondency would set in, and talk about suicide as the only alternative course of action was revived among the men.

Asada's novel may well describe the sequence of responses of the average Japanese prisoner of war to his new status: first, an overwhelming sense of shame at being captured, followed by efforts to commit suicide;[34] and then by a sense of relief that the enemy, contrary to his expectations, treats him humanely, and neither tortures nor kills him. But as the prisoners regained their strength and came in contact with other Japanese prisoners their attitude gradually changed. Instead of being grateful for being alive, they began to wonder why they had not been treated in the manner which they expected and which would have seemed appropriate in their own cultural context—cruelly, with the contempt due to individuals who had irrevocably disgraced themselves, their family and their country. Not all the prisoners, however, shared these sentiments: Asada describes the reactions of some of the other officers held at Cowra, which indicate clearly that these men had never wholeheartedly supported the precepts of the Military Field Code. "Lieutenant Kimura", for instance, who was at first the leader of the officers, "quite willingly became a P.O.W. and had his men taken prisoner along with him". He apparently persuaded his men to follow him "by assuring them that in the event of a court martial he would take full responsibility for the surrender".[35]

While some of the prisoners, then, found it possible to come to terms with their new status, others were too deeply indoctrinated with the precepts of the Military Field Code to accept a culturally alien interpretation of the status of prisoners of war "entitled to respect for their person and honour"[36] as offered by the Geneva Convention of 1929.

As the number of Japanese prisoners at Cowra increased, the tensions and strains among them became greater. That the heightened state of tension was not induced by mistreatment or victimization of the prisoners is confirmed by the reports of the delegate of the International Committee of the Red Cross in Australia, Dr Morel, who visited the camp at Cowra on four occasions before the incident of 5 August. He first reported on the conditions and treatment of the Japanese prisoners of war in July 1943, when he visited the camp at Cowra for the third time. At that time 340 Japanese enlisted men were held in B camp and thirteen Japanese officers in compound 3 of D camp. (A and C camps held Italian prisoners; there were Koreans and Formosans in compound 1 of D camp.) Dr Morel visited all four camps, "sans escortes et sans interprètes", and spoke to the prisoners without witnesses.[37] Neither the elected camp leaders nor individual prisoners voiced any complaints about their treatment or the conditions of internment. On the contrary, the leader of the Japanese officers, Captain Tsukuhara, asked Dr Morel to express their gratitude to Captain Lees, D camp commandant "pour son attitude correcte et bienveillante".[38]

Dr Morel observed that the Japanese officers, who had the right to employ batmen, had not availed themselves of this privilege; neither officers nor enlisted men had written letters or received letters or parcels. Both officers and enlisted men had asked for books and periodicals in Japanese, sports equipment, and musical instruments; furthermore, the enlisted men had inquired whether a Japanese-type bath could be installed and the copper cooking pots replaced with iron ones, which were "favourable à la bonne cuisine du riz".[39] In July 1943, then, there were no real indications of cruel treatment or victimization of prisoners.

Nor had the situation altered radically when Dr Morel visited Cowra in March 1944. There were now 439 enlisted men in B camp, 99 more than in July 1943 (the great increase to 1,104 the number in the camp at the time of the outbreak, must have taken place between the end of March and the beginning of August). There were now fourteen officers, owing to the arrival of Captain Nishio, who had replaced Captain Tsukuhara as the leader of the Japanese officers. Taking the number of disciplinary actions as an indication of the state of affairs in camp B, fifty-four reported breaches of discipline were noted by Dr Morel. Most breaches were absence from roll-call (thirty-nine cases, which were punished by twenty-one to twenty-eight days of detention), and two cases of "violence personelle".[40] One of these was punished by nine months detention, the other by twenty-eight days. All in all this report did not indicate that a great deal of unrest prevailed in B camp between July 1943 and March 1944.

The Australian Intelligence reports for the period tend to fill in some of the details of the problems that arose during that time. In April and again in September 1943, troubles arose among the inmates of B camp over the quality of food, cigarette rations, and untidy mess-kits. During the disturbances of September 1943 the Japanese prisoners retired to their huts, after voicing protests over watery soup, and refused to attend roll-calls. The following

demands were submitted by the prisoners' representative
to the commandant of B camp, Major Robert Ramsay:

> Weekly instead of daily hut inspection;
>   Cigarette rations forfeited for untidy kits should be restored;
> Walks outside the camp should be arranged;
> Paid work should be reinstituted;
>   AMF soldiers should be asked to remove their boots before
>   entering the Japanese sleeping huts;
> Japanese POW in detention should be released.[41]

Major Ramsay rejected these demands. After the prisoners
continued to refuse to obey orders "a show of strength",[42]
including a special squad armed with batons, re-established
order.

The Japanese officers were not involved in these incidents. However, the only reports concerning talk of suicide
or attempted suicide emanated from the ranks of the
officers. Lieutenant Naka, who had attempted to escape in
April 1943, threatened to commit suicide after he was
recaptured. Naka had been previously singled out by the
camp authoritives as an "obstructionist". His tendency
toward self-dramatization was reminiscent of Adachi's
behaviour during the Featherston incident; for instance, he
offered to demonstrate to the court of inquiry into his
escape how competent he was at escaping. Cigarette in his
mouth, he demonstrated how he jumped with apparent ease
over the barbed wire enclosures, arriving at the camp
perimeter in less than three minutes.[43] Another officer,
Sakeida, was detained after he refused to be photographed.
In detention he tried unsuccessfully to kill himself.[44]

These are the only cases of suicide attempts which have
been officially reported. However, cases of unsuccessful
attempts, such as those related by Clarke, which took place
in the hospital, may not have been conceived as such and
were not included in official reports. The Cowra prisoners
were not, according to Clarke's informant Tamagawa,
submitted to very strict discipline; "at one stage prisoners
were answering roll call from lying or sitting positions. 'The
Australians,' Tamagawa said, 'tolerated these capricious

habits and displayed tremendous patience—except in regard to shaving daily. On this they insisted."[45]

There were, however, opportunities to commit suicide of which the Japanese prisoners could have availed themselves if they were so inclined. For instance, new razor blades were issued to them weekly in return for the used blade, and table knives were part of each prisoners' mess-kit. But until 5 August razor blades and knives seem to have been used only for the designated purposes and not to conform with the injunctions of the Military Field Code.

Warnings of Impending Trouble

The number of prisoners continued to grow during the autumn months as the campaigns in the Pacific gained greater momentum, and it soon became apparent that the facilities at Cowra would become inadequate. In August 1944 there were 1,104 prisoners in B camp, which was intended originally to hold only 1,000. The Australian authorities were aware of the dangers inherent in this situation, for as early as 3 June 1944 a Japanese prisoner of Korean descent, Matsumoto, a new arrival at Cowra, had informed them of impending troubles. On arriving at the Cowra camp on 12 March, 1944 Matsumoto had overheard a conversation between the Japanese camp leader of B camp and some of the new arrivals:

> What the old timer said to the newcomers after they exchanged greetings, is, in a nutshell—here the POW have banded themselves together; and breaking out over the wire entanglements, intend to take the Regiment over by storm. We shall take arms and after we have taken them, have a plan to pit ourselves against them.[46]

This information was taken very seriously and forwarded to GSI, Victoria Barracks, Sydney. The garrison was subsequently reinforced with modern automatic weapons; a continual watch was maintained on the prisoners in B camp, and new alarm orders were drafted and issued to all camp commandants. However, "it was too late to square the circle of the perimeter so that garrison fire would not be as great a menace to the garrison as it would be to enemy prisoners",[47] for anyone firing across a circle of only seven hundred metres in diameter with modern automatic weapons would be as likely to hit something on the other side of the circle as to hit something within the circle. The camp authorities were fully aware of the danger and had worked out plans to minimize this particular risk.

The camp authorities had also taken note of the Featherston incident; for at an earlier period, April 1943, when the representative of the prisoners in B camp had asked for a supply of egg-shaped stones to mark out the racetrack of B camp, the camp authorities, bearing in mind the experiences at Featherston Camp, where stones had served as weapons, refused the demand. Yet "a subsequent search of the huts disclosed a large *cache* of stones".[48]

However, a request for more garden tools submitted to the camp commandant during the early summer of 1944 was complied with, for the Japanese prisoners of B camp tended their small vegetable plots with great devotion. Their state of health and spirits had shown a marked improvement. Good food, medical care, and outdoor exercises such as playing baseball, wrestling, and physical fitness training had brought about their recovery. Timms describes the behaviour of the prisoners at this stage as not "openly defiant as a whole, or rebellious or disobedient in the mass, but the wind of ill-concealed and sullen hostility was already carrying the straws of their intransigence".[49]

The camp authorities noted with concern the increasing emphasis placed on physical fitness training during the recreation periods, as well as the increased energy with which they looked after their gardens. They were not deceived by the apparent innocence of the B camp's inmates' activities. The camp commander of No. 12 Prison of War Group, Cowra, had completed arrangements with the commandant of the Recruit Training Centre, two miles away, to keep watch from retreat to reveille; the firing of red flares would indicate danger and a state of alert, which was to be acknowledged with green flares. The stage was set for a major confrontation.

The Outbreak

In accordance with the terms of the Geneva Convention in 1929, "in the event of transfer, prisoners of war shall be officially informed in advance of their new destination".[50] Thus on Friday 4 August 1944 Major Ramsay, the camp commandant of B camp, summoned the camp leader, Sergeant-Major Kanazawa, the assistant camp leader, Sergeant Kojima, and the former camp leader, Sergeant Pilot Minami, who spoke English, and informed them that the prisoners of war designated on a nominal roll then supplied to them, comprising Japanese prisoners of war below the rank of lance-corporal, would be transferred to Hay Prisoner of War Camp on Monday, 7 August 1944.[51] Minami, after examining the list of prisoners who were to be transferred, remarked: "Very bad business. Why can't we all go?"[52] Major Ramsay informed the Japanese that this matter had been decided by higher authority and could not be further discussed.

We shall now look at succeeding events from both sides of the wire. As far as the garrison personnel were concerned, "nothing unusual was noted at the parade at 16.30 hours that day",[53] but they remained, nevertheless, on alert. As Major Timms, the camp commandant of C camp, puts it: "the sentries in towers and on catwalks were watching the compound shadows with lynx-like eyes. The long white fingers of the searchlights . . . kept feeling the pulse of the dark veins between the huts."[54]

The Japanese camp leader, Kanazawa, had called an emergency meeting of hut leaders when he returned from the meeting with Major Ramsay. The hut leaders agreed unanimously "to oppose this separation [of ORs from NCOs] even at the cost of death".[55] The decision to stage an outbreak was arrived at around midnight, and it was agreed that the action would begin shortly before 2 a.m. The notion of "unanimity" in the Japanese decision-making process is discussed at a later stage, but it may be useful here to note Flight-Sergeant Yoshida's statement about the hut leaders conference: "No one liked the idea, but it was decided unanimously by the camp leaders and all others that the time to die, which had been our desire right along since the day of capture, had arrived."[56]

Thus the tension was mounting on both sides in the moonlit tranquillity of the silent camp. Suddenly a Japanese prisoner, whose name will never be known, climbed over the inner fence and raced towards the outer gate leading to Broadway. The harsh, strained voice was evidently giving a warning; the prisoner "was weeping and appeared to be in great fear" and although he was speaking in Japanese, he was heard to use some English words, "such as 'strike', 'calaboose', and 'come' ".[57] But before the guards could withdraw him from the compound, a trumpet sounded, loud yelling of "banzai" was heard, as the Japanese prisoners made a rush towards the perimeter fences.

The Japanese huts were blazing, the fire providing almost the only light, for during the first volley from the gun emplacements, "an unlucky ricochet had cut the feed line".[58] The Japanese attacked the wire fence in two places on the perimeter and in several places on Broadway. "They were carrying blankets and baseball bats, staves and improvised clubs and other weapons, dining and kitchen knives which had been specially sharpened or serrated. They wore baseball and specially prepared gloves, towels and pads of toilet paper as protection for hands, whilst escaping over the barbed wire. Blankets were thrown on the wire to facilitate escape."[59]

The Japanese then split into four parties of two hundred to three hundred, each party seemingly heading towards a different objective. One group endeavoured to overpower the crew of a Vickers gun, killing two Australian servicemen; fortunately the gun jammed and the Japanese were unable to make use of it. Over three hundred Japanese escaped through the breaks in the perimeter, while about fifty others forced their way into D camp—the Japanese officers' compound—"remaining within the huts until daybreak, when they were marched out".[60] One Japanese

Weapons found on Japanese prisoners after the breakout on 5 August 1944. (Photo: Australian War Memorial, Canberra)

Blankets and articles of clothing left on the barbed-wire fences after the riot. (Photo: Australian War Memorial, Canberra)

officer was killed, and another, Sub-Lieutenant Oikawa, was wounded during the riot, apparently when the mutineers entered the officers' compound; the officers, however, did not participate in the outbreak.

The prisoners who had escaped into Broadway divided into two parties, one turning north to storm the gates, the other south, but both groups were prevented by the fire from the watch towers from achieving their objective. Those who were not killed or wounded in these actions subsequently sought shelter in the open stormwater drains on either side of Broadway. Timms describes how a party of Japanese who had broken out of the perimeter of the camp endeavoured to attack C company, the garrison troops posted to C camp, from the rear; this tactical manoeuvre had been foreseen, "and the grim, tough men guarding this flank", stopped the assault. The deadly gun and rifle fire forced the Japanese to melt into the trees, but the Japanese had not yet given up; they "edged round on to the southern hill slopes. But the Bren reached them, cut more of them to pieces, and sent the stumbling, broken remnants out of sight in the moonlight."[61]

When daylight came, the Japanese put up a white rag and surrendered.

The Aftermath

"During the ensuing nine days 334 Japanese escapees in all were recaptured, of whom 25 were dead", by patrols of AMF personnel who scoured the surrounding countryside. Eleven of the dead had committed suicide by hanging, two others had thrown themselves in front of a passing passenger train, and a number of others had stabbed themselves to death. From the evidence it is quite likely that a number were killed by their compatriots.[62]

No civilians, either at Cowra or in the surrounding countryside, were molested in any manner, although some of the Japanese escapees reached lonely homesteads where only the wife was present at the time. "At Homewood, six miles from Cowra, three escapees came to a house occupied by Mrs Walter Weir. Mrs Weir's husband was away in his cattle paddock at the time, but the prisoners were well behaved and friendly. They sat on the side verandah to await the arrival of the Military Police while Mrs Weir served them scones and tea." There was, however, a military casualty during the search for escaped prisoners; an unarmed Australian officer, Lieutenant H. Doncaster, who led a small patrol, armed only with sidearms, was attacked by a group of prisoners and killed. From then on, patrols searching for escapees were armed and operated only in daylight.

Of the 1,104 Japanese in the camp, 234 were killed and 108 wounded; 138 prisoners, however, never left their huts and thus did not participate in the incident; 50 others broke into the compound of the Japanese officers and remained in the officers' huts until the next morning. There were other indications that the decision to stage the outbreak was not supported by all members of the prison community: On 5 August and again on 7 August, very similar notes written in English and Japanese characters were found tied to a stick in the hospital compound. All the notes were signed "Y.S." and gave warnings of impending trouble within B camp and made allegations of culpability against Matsushima.[64] Another note of a similar nature was found on Matsushima, who testified at the proceedings of the court of inquiry that he himself had written these notes "in the hope of bringing suspicion upon himself" in order to be removed from B camp as a potential troublemaker.[65] This would have prevented him from participating in the planned outbreak.

But there is a further complication in connection with Matsushima's notes which tends to cast doubt on the credibility of his explanations. On the morning of 9 August 1944, a Japanese prisoner of war was carried out, dead, from B camp by other Japanese prisoners of war. He had a rope around his neck and had died of strangulation. The body was identified as that of Sergeant-Major Yoshio Shimoyama. The name corresponds with the initials Y.S.

Some of the burnt huts after the riot. (Photo: Australian War Memorial, Canberra)

Burial of Japanese prisoners of war killed in the Cowra outbreak. (Photo: Australian War Memorial, Canberra)

mentioned in Matsushima's notes. Matsushima claimed that
he used the initials Y.S. by coincidence.[66]

Asada's account throws some light on this incident, but
does not explain it entirely. The death of Shimoyama
resembles in many details that of "Flight-Sergeant Tobé",
one of the leaders of the extremist elements in B camp
who were "keen to remove the shame of imprisonment by
carrying out an unarmed attack."[67] Anyone who spoke
against such a course of action was designated a coward
by Tobé and his followers, and while "all feared death,
[they] feared the name coward even more. They wanted
to appear patriotic, loyal soldiers before the world and they
could not have it said that they would suffer any shame
in order to preserve their lives."[68] Some of the other hut
leaders had allowed servicemen to make up their own
minds whether they intended to participate in the action
or not, although "it took a lot of courage to express such
an opinion, if it conflicted with the feeling of the majority".
'Tobé', however, "refused to acknowledge the right to such
freedom" of choice.[69]

However, while Tobé had been one of the men who most
vehemently advocated breaking out and who "had coerced
the sick and the wounded into committing suicide", he had
played a somewhat miserable role during the actual break-
out, for he was apparently too drunk or too afraid to lead
his section. The survivors of the attack felt very bitter
towards him, and openly voiced their criticism. Tobé finally
"fled to the boiler room to hang himself—a death mourned
by no one".[70]

Not only had opinions between the NCOs and men been
divided but, according to Asada, all the officers, except for
"Captain Kaji", were against the plan. Again Asada's
account is substantiated by actual events. Captain Nishio,
the medical officer (like Kaji in the novel) was elected leader
of the officers a few weeks before the incident, after the
former leader of the officers was discredited because of the
rumours of his deliberate surrender to the enemy. On 16
July, according to Australian Intelligence reports, Nishio

was detained for offensive behaviour and was still in a prison cell on the night of the outbreak. Captain Kaji, the protagonist of the novel, was only put in solitary confinement on the day before the outbreak and thus was also unable to participate in the incident.

The role of the Japanese officers in the events immediately following the outbreak appears to be somewhat ambivalent. In sharp contrast to their previous attitude of non-involvement, they now played an active role on the official and on the unofficial level. On 5 August 1944, the camp authorities received a communication signed by twelve Japanese officers stating: "In view of the fact that it is clear that we officers assisted in the incident among the Japanese NCOs and ORs at dawn on August 5, 1944, we request death by shooting of all of us officers."[71]

On the other hand, five officers, including Captain Nishio, who were held in detention addressed a clandestine note, written in Japanese characters on sanitary paper, to Sergeant-Major Kanazawa, the former leader of B camp, who had been relieved of his position and was held in the detention block. The message, which was intercepted, was intended as an instruction advising Kanazawa on the form of evidence and the explanations he was to offer to any court of inquiry.[72] They suggested that the impending transfer should be used as the pretext for the mutiny and to frame his evidence in such a manner that it would appear that the plan for a mass escape was spontaneously embarked upon and was not carried out according to a premeditated plan.

The officers further referred to a recent newspaper account of the riot at Featherston, indicating that these events may have exerted some influence on the Cowra prisoners. Advising Kanazawa not to answer questions that were to his disadvantage, they suggested that he should stress that the aim of all the participants in the outbreak had been to die by rushing the wire entanglements.

From the content of the official communication, one could deduce that the Japanese officers, realizing that reports of the incident would eventually reach Japan, endeavoured to create the impression that they shared responsibility for the outbreak with the enlisted men. However, even as far as this communication is concerned the decision to write and sign it may not have been truly unanimous. For Sub-Lieutenant Oikawa, whose signature heads the list of officers signing this declaration, testified on 14 August 1944, from his hospital bed: "I had nothing to do with the incident, but I would like to know why I was shot while sitting in the hut."[73]

Comparison of Events at Featherston Camp and at Cowra

The remaining chapters of this book are devoted to an analysis of the underlying causes for the behaviour of the Japanese prisoners at Cowra and to offering some explanations for the events outlined above. It might, however, be useful at this stage to highlight some of the most conspicuous differences between the incidents at Featherston and Cowra.

The situation at Cowra differed in several important respects from that prevailing at Featherston Camp. First, a considerably larger number of prisoners were involved —over 900 compared with only 240 who participated in the Featherston incident. Second, while the prisoners involved in events at Featherston were largely a homogeneous group, comprising naval ratings, the Cowra prisoners were drawn from the army, the navy, the air force, and the merchant marine. Third, the Japanese officers who played an important role in the Featherston incident were naval officers who may have previously commanded at least some of the ratings in battle; the fact that enlisted men and officers belonged to the same service is likely to have induced the ratings to look to the officers as their natural leaders. These men may have demanded that the officers set an example and commit suicide, thus conforming to the

Military Field Code; the officers, feeling threatened, had asked the camp authorities for protection and then suggested that one of them should be detailed to maintain discipline among the men. On the other hand, the officers might have engaged in duplicity from the outset, developing a strategy designed to persuade the camp authorities that they could be trusted. Adachi's offer to supervise the raising of fatigue parties in the enlisted men's compound could therefore have served to organize a rebellion more effectively.

The Australian authorities at Cowra were thus forewarned that Japanese officer prisoners might play a crucial role, and took great care effectively to separate the officers from the enlisted men. However, the Japanese officers at Cowra seem to have had no previous close connection on the military level with any groups of enlisted men. Unlike the Featherston officers, they had not availed themselves of the services of batmen, preferring to keep themselves to themselves and to maintain their own compound.

Fourth, the level of indoctrination with the precepts of *kokutai no hongi* and of the Military Field Code appeared to be different not only between officers and enlisted men at Cowra, but also among the NCOs and ORs in B camp. The naval ratings at Featherston, on the other hand, formed a more closely integrated group, not only because they belonged to the same service, but because of the presence in the camp of some five hundred members of the work units, whom they regarded as inferior. These prisoners had not fought with the same dedication at Guadalcanal and had freely surrendered to the enemy; at Featherston they had complied with the orders of the enemy and performed the tasks assigned to them. The different status and attitudes of the two groups is likely to have effected a higher level of unity among the naval ratings.

Fifth, the global military strategy at the time of the Featherston incident in February 1943 differed greatly from that prevailing in August 1944. Although the Japanese defeat at Guadalcanal could have been construed as foreshadowing eventual Allied victory in the Pacific theatre of operations, nevertheless in 1943 the Axis forces in Europe were still on the offensive. By 1944, however, the Axis forces were fighting with their backs to the wall in Europe, and the Japanese had suffered a crushing defeat at Saipan in July 1944. The extent to which these events may have influenced the attitudes of guards and prisoners respectively will be discussed later.

Sixth, and lastly, the conflict between the authorities and the prisoners at Featherston had focused on a particular issue—the nature of the tasks to be performed by the Japanese prisoners—which led irrevocably to the final confrontation. Neither Adachi nor the adjutant, representing the opposing factions, seems to have wished to precipitate the final tragedy. The adjutant gave Adachi four opportunities to withdraw with his honour untarnished, for even an unarmed Japanese naval officer is no match for four armed guards. Adachi, on the other hand, retired to a hut and displayed some hesitation before permitting the confrontation to escalate into violence. The dénouement only came when both men had manoeuvred themselves into positions where either would have lost face if they had made any attempt at a compromise.

No such sequence of events marked the incident at Cowra; there was no conflict over a single issue, no dramatic confrontation. The violent outbreak of 5 August 1944 appears to have resulted from more complex factors, and it is therefore unlikely that any single explanation will be found to account for the actions of the prisoners. The behaviour patterns of the Japanese prisoners of war, which ranged from non-involvement to suicide, must now be examined in the light of the traditional features of their culture and their personality structure and value orientations.

Notes

1. W.W. Mason, *Official New Zealand War History, 1939–45: Prisoners of War* (Wellington: Government Printer, 1954), p.357.
2. International Committee of the Red Cross, "Prisonniers de guerre japonais en Nelle Zélande, 1942–1945: conditions générales de captivité, incidents, évasions, mésures disciplinaires", mimeographed (Geneva, 4/1/77/GD), p.2.
3. Ibid., p.4.
4. New Zealand, Military Forces, "Proceedings of a Court of Inquiry on Mutiny at Prisoner of War Camp, Featherston, 25 February 1943", mimeographed (National Archives, Wellington, 1943), p.106.
5. Mason, *Prisoners of War*, p.357.
6. Commonwealth Archives Office, Canberra, CRS A1608, item AK/20/1/1, cable of 23 March 1943.
7. Ibid., cable of 26 February 1943, p.2.
8. Ibid.
9. Ibid., p.3.
10. Ibid.
11. Ibid.
12. Mason, *Prisoners of War*, p.358.
13. Ibid.
14. Manley O. Hudson, ed., *International Legislation*, vol.5 (Washington: Carnegie Endowment for International Peace, 1936), p.37.
15. Ibid., p.36.
16. Ibid., p.35.
17. New Zealand, Military Forces, "Court of Inquiry on Mutiny", p.20.
18. "Although copies of the Geneva Convention of 1929 in English were always available there were no translations into Japanese until after the incident" (Mason, *Prisoners of War*, p.359). Bossard reported that when he visited the camp in September 1943 the convention had been translated by the camp interpreters with the help of some of the English-speaking captives. Handwritten copies in Japanese characters had been prepared, and each camp representative had been given an exemplar. The International Committee of the Red Cross also prepared official translations of the convention into Japanese, and by January 1944 two copies of that translation were transmitted by Bossard to the New Zealand authorities, who distributed a number of photocopies of the original among the prisoners (CICR, 1977:1).
19. New Zealand, Military Forces, "Court of Inquiry on Mutiny", p.155.
20. Australia, Prime Minister's Department, Correspondence Files S C series, cable of 23 March 1943.
21. New Zealand, Military Forces, "Court of Inquiry on Mutiny", p.114.
22. Ibid., p.256.

23. L. Hetherington, "Kenneth Mackenzie: Poet Novelist" (MA thesis, University of Sydney, 1972), pp.76–77.
24. Hugh V. Clarke, with Takeo Yamashita, *To Sydney by Stealth* (Sydney: Horwitz, 1966), p.8.
25. Hugh Clarke, *Break-Out!* (Sydney: Horwitz, 1965), p.38.
26. Ibid., p.39.
27. E.V. Timms, "The Blood Bath at Cowra", in *As You Were!: A Cavalcade of Events with the Australian Services from 1788 to 1946* (Canberra: Australian War Memorial, 1946), p.176.
28. Commonwealth Archives Office, Canberra, AA1973/254, p.121.
29. Timms, "Blood Bath at Cowra", p.176.
30. Clarke, *Break-Out!*, p.42.
31. Teruhiko Asada, *The Night of a Thousand Suicides* (Sydney: Angus and Robertson, 1970), p.2.
32. Ibid., p.24.
33. Ibid., p.17.
34. Tamagawa, one of Hugh Clarke's Japanese informants, arrived in Cowra with a rifle bullet still embedded in his stomach and asked only to be left to die. He was placed in hospital and operated on four times; he had to be tied to his bed by his hands and feet to prevent him from harming himself. He tried repeatedly to kill himself (Clarke, *Break-Out!*, pp.48–49).
35. Asada, *Night of a Thousand Suicides*, p.62.
36. Hudson, *International Legislation*, pp.26–27.
37. Commonwealth Archives Office, Canberra, CRS A989, item 43/925/1/30, pt. 2, p.1.
38. Ibid., p.2.
39. Ibid., p.18.
40. Commonwealth Archives Office, Canberra, CRS A989, item 44/925/1/140, p.15.
41. Australian War Memorial, Canberra, CRS A2663, item 780/10/3, 18 April 1943.
42. Ibid., 12 September 1943.
43. Ibid., 13 June 1943.
44. Ibid., 18 April 1943.
45. Clarke, *Break-Out!*, p.46.
46. Commonwealth Archives Office, Canberra, AA1973/254, exhibit F.
47. Timms, "Blood Bath at Cowra", p.176.
48. Australian War Memorial, Canberra, CRS A2663, item 780/10/3, 18 April 1943.
49. Timms, "Blood Bath at Cowra", p.177.
50. Hudson, *International Legislation*, pp.34–35.
51. Commonwealth Archives Office, Canberra, AA1973/254, p.6.
52. Ibid.
53. Ibid.
54. Timms, "Blood Bath at Cowra", p.178.

55. Australian War Memorial, Canberra, CRS A2663, item 780/3/2.
56. Ibid.
57. Commonwealth Archives Office, Canberra, AA1973/254, p.6.
58. Timms, "Blood Bath at Cowra", p.179.
59. Commonwealth Archives Office, Canberra, AA1973/254, p.6.
60. Ibid., p.7.
61. Timms, "Blood Bath at Cowra", p.180.
62. Commonwealth Archives Office, Canberra, AA1973/254, p.8.
63. Clarke, *Break-Out!*, p.80.
64. Commonwealth Archives Office, Canberra, AA1973/254, p.8.
65. Ibid.
66. Ibid.
67. Asada, *Night of a Thousand Suicides*, p.87.
68. Ibid., p.88.
69. Ibid., p.92.
70. Ibid., p.104.
71. Commonwealth Archives Office, Canberra, AA1973/254, exhibit BB.
72. Ibid., p.9.
73. Ibid., p.129.

3
Cultural Continuity in a Changing Society

To gain a proper understanding of the action of Japanese prisoners of war, it is important to consider the ethos underlying their behaviour patterns—*bushido* and *kokutai no hongi*. While both can be regarded as essentially codes of secular morality, their sources are deeply embedded in the Japanese belief system. Ruth Benedict suggests that *bushido* is a term which has been popularized in the twentieth century to "designate traditional Japanese ideals of conduct",[1] but in fact the term *bushido* was already used in the tenth century to subsume the moral principles regulating the behaviour of the samurai class. It is a concept which has envolved over time from *ethereal bushido*—akin to the medieval European notion of chivalry—to *traditional bushido* during the feudal age, and then to the modern form of bushido, which I shall refer to as *militant bushido*.

Kokutai no hongi evolved in the nineteenth century and became "the most potent concept in modern Japanese nationalism",[2] synthesizing elements of Shinto mythology, Confucian ethics, and the martial spirit propagated by *bushido*. *Kokutai* reached its apogee in the twentieth century with the publication in 1937 of *Kokutai no Hongi* (Fundamentals of Our National Polity), which set the ideological course for the Japanese people. This short work, of which two million copies were sold, was used as the basic text of study in schools and military training establishments, with the purpose of creating a culturally homogeneous population which would conform to the precepts enunciated by *kokutai no hongi*.

Japanese Historical and Cultural Developments

Like many insular people, the Japanese tend to regard themselves as unique, a race apart, claiming lineal descent from the gods, not only for the imperial dynasty, but also for the Japanese people as a whole. The origin myth and other early Japanese legends are contained in two great narrative chronicles, the *Kojiki* and *Nihongi*, which were compiled in the eighth century, a period when Japanese writers were strongly influenced by Chinese cultural traditions. Although many of the myths and legends recounted are anachronistic and often selected by the compilers with a view of confirming the political and religious claims of the ruling dynasty, they incorporated many significant elements of Japanese culture.

The Origin Myth

At the beginning was nothingness. Then a number of gods were born on the Plains of Heaven; they did little but exist until the advent of a divine male and female pair called Izanagi and Izanami. "Izanagi dipped a heavenly jeweled spear into the deeps and the drops that fell from it as he withdrew it formed the islands of Japan".[3] Izanagi and Izanami later brought forth the Sun Goddess, Amaterasu, who was appointed by her father to rule over the Plain of Heaven, and Susano-o, the unruly Storm God, who was granted domain over the Sea Plains. Susano-o is cast in a role which has a great significance for anyone endeavouring to understand the Japanese personality structure: he is represented as the veritable *enfant terrible* among the pantheon of gods, and the ancient chronicles recount many of his misdemeanours and impetuous acts with great relish and, one suspects, a certain amount of admiration for his unorthodox behaviour.

From the very beginning, Susano-o manifested his dissatisfaction with the distribution of domains made by his father, Izanagi. He disregarded the latter's commands and committed a number of acts which were offensive to his sister, Amaterasu, and challenged her authority. His powerful breath broke the fences between her carefully laid-out rice fields, and he chewed up his sister's precious ornaments. However, when he produced the "imperial offspring" from his mouth, Amaterasu claimed the offspring as her own, on the grounds that he was created out of her own personal possessions. Thus the Japanese origin myth tends to reverse the male and the female contribution to the process of reproduction, adding yet another dimension to the fundamental question which according to the French anthropologist Claude Lévi-Strauss has exercised the curiosity and imagination of people of all ages: How can *one* be born from two? How is that we have not only one procreator, but a mother and a father?

The Storm God's antics finally exhausted Amaterasu's patience: the last straw was when he threw a piebald horse into the window of the house where his sister was supervising her weaving women, who were engaged in fashioning garments for the deities. This strange and unexpected act terrified the women, "and caused them to prick themselves in a shocking manner".[4] The Sun Goddess retaliated by retreating to her cave, slamming the door and thus plunging the world into darkness.

The remaining gods banded together and, by appealing to Amaterasu's vanity—a mirror and five hundred curved jewels, which later became parts of the imperial regalia, were used to entice the Sun Goddess from her hiding place —succeeded in restoring the previous state of affairs. Susano-o, however, as punishment for the cavalier treatment he had accorded his sister, was expelled from the heavens. After many adventures he settled in Izumo, in Western Japan, where he married Princess Inada, the daughter of two earthly deities. The offspring of the pair are regarded as the first inhabitants of Japanese stock to dwell on Nippon.

Thus divine lineal descent is claimed not only for the imperial dynasty, which regards Amaterasu, the Sun

Goddess, as its ancestress, but also for all the Japanese people. The descendant of Amaterasu is, however, a god in his own right, and the individual merit, or *karma*, of a reigning Japanese monarch cannot be exhausted. Unlike the god-kings of South-East Asia, such as members of the Cambodian royal dynasty, whose *karma* acquired in previous lives is the essential factor which makes a man a king but which also when it is exhausted contributes to his downfall and replacement by a rival who has acquired sufficient merit, the Japanese imperial family holds its lofty position in perpetuity. Thus Shinto mythology laid the basis for the claim that the Japanese imperial dynasty was indeed unique and superior to all other dynasties, for the reigning emperor is at all times the only legitimate ruler and can never be removed from his exalted position or forfeit it under any circumstances.

In keeping with the origin myth, the emperor is also regarded as the "head of the 'national family'"[5] for all Japanese are related to him by blood; in other words Susano-o is regarded as the procreator of both the imperial dynasty and the Japanese people. This may explain, to some extent, why such wholehearted credence was given during World War II to slogans like "the Emperor and the People are One".[6]

The notion of the uniqueness and superiority not only of the imperial dynasty but also of the Japanese people therefore is deeply embedded in Shinto mythology. While Shinto beliefs incorporate many features of Chinese cosmology, such as the explanation offered for the distribution of the heavenly domain between the Sun Goddess and the Storm God in accordance with yin and yang principles,[7] it comprises cults of diverse origins. Shamanism, fertility cults, and the worship of ancestors, but above all the worship of nature and in particular of some typically Japanese topographical features such as Mount Fuji, give Shinto a peculiarly Japanese flavour.

Buddhism was introduced to Japan in the seventh century A.D. and gradually became the religion of the imperial court and nobility, although Shinto continued to remain the belief system of the common people. Even the court, however, accorded recognition to the Shinto gods, who were associated with "natural phenomena—rain, drought, earthquakes, etc.".[8] By the early tenth century, "more than 6,000 Shinto shrines were enumerated where annual offerings were to be made by the court or the provincial governments".[9]

Buddhist ceremonies and Shinto ritual fused over time; incantations, ritual fire ceremonies, charms, and methods of instruction were adopted from Buddhism. These alien features became so much a part of Shinto that "even purists later considered them to be part of the religion in its pristine form".[10] However, before Shinto became the true national faith of Japan during the late Tokugawa period, it absorbed in addition some of the philosophical concepts of Confucianism as well as elements of Neo-Confucianism and Zen Buddhism. During the seventeenth century, the Neo-Confucian emphasis on the study of history as revealing constant laws of human behaviour and political morality encouraged a new interest in the study of native religious traditions and Shinto mythology. The ensuing revival of Shinto beliefs focused attention on the legitimacy of imperial rule and the unbroken succession of the reigning dynasty, rekindling loyalty to the throne and preparing the way for the imperial restoration in the nineteenth century.

Early Cultural Influences

Japan's geographical position as an island separated by a large body of water from its nearest neighbours on the Asiatic mainland has greatly influenced her history and cultural development. While her population as well as her culture emanated largely from the Asiatic mainland, she was at no time subject to an uninterrupted stream of cultural influences. Her contacts with the outside world were irregular and spasmodic, periods of intensive cultural interaction alternating with periods of almost complete isolation.

Nor were the main streams of cultural innovations which came from India and China by way of Korea forced upon the Japanese by invasion and conquest. The Mongols, Asiatic hordes who had occupied a large part of China and Korea, came nearest to invading Japan in the thirteenth century. They were, however, repulsed by the Japanese people, who for a brief time forgot their internal dissensions and united to drive out the common enemy. It is believed that this was achieved with the assistance of supernatural forces, for according to legend a divine wind—the *kamikaze*—arose and drove the Mongol fleet back to the mainland.

Thus for some centuries Japan enjoyed periods of relatively undisturbed cultural development. The imperial dynasty first governed the country from Nara, subsequently moving in the eighth century to Kyoto. The emperors were absolute monarchs, regarding people and land as their private property, and had the power of life and death over their subjects. The great aristocratic families of the country served the imperial dynasty loyally and supported its efforts to maintain a balance of power at the court.

Over time, however, members of the Fujiwara family began to occupy the most important positions as advisors of the emperors, and on many occasions provided consorts for the reigning emperors. The rise of the Fujiwara family to pre-eminence at court was fiercely opposed by the Taira, Tachibana, and Minamoto families; but after 986 A.D. the Fujiwaras won a decisive victory over the rest of the court nobility. From then on, for the next hundred years, their power remained virtually unchallenged, and few court appointments to high office could be made without their approval. The Fujiwaras did not usurp the imperial prerogatives; on the contrary, they reigned in the name of the emperors, who retained their position as political and spiritual leaders of the country.

The court nobility's rise to power was accompanied by the growth of proprietary domain. The lands which had been assigned to the nobles as rewards for officially supporting the dynasty eventually became their possession in perpetuity. Court families benefited greatly from the ample flow of goods and services from their landed properties and, freed from financial preoccupations, devoted their energies to the creation of an aristocratic culture which epitomized for the Japanese people the ideal of courtly life and moral values.

The Heian Period (794–1191)

During the Heian period, Chinese cultural influences were largely assimilated and a typically Japanese culture began to evolve. The culture developed by the court nobility was creative, highly individualistic, and largely unrepressed. A distinctive style of architecture came to the fore, and painting and literature flourished. The introduction of *kana*, a native phonetic syllabary, greatly simplified the writing of the Japanese language, which had until then been very cumbersome owing to the use of unmodified Chinese characters.

While the men of the court nobility remained deeply involved in the grave study of the Confucian classics and tended to "look down upon poetry and romances" composed in the native language,[11] the court ladies used the new medium to give free play to their emotions and instincts. Lady Murasaki (975–1031), in her *Tale of Genji* and Sei Shonagon in *The Pillow Book* expressed their thoughts and feelings in a free flowing, uninhibited style, providing us with a detailed description of court society.

The court nobility was preoccupied with cultivating *miyabi*, the quiet pleasures of refinement and sophistication. Aristocratic tastes became attuned to the beauty of nature: to enjoy the falling of cherry blossoms, the reddening of the autumn leaves, the elusive perfume of a rare wood or the delicate blending of colours in their kimonos. In love as in art a hierarchy of values prevailed, which permeated every facet of social life at court. While court society could be regarded as a small enclave of refinement and sophistication, in a country "otherwise marked by ignorance and uncourtliness"[12] these specifically aristocratic standards of behaviour and values were transmitted over time to the provincial nobility, from among whom the warrior class—the samurai—evolved.

During the eleventh and twelfth centuries the court nobles had to resort increasingly to the services of the provincial warriors to defend their interests against the power of the great Buddhist monasteries, or to assist them in disputes, which frequently arose among court factions. The moral values of the court nobility, such as devotion to women, pursuit of aesthetic beauty, protection of the weaker and poorer, a sense of *noblesse oblige*, which emphasized veracity and sincerity, as well as scrupulous adherence to the principles of justice—the essence of ethereal bushido—were gradually amalgamated with the martial values of the warrior class. With the advent of the provincial aristocracy in court circles, devotion to the arts of war, a readiness for self-sacrifice and intense loyalty to the feudal master, and the notion of Spartan indifference to suffering and death became an intrinsic part of the code of ethereal bushido.

The Civil Wars (1192–1571)

Gradually the warrior class took over the effective exercise of power from the court nobility. The Taira and Minamoto families were locked in bloody struggles during the second half of the twelfth century; finally the Minamoto family gained supremacy and Yoritomo Minamoto, styling himself *shogun* in 1192, took over the military control of the country. He made peace with the powerful Buddhist monks and restored to the court nobility the lands they had lost during the years of strife; but he refrained from seizing the imperial throne and permitted the emperor and the Fujiwara family to continue "their sham civil government"[13] from Kyoto.

Yoritomo set up his own military administration, the *Bakufu*, in Kamakura, not far from the present capital, Tokyo. Thus, there were actually two administrative centres, each with their own organization of officials, and each in their own capital, operating side by side. This dual form of government established by Yoritomo lasted for a period of more than six and a half centuries until the middle of the nineteenth century. But Yoritomo's descendants were unable to retain control of the military administration, and during the thirteenth and fourteenth centuries civil wars raged through the country while such great military families as the Hojo and the Ashikaga strove for power.

It was during this period that Japan was seriously threatened by a foreign invasion. The Mongols were, however, turned back in 1274. For a brief period the peril to the nation created a sense of national unity, but shortly afterwards civil strife broke out again. Private feuds added to the disorder, and all centralized authority seemed doomed to ineffectiveness. Meanwhile the power of individual families grew; away from the capitals, and with the support of their loyal samurai, the feudal lords set up increasingly independent domains.

During this period of civil wars, both the effective power and the economic position of the imperial family were further eroded as the feudal lords, the *daimyō*, gradually absorbed into their domains many of the estates from which the imperial family had derived its revenue. One emperor is said to have been "reduced to selling his calligraphy on the streets" of Kyoto to eke out a precarious existence.[14]

The incessant changes which marked this period of virtual anarchy from the twelfth to the sixteenth century did not, however, stultify the development of Japanese economic, social, and religious life; only in the political sphere did "the powerful centrifugal tendencies of feudal society"[15] prevent an orderly pattern of development. In these times of national chaos, low ranking men of merit and ability had had a better chance of winning recognition and power than in peaceful times, when noble birth was a precondition for high office. It is thus significant that the three vigorous leaders who successively arose to unify Japan and mould her into a highly centralized state came from the lower ranks of the warrior class and even the peasantry.

The Tokugawa Period (1571–1867)

During the sixteenth and seventeenth centuries, Nobunaga (1534–1582), Hideyoshi (1536–1598), and Ieyasu Tokugawa (1542–1616) successively became leaders of their nation. Ieyasu, who is characterized as "less impetuous than Nobunaga, less colorful and dramatic than Hideyoshi"[16] surpassed them both in foresight and political acumen. Having risen from the lower ranks of the gentry while serving in Nobunaga's armies, Ieyasu was able to climax his military victories by the achievement of a lasting peace. His family, the Tokugawa, subsequently retained unbroken control of the shogunate until 1867, providing the longest period of peace and relative prosperity that Japan had known in recorded history.

Like earlier shoguns, the Tokugawa left the "age-old fiction of imperial rule undisturbed".[17] While keeping the imperial family and the court nobles under strict surveillance and control, they re-established the economic viability of the court by generous financial treatment. The emperor's position as the symbolic representative of the nation had remained unassailable, even during the prolonged period of domestic strife. It has been suggested that the Emperor's role during this period could be equated with that of a Roman pope, who conferred honour upon the Bakufu and the feudal lords and was himself the centre of the traditional faith. The Tokugawa strategy of increasing the emperor's sanctity, by re-emphasizing the imperial dynasty's divine origin, barred the emperors effectively from concerning themselves with the material problems of Japan and the everyday duties of ruling the country.

The Tokugawa created a powerful, centralized administration in Yedo—later Tokyo—where they built an elaborate castle. To ensure the stability of the social order they created a rigorous hierarchy of four social classes. The top class consisted of warrior-administrators, a hereditary aristocracy, the samurai; the badges of honour of the samurai class were their long and short curved swords. They also wore distinctive clothing, the *hakama*, or skirt which formed the lower portion of the official dress of the samurai, and a distinctive hairstyle, the *chomage* or topknot.

The other three classes were peasants, artisans, and merchants. The peasants, who during the protracted civil wars had been armed, were deprived of their weapons under the rule of Hideyoshi, who although himself from peasant stock, made fighting the exclusive prerogative of the hereditary samurai class. In addition, the Tokugawa introduced prohibitions with regard to changes of status, residence, and allegiance to the feudal lords, leaving it to the latter to regulate the activities and movements of the people in their domain, thereby creating a rigid and oppressive social system which endured until the mid-nineteenth century.

While the feudal lords, the *daimyō*, were allowed virtual autonomy over their domains, the Tokugawas worked out a careful system of controls to prevent any of them from becoming a military threat to their administration. Each *daimyō* for example, was required to maintain a residence in Yedo, where he had to spend six months of every year. When he returned to his estates, his wife and other members of his family had to remain behind, as "hostages", thus ensuring his loyalty. The upkeep of a permanent residence in Yedo, as well as the costly journeys from his estates to the administrative centre, caused a considerable drain on the feudal lord's resources, which further undermined his power to engage in conspiracies or warfare.

Another Tokugawa innovation was the creation of cadres of officials, the *metsuke*, who acted as censors "ferreting out cases of maladministration" on the part of administrators appointed by the government. The *metsuke* also functioned as a secret police force, "spying on all men or groups who could be a menace to Tokugawa rule."[18] Thus, the Tokugawas have the dubious distinction of developing as early as the sixteenth century an extensive and effective secret police system and making it an important organ of state.

The early Tokugawa rulers took drastic measures to

ensure the stability of the social order and the continuity
of their regime. While freedom of action and movement
as well as a measure of social mobility had characterized
both the Heian period and the time of civil strife, the
initiative of the individual Japanese was severely restricted
during the Tokugawa period. The Tokugawa government
practically stifled normal social and economic development,
and deliberately isolated the Japanese people from the rest
of the world. In 1637 the Bakufu decreed that no Japanese
subject should leave the country, or having left it, should
be allowed to return. Death was the penalty for any attempt
to disobey these rules, and to ensure the full enforcement
of the law, the building of ships large enough to make
voyages overseas was forbidden.

The traditional form of bushido evolved during the
Tokugawa period. In times of peace and internal stability
the high value placed on such virtues as martial excellence,
courage in battle, and indifference to danger and death
tended to decline. The warrior classes had made a veritable
cult of their swordsmanship, glorying in a life of constant
warfare, a behaviour which was no longer encouraged. The
purely military role of the samurai class was further
challenged by the new emphasis on the acquisition of
knowledge. Hayashi Razan (1583–1657), the great Confucian scholar of the early Tokugawa period, encouraged the
warrior class to provide not only martial but also moral and
intellectual leadership. He suggested that it was no longer
sufficient for the "ideal type" samurai to perfect himself
in the art of warfare and neglect his education and the
cultivation of his intellect. This trend was further encouraged by the Tokugawa regime, which needed a large
number of educated bureaucrats to administer Japan in an
orderly fashion during the years of peace.

Yamaga Soko (1622–85), one of Hayashi Razan's brilliant
students, reinterpreted his teacher's Confucian concepts,
adapting them more closely to Japanese requirements. In
his study *The Way of the Samurai* he outlined the lofty
mission of the warrior class, as he conceived it. Yamaga

emphasized the samurai's obligation to set a high example of devotion to duty, and to "serve his lord with the utmost loyalty and in general to put devotion to moral principle (righteousness) ahead of personal gain".[19] He provided not only the first systematic exposition of the warrior code but also a philosophical basis for the behaviour patterns and values of Japanese feudal society.

Hayashi's and Yamaga's writings contributed significantly to the transformation of the warrior class from a purely military aristocracy to one of increasing political and intellectual importance, which finally, in the nineteenth century, provided the leaders who initiated the reform of the feudal government. They played an important part in the subsequent modernization of Japan. Yamaga also revived the study of Japanese native traditions, focusing on the uniqueness of the divinely created imperial dynasty. In *The True Facts concerning the Central Kingdom* he set out to prove that his own country, rather than China, was the centre and zenith of all culture. He based his claim on the fact that Japan was divinely created and ruled over by an imperial line coeval with heaven and earth. The truths of Confucius had been revealed to the divine ancestors of the imperial line, and only the Japanese had been true to the highest concepts of loyalty and duty of their dynasty. Only Japan had enjoyed unbroken rule by its dynasty, while in China, dynasties had come and gone and Confucian teaching itself had been corrupted beyond recognition.

Yamaga did not clamour for any change in the status of the emperor, having no intention of undermining the authority of the shogunate; instead he contended that the recognition by Japan's successive military rulers of the imperial sovereignty had ensured the continuity of the imperial dynasty. However, as opposition to the arbitrary exercise of power by successive shoguns grew in later centuries, Yamaga's devotion to the imperial house gained increasing political significance, particularly among those sections of the population who sought to put the ethos of bushido at the service of the emperor rather than at the exclusive disposal of the feudal lord.

Yamaga's writing also exerted great influence on one of the most dramatic episodes in the history of Japan, which occurred in the early eighteenth century. The leader of the Forty-Seven Ronin, whose exploits greatly affected the emotional climate of Japan for the next two centuries, was Oishi, one of Yamaga's students, whose conduct exemplified the ideals of bushido. The gist of the story of the *Forty-Seven Ronin*, which continues to be enacted in contemporary Japan not only on the *kabuki* stage and in puppet theatres but also in the cinema and on television, may be summarized as follows: a *daimyō*, Asano, was involved in a sword fight with another feudal lord, Kira, who had insulted him. The fight took place in the shogun's castle. Asano, who had succeeded in wounding Kira, is condemned by the shogun to commit *seppuku*—ceremonial suicide— for baring a weapon in the shogun's palace and breaking the peace imposed by the Tokugawa government, considered very grave offences.

Asano obeys the shogun's command and commits *seppuku*. Forty-seven of his principal retainers, who are now *ronin*—masterless warriors—pledge themselves to avenge their master. Under the leadership of Oishi, they leave their homes and families and stoically suffer humiliation and deprivation. After two years of patient watching and waiting, the ronin triumph over hardship and misfortune; they force their way into Kira's mansion on a snowy February morning in 1703 and kill their master's enemy. Having presented Kira's head ceremonially at Asano's tomb, the ronin give themselves up to the authorities.

Although the ronin had behaved in accordance with the code of bushido and in terms of Confucian ethics, which prescribe that no man should allow the unjust death of a father or immediate superior to remain unavenged, Oishi and his followers broke the rules imposed by the Tokugawa government. They therefore had to be punished, although the entire Japanese population tended to regard them as heroes. The shogun, after long deliberation, decided that only a sentence imposing honourable suicide would meet both the requirements of feudal law and the tenets of the warrior code of ethics.

The Forty-Seven Ronin accordingly committed *seppuku*, and to this day their tombs, adjacent to Asano's, are places of pilgrimage for thousands of Japanese; their memory is still venerated, for their self-sacrificing loyalty and single-minded efforts to avenge their master became the model for the appropriate conduct of members of the samurai class. It seems paradoxical, however, that this episode should have occurred during the prolonged period of peace when the standards of martial excellence of the samurai class had begun to diminish. Clearly a conflict existed between the emotional commitment of the warrior class and the system of ethics propagated by Hayashi and Yamaga, who had attempted to adapt the traditional feudal values to the needs of a stable and peaceful society.

During the prolonged period of peace—interrupted only by the dramatic episode of the Forty-Seven Ronin—on the one hand the standards of loyalty and martial excellence declined among the samurai, while on the other hand the change from a rice economy to a money economy greatly undermined their financial position. In the early Tokugawa period, rice had become "the principal means of exchange";[20] the samurai class, in particular, had been paid their stipend in rice by their feudal lords. However, during the long years of peace, internal commerce began to flourish; trading centres such as Osaka, Nagasaki, and Sakai grew and prospered, and the affluence of the merchants and artisans in the towns increased. Rice proved too cumbersome a means of exchange and was gradually replaced with silver and copper coins. As the seventeenth century progressed, members of the warrior class increasingly traded their rice for cash with the town merchants, from whom they bought manufactured goods.

However, the price of rice was subject to fluctuation, and soon many samurai were deeply in debt to the merchants,

who had grown in number as well as in wealth. The
government, greatly concerned with upholding a static
hierarchic society, tried from time to time to curb the
growing affluence of the city merchants by outright
confiscation of their property or by the "cancellation of
samurai debts".[21] While the samurai continued to look
down on the merchant class as socially inferior, even when
heavily in debt to them, the merchants gradually began to
acquire some of the social privileges which usually accompany economic power. Many merchants and artisans endeavoured to achieve samurai rank by marrying their
daughters into samurai families or by arranging for their
sons' adoption into impoverished samurai families, not
unlike the social climbing described in Molière's *Le
Bourgeois Gentilhomme*. Outright purchase of rank became quite usual, and G.B. Sansom suggests that by about
1850, if not before, there was a regular tariff for the entry
of a commoner into a samurai family.[22]

The life of the peasant, which had been wretched enough
in earlier periods, was now rendered almost unbearable by
fluctuating prices of rice and by the rising standard of living
among all classes but his own.[23] Now there was hardly any
surplus left after paying the feudal landlord's taxes, which
had to be in money instead of in rice; many fell into debt
and migrated to the towns in search of other employment.
The decline of the rural population caused great concern
to the Tokugawa regime, which decreed that all peasants
must return to their native villages. Such decrees, repeated
at intervals until 1843, did not, however, prevent men from
deserting their farms, since hardly any punishment could
be worse than the life they were forced to lead in the rural
environment.

During the late Tokugawa period, therefore, a certain
blurring of the hierarchical class distinctions occurred;
many of the farmers had become artisans or small shopkeepers; merchants and artisans acquired wealth and prestige. Some of the commoners had achieved samurai rank
while the samurai class lost some of the economic advan-

tages of its privileged position. The attempts of the Bakufu
to stabilize the social order, however, proved unsuccessful:
peasant uprisings became more frequent after 1714, when
ineffective measures to stabilize the price of rice for the
benefit of the *daimyō* and the samurai brought the rest of
the population to the verge of starvation and resulted in
food riots. Although it issued oppressive edicts, the Bakufu
failed to guide the tradespeople into frugal paths,[25] for the
habit of living comfortably was by then too well ingrained
among the town merchants to be checked. When external
display was forbidden and richly dressed merchants were
arrested, the townspeople proceeded to spend their money
on less obvious but even more costly splendours.[26]

By the middle of the nineteenth century the power of
the Tokugawa regime was rapidly declining. The chaotic
economic situation, the revived theory of imperial rule, and
the intervention of external forces combined to bring about
the downfall of the feudal order. Official encouragement
of the study of history and native religious traditions by
the Tokugawa government contributed to the emergence
of scholars who began to question the legitimacy of indirect
rule by shogun. The political influence of the Mito school
—founded in the seventeenth century by the Tokugawa
regime with the purpose of compiling an official history
of Japan—increased in the eighteenth and nineteenth
centuries. Dedicated to the restoration of the emperor and
the expulsion of all foreigners, their simple and forceful
doctrines were dramatized in such slogans as "Revere the
Emperor, Repel the Barbarians", and "Loyalty to sovereign
and loyalty to parents are one in essence".[27] These were
widely disseminated and had a strong appeal to the nation.

In the atmosphere of impending crisis that pervaded
Japan in the mid-nineteenth century, such slogans were to
prove "remarkably effective in rallying nationalistic sentiments around a single center, the imperial house".[28] The
clarion call for action was taken up by Yoshida Shoin
(1830–1859), who claimed that only the divine descendant
of the Sun Goddess, Amaterasu, could unite the nation and

deal effectively with the Western "barbarian". Yoshida Shoin represents an important link between the old order and the new. He inherited from his father, who was the principal of a military academy, a deep devotion to the precepts of Yamaga Soko, whose concept of bushido was extolled in the family's school.

Even more decisive, perhaps, was the influence on Yoshida of Mencius, whose strong idealism and assertion of the intrinsic worth of the individual instilled in him "a lively sense of his own mission in the world and an impatience with all external restraints".[29] He proclaimed that it was Japan's divine mission to turn back the challenge of the West and to found a world empire. Yoshida may be regarded as one of the first modern Japanese revolutionaries, advocating the restoration of the imperial dynasty and the overthrow of the feudal aristocracy together with the raising of the status of the common man and the revival of the ethos of traditional bushido.

But the primary concern of Yoshida and his followers was not to overthrow the social order but rather to revitalize the national leadership and to dramatize, by some spectacular act of bravery, the need for selfless loyalty and devotion to the emperor and the nation. Accordingly, he conceived of a plan to assassinate the emissary of the shogun, whose mission was to secure the emperor's approval for a treaty with the United States. The plot was, however, discovered, and Yoshida imprisoned. He was beheaded in 1859, at the age of thirty, and subsequently became a hero to a whole generation. The "Big Three" of the Meiji era, Kido Koin and Ito Hirobumi (the framers of the Constitution) and Yamagata Aritomo (the founder of the modern Japanese army), were some of Yoshida's disciples. Inspired by his example, they devoted themselves to the restoration of imperial rule and the modernization of Japan.

The threat of outside intervention, however, can be regarded as the immediate reason for the overthrow of the Tokugawa regime. The United States, England, and Russia (as well as other European nations) had sent numerous expeditions in the eighteenth and nineteenth centuries to persuade Japan to open her door to traders. In 1853–54 America sent a considerable force under Commodore Perry, who demanded—and eventually achieved—the inauguration of trade and diplomatic relations. The Tokugawa regime in Edo was confused when confronted by the armed might of Perry and did not know how to cope with the situation. Then, for the first time in over six hundred years of military rule, the emperor was consulted.

Emperor Komei and the court nobility in Kyoto favoured confrontation with the foreigners. Their slogan became "Repel the Barbarians". However, faced with the reality of well-armed warships, the Edo government was incapable of implementing this policy and decided to open up the country in order to avoid bloodshed and humiliation. Thereafter the forces arrayed against the government proved too powerful. The movement calling for the restoration of imperial rule became a groundswell which forced Keiki, the last Tokugawa shogun, to resign. In 1867 he voluntarily surrendered his powers to Emperor Komei.

The Meiji Era (1868–1912)

Emperor Meiji acceded to the throne in 1868, after the death of his father. Modest and reserved, but very conscientious about attending to matters of state, he relied heavily upon his advisers, the youthful and progressive leaders of the Western Clans (the Satsuma, Choshu, Tosa, and Hizen, who had long been the most influential rivals of the Tokugawa regime). One of his first acts was to move the court from Kyoto, where the imperial dynasty had resided for over a thousand years, to Edo, which was renamed Tokyo. By moving into the Tokugawa castle and designating it as the Imperial Palace, Emperor Meiji indicated that the period of dual rule initiated by Minamoto Yoritomo in the twelfth century had come to an end. The new constitution was promulgated in 1868, and was further amended in 1889. Kido and Ito realized that feudalism had to be abolished if the emperor was to fully and effectively assume the powers formerly held by the shogun. Kido, a Choshu samurai and an extremely able negotiator, persuaded the *daimyō* voluntarily to surrender their domains to the emperor as a patriotic gesture. The country was then subdivided into new political divisions (*ken*), and governors were appointed by the centralized government to administer them. The Meiji regime also abolished the hierarchical class system established by the Tokugawas, stripping the samurai of their social, economic, and political privileges. In order to ensure the co-operation of the former *daimyō* and samurai with the new imperial regime, however, generous financial compensation in the form of government bonds was arranged.

The introduction of universal military conscription in 1872 deprived the samurai of their former "martial uniqueness"—until then they had been the only social class permitted to engage in military pursuits. By that time, however, members of the former samurai class were serving with the new government, where, owing to their superior education, they rose gradually to high positions within the Meiji bureaucracy. Others used the financial settlements provided by the government to engage successfully in business and trade, while others again were attracted to the ranks of officer corps of the newly established peasant army and navy.

But not all former samurai had been able to adapt themselves to the Meiji new order; the grievances of many were aggravated by an imperial edict forbidding anyone other than policemen or members of the regular armed forces to carry swords, which had been the badge of honour of the samurai. Their dissatisfaction manifested itself in several revolts, the most serious of which was led in 1887 by Saigo, who as a member of the Satsuma clan had been one of the staunchest supporters of the restoration of imperial rule. Disturbed by the treatment accorded the old warrior class and convinced that the process of rapid modernization would undermine traditional Japanese values, Saigo conceived it his duty "to try, by whatever means he had, to rescue his sovereign and the divine mission of Japan".[30]

The notion of saving the emperor from his "selfish and corrupt" advisors is a recurring theme in Japanese rebellions. The abortive mutinies by junior officers of the armed forces in March 1931, May 1932, and February 1936, as well as the unsuccessful *coup d'état* staged by the "young tigers" of the Eastern Army's general headquarters staff on the eve of the emperor's surrender broadcast on 14 August 1945, were not directed against the emperor but against the "traitors around the throne" who had misled him.[31]

During the nineteenth century the notion of loyalty and devoted service to the feudal lord was replaced by an equally intense loyalty to the imperial dynasty and the emperor. As the samurai had ceased to function as a social class exclusively devoted to military or administrative duties, their value patterns had begun to permeate other sectors of the population with which they were closely associated in their new occupations: the professions, business, and industry. The high value, however, which had been accorded to obligations to the feudal lord, was now accorded to service to the emperor and the nation.

Under the reign of the emperor Meiji, who had declared in the Charter Oath of 1868 that "knowledge shall be sought throughout the world so as to strengthen the foundations of imperial rule",[32] Japan became a modern nation. By 1914, the eve of World War I, she had almost caught up with Western technological and industrial development, and moreover she had become an important trading nation and possibly the most formidable military power in Asia, particularly after her victory over the Russian military forces at Port Arthur in 1904.

The Post-Meiji Era

Emperor Meiji died in 1912 and was succeeded by his son, Emperor Taisho, who ruled in name only. He is said to have been feeble-minded and unable to make decisions, which provided the opportunity for the cabinet and the

military establishment to exercise actual power. In 1926
Emperor Hirohito, his son, acceded to the throne. The
political significance of the imperial dynasty began gradually to diminish after Emperor Meiji's death; the ranks of
his advisors, the *genro*, who had served him with such
distinction, were decimated by death and assassination. Ito,
who framed the Meiji constitution of 1889, was assassinated
in 1909. Yamagata, the founder of the Japanese modern
army, and who had twice been premier, died in 1922.

A new generation of decision-makers, statesmen, generals, admirals, and bureaucrats had come of age since the
Meiji Restoration. The maintenance of imperial rule, except
as a symbol of national unity, was no longer the primary
concern of this group. The Japanese throne was thus once
again eliminated from the political arena and confined to
a largely ceremonial role. Actual power resided with the
cabinet, which included the heads of the army and navy,
who became increasingly subject to the influence of extra-
governmental pressure groups, such as the *zaibatsu*—the
great business empires—and to ultra-nationalist, patriotic
organizations such as the notorious Black Dragon Society.
During the 1930s the military establishment gradually
monopolized their hegemony over the cabinet. In the late
1930s the cabinet and the emperor virtually functioned only
to sanction decisions made by the army and navy.

During World War I Japan fought on the side of the
Allies and took part in the Versailles Peace Conference of
1919. But the failure of the Japanese delegates to secure
the insertion of a racial equality clause in the Covenant
of the League of Nations "aroused bitterness in Japan,
especially in chauvinistic Army circles".[33] Despite the fact
that Japan was given a permanent place on the League
council and granted a mandate over the former German
possessions in the Pacific, as well as obtaining some important German trading concessions in the Chinese province
of Shantung, the Japanese felt that they were still not
regarded as "full equals by the nations of the West".[34] The
rejection of the racial equality clause served to strengthen

the military establishment in its persuasion that Japan's "weak-kneed diplomats were usually outwitted by unfair or underground coalition of the White Powers".[35]

Soon it became apparent that they were impatient with both the peace-oriented international negotiations abroad and the aims of representative government at home; by the early 1930s the military establishment had become convinced of the crucial need to protect Japan's special interests in China and the need to secure, for strategic and economic reasons, control over Manchuria. The junior officers, persuaded that their cautious seniors were unable to act with sufficient resolution, took matters in their own hands and initiated hostilities near Mukden. On 18 September 1931 the field command of the Kwantung Army provoked a confrontation with the Chinese forces and proceeded to take over Manchuria. Responsibility for the Mukden Incident was at the time attributed to the initiative of the junior officers wholly, who were said to have acted without the prior knowledge of their superior officers. Documents published after World War II indicate, however, that the senior officers of the Kwantung Army as well as the General Staff and the War Ministry in Tokyo were at least sufficiently predisposed, if not actually party to the action, not to interfere once the action had started.

The Japanese thrust into Manchuria was carried out in defiance of Japan's international agreements, and the League of Nations consequently appointed the Lytton Commission to investigate the situation that had arisen in Manchuria. While the report of the commission was equivocal—Japan was not actually named as the aggressor—the League voted almost unanimously against recognition of the Japanese puppet state of "Manchukuo". Japan subsequently withdrew from the League of Nations in 1932, unwilling to be hemmed in any longer by a network of international treaties and agreements.

The apparent success of Japan's action in Manchuria was reflected by the changing national mood in Japan. The feeling of resentment against the rest of the world, which had implicitly criticized Japan's occupation of Manchuria, grew, and the ultra-nationalist elements now gradually gained the upper hand and more and more began to shape domestic as well as foreign policy. Against this background of growing nationalism and militarism, *kokutai* reached its apogee. By 1937 it became the vehicle inculcating into the entire population of Japan such values as the divine origin of Japan and its imperial dynasty, her uniqueness and moral superiority, and her mission to establish a world empire.

Adherence to the precepts of *kokutai* as outlined in the book *Kokutai no Hongi*, was rigorously enforced in the late 1930s. R.K. Hall in his study *Kokutai no Hongi: Cardinal Principles of the National Entity of Japan*, notes that in 1937 approximately 300,000 copies of this small book were distributed to the teaching staffs of both public and private schools from the university level to the lower cycle of elementary schools. It was used as a textbook and as approved supplementary reading; teaching staffs were compelled to form self-study groups and to read and discuss the material contained in *Kokutai no Hongi*. It was constantly referred to in public speeches and was quoted at great length at the ceremonies marking national holidays. The study of *Kokutai no Hongi* was pursued with equal vigour during military training. The Peace Preservation Law of 1925, which legislated against dangerous thoughts, was enforced with renewed vigour. The power of the police to supervise and control the behaviour of the Japanese people, first introduced by the Tokugawa regime, had continued unabated during the Meiji government and now reached its zenith.

By 1937 the clash between China and Japan, which had been impending since the early 1930s, escalated into fully fledged war; the well-prepared and equipped Japanese army seized Shanghai, Nanking, and Hankow in quick succession, obtained control of the Yangtze River and seized most of the Chinese railway system. In October 1938 the Japanese moved into Canton and pushed inland to intercept some of the traffic between French Indo-China and the unoccupied regions of China.

Although the Japanese expected resistance to crumble after these decisive defeats, the Chinese continued to resist, successfully holding the invader at bay through guerilla warfare and occasional battles. The Japanese then changed their tactics and embarked on a slow process of war by attrition, progressively tightening the blockade off the Chinese coast. After the collapse of France in 1940, the weak Vichy government entered into an agreement with Tokyo, whereby Japanese troops moved into French Indo-China. This shut off another outlet to the sea for the Chinese.

The United States, which had opposed Japanese expansion into China and had hoped to restrain Japan during the Manchurian Incident through the moral censure administered by the League of Nations, also participated in the Brussels Conference of 1937, which called upon China and Japan to settle their differences in a peaceful manner. But Japan ignored the American initiative. Later, when the American embargo on the sale of scrap-iron and oil to Japan and the repudiation of the US–Japanese Commercial Agreement should have warned Japan of the seriousness with which the United States viewed Japanese aggression, the Japanese government gave its defiant answer by announcing plans to create a "new order in Asia", the Greater East Asia Co-Prosperity Sphere.

It now became clear that Japan had embarked on a course of action which could only end in a confrontation with the United States and the Allies, for her territorial ambitions now extended far beyond China to the conquest of British and Dutch possessions in South-East Asia. The formal decision to attack the United States was taken by the Japanese at the Imperial Conference in September 1941. On that occasion Emperor Hirohito, who had endeavoured on several occasions to restrain the aggressive, expansionist designs of the military leaders, indicated his disapproval of this proposed course of action by reading a brief poem, composed by his grandfather, Emperor Meiji. The poem spoke in allegorical terms of the emperor's concern over

the shrieking gales and roaring waves that disturbed the
calm of the sea, inasmuch as the emperor had regarded
the inhabitants of all four seas as brothers.

> When I regard all the world as my brothers,
> Why is it that its tranquillity should be so '
> Thoughtlessly disturbed.

Lester Brooks suggests that "though the military realized
that this was a reproach", it had scarcely more effect on
them than if the Emperor had pulled a fan from his
pocket".[36]

Emperor Hirohito, a man of scholarly tastes with a special
interest in marine biology, performed his largely ceremonial
role with great dignity. He was seemingly in no position
to "countermand or contradict": his function was merely
to listen, look, and approve, but not to "criticize, modify,
or veto".[37] A controversial study by L. Bergamini, *Japan's
Imperial Conspiracy*, suggests that Emperor Hirohito actually ruled pre-war Japan by cleverly manipulating his
civil and military advisors. The author's contention that
Hirohito was the "will" behind Japan's aggressive policies
which culminated in the attack on Pearl Harbour in
December 1941 and the war against the Allies is largely
unsubstantiated by documentary evidence and is con-
tradicted by a large body of scholarship.

On the contrary, ample documentary evidence exists to
indicate that the emperor reprimanded General Minami
and General Kanaya during the Manchurian Incident of
1931, and is said to have demanded that the officers
involved in the events should be disciplined. Takehiko
Yoshihashi, in his study *Conspiracy at Mukden*, reports that
the emperor reprimanded the two generals with the terse
words "Hereafter take heed".[38] However, the army continued to defy Hirohito and the civil authorities, and
proceeded with its plans to occupy Manchuria and to go
to war with China. The emperor's intervention in September 1941 during the Imperial Conference equally failed to
deter the Japanese military establishment from its projected

course of action. Although the Japanese continued to negotiate with the United States until the very eve of their surprise attack on Pearl Harbour, on 7 December 1941, the fateful decision to wage war had been taken already.

Japanese military strategy in World War II succeeded initially, perhaps even beyond the expectation of the Japanese High Command. The surprise attack on Pearl Harbour almost, but not quite, destroyed the American Fleet in the Pacific. By March 1942 Japan not only had conquered the Philippines but had overrun Malaya and Indonesia and had captured such strongholds as Singapore and Hong Kong. By May 1942 they had occupied almost all of Burma and were considering the conquest of India. In the Pacific theatre Japanese forces were in New Guinea, poised for an attack on Australia.

But the attack without warning on Pearl Harbour united the American people, instilling in them a fierce determination to crush Japan and revenge that "day of infamy". America joined the Allied war effort in all theatres of war, and the initial sequence of defeats was ultimately turned against the Axis powers and Japan by the mobilization of the massive military and industrial capacity of the United States. Japan suffered her first naval defeat during the battle of the Coral Sea in May 1942, and another at Midway in June of that year; her land forces were annihilated after bitter fighting at Guadalcanal. Several strategic islands in the Gilberts and Marshalls were reoccupied by the Allies, who succeeded by the capture of Saipan in the Marianas in June 1944 in assuring themselves of an air base from which Allied bombers could systematically attack Japanese cities. A single incendiary attack on Tokyo on 10 March 1945 is estimated to have killed over a hundred thousand people.

By the summer of 1945 the Japanese High Command realized that Japan was beaten, but the government as well as the military establishment were still unwilling to accept the terms of the Potsdam Declaration, which stipulated unconditional surrender. A rapid sequence of events, however, forced their hand: on 6 August 1945 the United States dropped the first atomic bomb on Hiroshima, with devastating effects; on 8 August the Russians declared war on Japan and invaded Manchuria; and finally on 9 August, the Americans dropped a second atomic bomb on Nagasaki, destroying much of the city. It now remained only a matter of finding a face-saving formula, which would permit the imperial house to continue to lead the nation. As Robert Butow, a perceptive observer, put it in *Japan's Decision to Surrender*:

> The one thing they could not do was sign a death warrant for the imperial house. If the Allies meant to wipe out, in one stroke, an imperial institution tenaciously rooted in the mind and soul of every true Japanese, . . . if they sought to deny to His Majesty's subjects the very polity upon which they rested their claims to being Japanese, then even the most ardent advocates of peace would obediently fall into step behind the fanatics rather than ever lend their support to an act so despicable that the record of it would soil their names forever and would render them the most reviled figures in all Japanese history.[39]

While some military fanatics united in one last effort to protect the emperor and to preserve the national polity, Prime Minister Suzuki had been forced to appeal on two occasions to the emperor to decide between the two opposing factions of the cabinet. The high value of harmony and unanimity which characterizes the Japanese decision-making process finally prevailed. The emperor, in an unprecedented step, agreed to address the nation over the radio on 15 August 1945, having previously declared himself satisfied with the equivocal Allied reply, which had not indicated an outright rejection of the demand of the Japanese government to retain the emperor. "After pondering deeply the general trends of the world and the actual conditions obtaining in Our Empire today," he announced, "We have decided to effect a settlement of the present situation by resorting to an extraordinary measure . . ."[40] Edwin O. Reischauer observes accurately that the mystical

concept of the imperial will had been much used by the
military extremists in shaping Japan's domestic and foreign
policy since the 1930s. It is thus "a strange irony of history
that the one clear expression of a Japanese Emperor's will
since ancient times sealed the doom of that dictatorship".[41]

The Evolution of the Ethos of Bushido

Inazo Nitobe, the Japanese Quaker scholar, in his study
Bushido, the Soul of Japan enumerates the most characteristic attitudes engendered by bushido: a sense of rectitude,
justice, courage, benevolence, the feeling of distress, po-
liteness, veracity, sincerity, self-control, honour, and above
all the duty of loyalty. These attitudes are identical with
those subsumed under the term chivalry in medieval
Europe and characterized "*le chevalier sans peur et sans
reproche*". Encouraging the striving towards greater
refinement and sophistication, the precepts inherent in
ethereal bushido were eminently suited to guide the behaviour of the court nobles and the aristocracy in a peaceful
age—the Heian period.

These aristocratic standards of behaviour not only permeated the attitudes of the provincial warrior class, which
in the eleventh and twelfth century was increasingly called
upon by the court nobility to defend its interests, but also
influenced other sectors of the Japanese population. The
sense of enjoyment of the beauties of nature which has
characterized the Japanese people through the ages can be
traced back to ethereal bushido, as also can their preoccupation with aesthetic pastimes such as painting, calligraphy,
and the writing of poetry. Even the last messages of
kamikaze pilots referred frequently to their nostalgia for
the sight of the falling cherry blossoms and equated their
imminent death with the setting of the evening sun.

As the provincial warrior class gradually began to exercise
actual power in the name of the emperor and the court
nobility and set up its own administrative centre in

Kamakura, the values that emphasized the capacity for personal loyalty, the importance of family ties, and a Spartan indifference to suffering and death gradually eclipsed those with an emphasis on refinement and *noblesse oblige*. During the thirteenth and fourteenth centuries these warrior factions engaged in bloody internecine warfare, forming and re-forming alliances—for the values of a cultured, peaceful society had little relevance under these circumstances.

In the sixteenth century the Tokugawa regime brought peace and stability. It was no longer sufficient for the warrior class to master the arts of war; the new social order had engendered a need for an educated, disciplined bureaucracy and a submissive, loyal, and industrious population. Hayashi Razan, and later his student Yamaga Soko, adapted the notions of ethereal bushido, as well as its martial values, to suit the requirements of the new social order. In *The Way of the Samurai* Yamaga skilfully amalgamated these precepts with Neo-Confucian notions such as trust in fate, quiet submission to the inevitable, disdain of life, and acceptance of death and revived important elements of Shinto mythology, such as reverence for the divinely created imperial dynasty.

The *Hagakure*, compiled *c.* 1717, is perhaps the most comprehensive manual of traditional bushido and extols the virtues of "frugality, loyalty and filial piety, courage, self-possession and, above all, benevolence". As J.J. Spae puts it, the values emphasized in the *Hagakure*, although "clothed in Confucian garb", have absorbed a distinct bathos, which emanates from their Shinto origin.[42] The most telling sentence in the *Hagakure*—"bushido consists of dying"—exalts death as an act which transcends all human striving; the notion that a "glorious death", a meaningful death, has a higher value than a meaningless life became one of the core values of militant bushido and *kokutai*.

The values diffused by traditional bushido were ideally suited to the purposes of the Tokugawa government: the development of a loyal, educated aristocracy, which could

administer the country efficiently and would unquestioningly carry out its orders, and of an industrious, frugal,
submissive peasantry and merchant and artisan classes,
which by their efforts would provide the means to uphold
the rigid social structure. Together with the enforced
isolation of Japan from the rest of the world, the ethos of
traditional bushido underpinned the *status quo* promulgated by the Tokugawa regime for many centuries. But
chaotic economic conditions gradually broke down the rigid
class structure—peasants became artisans, merchants on
acquiring wealth succeeded in acquiring samurai rank, and
members of the samurai class lost some of their status. These
changes weakened the power of the Tokugawa regime.

It was, however, the revived theory of imperial rule and
the demands by Western powers for Japan to open her door
to trade and diplomatic relations that contributed to the
demise of the Tokugawa regime. Japan had been governed
since the eleventh century by indirect rule. The shogun had
exercised power in the name of the emperor, first from
Kamakura and later from Edo, while the emperor, who
continued to live and hold court in Kyoto, remained the
symbolic and spiritual leader of the nation. But the revival
and study of Japanese traditions and Shinto mythology
initiated by the Tokugawa government brought scholars to
the fore who clamoured for the restoration of the imperial
rule and the end of indirect rule by shogun.

While the ethos of militant bushido evolved in the first
instance to provide a philosophical basis for the reform of
the feudal government, it proved a progressively more
powerful value system, which united the nation in the face
of external threats. Loyalty to the emperor now superseded
total devotion to the service of the feudal lord; the notion
of filial piety and the sense of obligation towards family,
nation, and imperial dynasty became the dominating values
of militant bushido. And with the increasing emphasis on
her uniqueness and moral superiority engendered by the
revival of Shinto, Japan's sense of mission evolved.

Yoshida Shoin proclaimed that Japan was divinely ordained to lead the world and found a world empire, a notion that fired the imagination of the population and exerted a great influence in the twentieth century on the ultra-nationalist elements which advocated aggressive, expansionist policies. Militant bushido, however, was no longer the exclusive ethos of the aristocracy and the warrior class. The Meiji Restoration in 1868 had abolished the hierarchical social system established by the Tokugawas and by the introduction of universal military conscription in 1872, and the Imperial Rescript on Education in 1890 endeavoured to attract all sections of the population to the service of the nation. Incorporated in *kokutai no hongi*, the national polity, the values inherent in militant bushido were widely disseminated by successive governments and inculcated into the entire Japanese population.

This brief excerpt from the *Fundamentals of Our National Polity* illustrates clearly how militant bushido was adapted to serve as a vehicle for the indoctrination of the Japanese people in the period before World War II:

> Our country is established with the emperor, who is the descendant of Amaterasu [the Sun Goddess] as her center, and our ancestors as well as we ourselves constantly have beheld in the emperor the fountainhead of her life and activities. For this reason, to serve the emperor and to receive the emperor's great august Will as one's own is the rationale of making our historical "life" live in the present; and on this is based the morality of the people.[43]

Kokutai no hongi equates loyalty to the emperor with reverence and defines obedience as "casting ourselves aside and serving the emperor intently. . . . Hence, offering our lives for the sake of the emperor does not mean so-called self-sacrifice, but the casting aside of our little selves to live under his august grace and the enhancing of the genuine life of the people of a State."[44]

The value patterns propagated by *kokutai* were widely diffused through the educational system with the aim of inculcating the ethos of self-effacement, disinterestedness, and obedience. The obligation of services to the nation, particularly through military service, was thus firmly impressed on Japanese youngsters. Joseph C. Grew suggests in *Report from Tokyo* that the indoctrination of Japan's youth with the values of *kokutai* involved not merely education or military training, but a conscious "shaping— a warping if you will,—of the mind", akin to brainwashing.[45] "The lower levels of education became increasingly a means to teach the people *what* to think rather than how to think," posits Reischauer,[46] suggesting that Japan pioneered the new techniques later generally used by totalitarian regimes to inculcate obedience and uniformity through a standardized and closely controlled education system.

The Modern Japanese Armed Forces

The introduction of universal conscription in 1872 by the Meiji government was a hard blow to the pride and morale of the samurai class, which until then alone had enjoyed the privilege of bearing arms and jealously guarded it. This had differentiated samurai from commoners. However, Yamagata Aritomo, who is credited with introducing universal conscription, and who was himself a Choshu samurai, did not envisage reducing the status of the warrior class as much as raising the peasant "to the dignity of the samurai".[46] From now on every subject would be expected to aspire to the high ideals of the warrior class and emulate their standards of behaviour.

It may be useful here to refer briefly to the behaviour of the samurai in combat, to illustrate clearly that this model had little relevance for the conditions of warfare prevailing in the nineteenth and twentieth centuries. In traditional society the samurai fought individually against one opponent at a time, engaging in personal heroics. A battlefield, therefore, tended to resemble groupings of separate combats rather than a generalized struggle. The "ideal type" samurai held his life "to be of no more value than a feather".[48] Facing conflict head on, he was at all times prepared to die unflinchingly in battle. Furthermore, hand-to-hand fighting with sharp, curved swords more often than not resulted in the death of one of the participants in the struggle.

To avoid capture in battle, the samurai often chose to commit suicide, because he believed that survival in captivity was not only "dishonourable and degrading, but generally bad policy, since prisoners were often tortured and otherwise wretchedly treated".[49] While Western medieval knights saw nothing dishonourable in seizure and incarceration by the enemy—which even sometimes enhanced a knight's reputation, as it did for Richard the Lion-Hearted—the samurai was prepared to kill himself rather than fall into enemy hands.

However, Yamagata's conception of the "citizen-samurai", as expressed in the Imperial Rescript to Soldiers and Sailors of 1882, adapted the precepts of bushido to a rapidly modernizing Japanese society. The emphasis was no longer placed on individual acts of heroism, nor on fanatical bravery, but rather on prudence, self-control, disciplined loyalty, and obedience to the commands of superior officers, the values stressed in the eighteenth-century manual of traditional bushido, the *Hagakure*. Thus the Imperial Rescript, which until 1941 prescribed the conduct of the members of the Japanese armed forces, states: "To be incited by mere impetuosity to violent action cannot be called true valor. The soldier and the sailor should have sound discrimination of right and wrong, cultivate self-possession, and form their plans with deliberation".[50] Respect due to superiors is emphasized, but superiors are also admonished to treat "their inferiors with consideration, making kindness their chief aim so that all grades may unite in their service to the Emperor". Harmonious co-operation as well as benevolence towards the enemy is stressed, for the Imperial Rescript cautions:

> Never to despise an inferior enemy or fear a superior, but to do one's duty as soldier or sailor—this is true valor. Those who

thus appreciate true valor should in their daily intercourse set
gentleness first and aim to win the love and esteem of others.
If you affect valor and act with violence, the world will in
the end detest you and look upon you as wild beasts. Of this
you should take heed.[51]

Under the leadership of officers who like Yamagata came
from Choshu samurai backgrounds, the modern Japanese
army was moulded into a dedicated and highly disciplined
force. The value of the conscript army was demonstrated
in their victory, under Yamagata's command, over Saigo's
samurai forces in 1887. Under the leadership of General
Nogi, the Japanese army subsequently distinguished itself
against the Russian forces in the Russo-Japanese war of
1904–5. However, an element of fanaticism which was no
longer in keeping with the precepts enunciated by the
Imperial Rescript now became progressively more promi-
nent. Tadayoshi Sakurai, whose account of the siege of Port
Arthur, *Human Bullets*, exemplifies the vainglorious spirit
of the "new samurai", describes his emotions, as he went
into battle: "To die under the flag of the Rising Sun and
to die while doing a splendid service to one's country and
one's Emperor was the wish and resolve in every heart".[52]

General Nogi, a dedicated soldier, who "held steadfast
to all that was best in the *samurai* tradition",[53] imposed
the highest standards of discipline upon his troops, both on
and off the battlefield; the slightest misdemeanour towards
civilian life and property was most severely dealt with.
According to Richard Storry both sides fought with remarkable courage and some chivalry. The Japanese treatment of Russian prisoners was regarded as more than
correct; it was generous as well as humane.

General Nogi is also renowned for his decision to observe
the custom of *junshi*, which was regarded as the supreme
manifestation of loyalty to one's superior. In ancient times
it had been customary when a ruler or great lord died that
certain of his retainers killed themselves, in order that they
might escort him to the next world. On the death of
Emperor Meiji in 1912 the general and his wife committed

seppuku in the traditional manner. Some Japanese scholars attributed Nogi's action to feelings of depression resulting from a recognition of his personal responsibility for the exorbitant loss of lives during the siege of Port Arthur. Others, however, interpreted his suicide note as a reminder to his countrymen of the high values inherent in traditional samurai virtues, which had tended to be increasingly neglected in recent times.

After World War I the paramountcy of the Choshu officers was gradually eroded. These older officers found it difficult to adjust to the changes that had taken place in modern warfare. A conflict similar to the clash between de Gaulle and the senior officers of the French army over the introduction of technological innovations arose between the junior and senior officers in the Japanese army. This was made worse by resentment that members of the armed forces who came from Choshu families were given preference in appointments and promotions. When Yamagata died in 1922, sweeping changes in personnel policies and technical equipment were introduced. Some of the Choshu officers were supplanted by officers who had no connection with the old samurai families, but were drawn from "the middle or lower middle class, which includes small landowners, small independent farmers, and small shopkeepers from rural areas and small towns"[54]. A struggle for leadership ensued, resulting in unrest and laxer discipline within the army. The new breed of officers were unable to enforce General Nogi's high standards of conduct, or to prevent *gekokujo*, "the overpowering of seniors by juniors".[55]

The Volunteers Act of 1927 further changed the social composition of the armed forces: now anyone who could support himself for one year and could pass the required examinations would be admitted to the rank of noncommissioned officer; thus the influx from the lower middle and lower classes was further accelerated. These noncommissioned officers rapidly established close ties with the peasant conscripts, with whose economic and political aspirations they could readily identify, since they themselves were only one step higher up the social ladder. The rural and small-town background of the "new samurai" engendered paternalistic relationships with the other ranks, who in turn gave their officers loyal support.

Following World War I the armed forces were faced with growing unpopularity in the community and diminishing power in the government. "Army prestige in Japan then reached so low an ebb that officers changed into civilian clothes when appearing in public"[56]. This temporary loss of prestige can largely be attributed to the unproductive intervention of the Japanese forces on the side of the Allies in Siberia in 1918. For Japan it was "a disillusioning military adventure": each Allied nation had committed itself to provide a force of seven thousand men for the purpose of encouraging "any efforts at self-government or self defence" in Russia, and to withdraw when order was re-established.[57] Japan , however, did not abide by the terms of this agreement—in November 1918, three months after the first troops had landed, she had stationed "73,400 men in Siberia"[58].

Bitter clashes between the civilian and military authorities caused by this costly intervention were sharpened by the effects of the post-war depression. Nevertheless, Japanese forces remained in Siberia long after the withdrawal of Allied forces in 1920, and left Sakhalin only in 1925. Civilian authorities responded to the defiant attitude of the military establishment by drastically reducing military budgets, a practice which continued until the early 1930s.

Resentment over these cuts in military expenditure was exacerbated by the cabinet's acceptance of the Washington Peace Conference decision of 1921–22 of the 5:5:3 naval ratio, giving the United States and Britain a naval strength of five capital ships to Japan's three. In 1928 Japan signed the Kellogg–Briand Pact which outlawed war; however, the Japanese diplomats failed to secure freedom of action in their own spheres of interest as did the British. At the London Naval Conference of 1930, the Japanese government, in the face of violent opposition from both the army and the navy agreed to continue the 5:5:3 naval ratio.

Dissatisfaction over conciliatory policies and awareness of the growing power of the party politicians and the "liberal" influences around the throne resulted in repeated attempts by junior officers of the army and, to a lesser extent, the navy to protest "against the corruption of the political parties" by terrorist actions.[59] The assassination in November, 1930 of Prime Minister Hamaguchi, who had signed the London Naval Treaty, was followed by those of Inouye, the finance minister who had opposed large army budgets, Prime Minister Inukai, and Baron Dan, of the Mitsui industries, in 1932. However, after the invasion of Manchuria in 1931 the popularity of the armed forces began to increase again; while they continued to defy the commands both of the civilian authorities and of the emperor, the population was "swept by a nationalistic euphoria" and supported the expansionist policies which eventually led to Japan's entry into World War II.[60]

It was during the war with China, in 1937, that the necessity arose to frame a new Military Field Code which would replace the Imperial Rescript of 1882. While the attempted *coups d' état* by officers of the armed forces in March 1932, May 1932 and February 1936 were destined to be frustrated, the chiefs of staff became increasingly aware that the standards of military discipline had fallen to a dangerously low level. After the abortive rebellion of 26 February 1936 the army and the navy launched a purge of extremist elements, holding that membership in external political or patriotic organizations was no longer compatible with military service. Abroad, too, disobedience and desertion had become widespread and the standards of behaviour of Japanese military personnel in respect of civilian lives and property were in striking contrast to those enforced earlier by General Nogi. The rape of Chinese women, the arbitrary killings of civilians, and the looting of civilian property culminated in the "massacre of Nanking" in 1937, which was described by Lord Russell in *The Knights of Bushido* in the following terms:

On 12th December the Japanese troops stormed the south gate and most of the Chinese troops escaped through the northern and western gates . . . All resistance had ceased. The Japanese troops were then let loose like the hordes of Genghis Khan to ravish and murder . . . Small groups of Japanese soldiers roamed all over the city night and day. Many were crazed with drink, but no attempt was made by their commander or their officers to maintain discipline among the occupying forces. They looted, they burned, they raped and they murdered. Soldiers marched through the streets indiscriminately killing Chinese of both sexes, adults and children alike, without receiving any provocation and without rhyme or reason.[61]

The drafting of a new military code became now a matter of urgent concern; the Army Education Corps and the Ministry of War began to frame new standing orders on discipline and morale, overriding objections from a minority group who considered Emperor Meiji's Imperial Military Orders were sufficient to deal with the problem.[62] The draft of the new code was completed in the autumn of 1940, and the author, Toson Shimazikazi, was entrusted with the task of expressing it in appropriately jingoistic terms.

The new Battlefield Commandments or Military Field Code, prohibited all members of the Japanese armed forces from surrendering to the enemy, but exhorted them to kill themselves or charge the enemy in a final, suicidal attack. While the Battlefield Commandments did not represent an entirely new departure (in traditional society, samurai avoided capture by the enemy and frequently preferred to resort to self-destruction), the origins of this innovation can be largely traced to the low state of discipline and morale prevailing among the Japanese forces fighting in the 1930s on the Asiatic mainland.

Two important factors can be advanced to explain the deterioration in the standards of conduct of the armed forces: first, the junior officers' practice of endeavouring to overpower their seniors and their tendency to regard the upper echelons of the armed forces as too irresolute and too conservative; and second, the factionalism that infected the entire armed forces, junior officers as well as senior officers constantly forming and re-forming alliances to support different courses of action. An army which had embarked on shaping foreign policy by *faits accomplis* and which could no longer be effectively controlled by the civilian government or the emperor was unlikely to be a disciplined force. While the High Command in Tokyo did not openly support either the radical ideology or the expansionist policies of the junior officers, they used these as a means of exerting pressure on the government to introduce political changes which would enable the generals and the admirals to play an increasingly important role in the decision-making process.

To sum up: The conduct of the Japanese fighting forces was regulated in the nineteenth century by the Imperial Rescript to Soldiers and Sailors of 1882, which was primarily based on the ethos of traditional bushido. In the twentieth century the values propagated by militant bushido, such as the "uniqueness" and superiority of Japan, loyalty to the emperor, and Japan's divine mission in the world, permeated the ethos of the fighting forces. Finally, in 1941 the new Battlefield Commandments added yet another dimension to the high values accorded to obedience and conformity by *kokutai*, reviving to some extent standards of behaviour which had been exclusive to the samurai class in traditional society. Thus the core features of Japanese culture adapted themselves to the changing social and economic circumstances, displaying a remarkable continuity of cultural traditions.

The cumulative effects of this "cultural conditioning" process on the individual soldier or sailor are difficult to assess: while the indoctrination of individuals began at a very early age, continued through the school years, and was further intensified during the period of military training, it tended to be internalized in different ways. While it appears most members of the armed services gave at least lip service to the values propagated by the new Battlefield

Commandments, obedience to its commands was by no means unanimous, for it seems likely that certain facets of the Japanese personality structure and value orientation militated against total compliance.

Notes

1. Ruth Benedict, *The Crysanthemum and the Sword* (London: Routledge and Kegan Paul, 1967), p.223.
2. Hall, R.K., *Kokutai no Hongi* (Cambridge, Mass. Harvard University Press, 1949), p.10.
3. John F. Embree, *The Japanese* (Washington: Smithsonian Institution, 1943), p.2.
4. Ibid., p.3.
5. Lester Brooks, *Behind Japan's Surrender* (New York: McGraw-Hill, 1968), p.97.
6. Ibid.
7. Yin denotes affinity with the earth, yang with heaven. Maurice Freedman suggests that yin and yang are opposite but complementary principles and, when present in the correct ratio, are believed to ensure the concentration of the divine breath (M. Freedman, *Chinese Lineage and Society* [London: Athlone, 1966], p.123).
8. Ryusaku Tsunoda, Wm. Theodore de Bary, and Donald Keene, comps., *Sources of Japanese Tradition* (New York: Columbia University Press, 1964), vol.1, p.261.
9. Ibid., p.262.
10. Ibid., p.263.
11. G.B. Sansom, *Japan: A Short Cultural History*, rev. ed. (London: Cresset, 1962), p.239.
12. Tsunoda, de Bary, and Keene, *Sources of Japanese Tradition:*, vol.1, p.174.
13. Edwin O. Reischauer, *Japan Past and Present*, 3rd ed. (London: Duckworth, 1964), p.48.
14. Ibid., p.69.
15. Tsunoda, de Bary, and Keene, *Sources of Japanese Tradition*, vol.1, p.302.
16. Ibid., p.322.
17. Reischauer, *Japan Past and Present*, p.87.
18. Ibid., p.86.
19. Tsunoda, de Bary, and Keene, *Sources of Japanese Tradition*, vol.1, p.386.
20. Richard Storry, *A History of Modern Japan* (Harmondsworth, Mddx.: Penguin, 1960), p.73.

21. Ibid., p.74.
22. Sansom, *Japan*, p.526.
23. Ibid., p.518.
24. More than fifty peasant uprisings are mentioned in published historical works after 1714 and there are manuscript accounts of hundreds more (Sansom, *Japan*, p.522).
25. Sansom, *Japan*, p.474.
26. Ibid.
27. Tsunoda, de Bary, and Keene, *Sources of Japanese Tradition*, vol. 2, p.85.
28. Ibid., p.96.
29. Ibid., p.109.
30. Frank Gibney, *Five Gentlemen of Japan* (New York: Farrar and Strauss, 1953), p.88.
31. Brooks, *Behind Japan's Surrender*, p.375.
32. Tsunoda, de Bary, and Keene, *Sources of Japanese Tradition*, vol.2, p.137.
33. Hillis Lory, *Japan's Military Masters* (New York: Viking, 1943), p.123.
34. Storry, *History of Modern Japan*, p.162.
35. Lory, *Japan's Military Masters*, p. 123.
36. Brooks, *Behind Japan's Surrender*, p.97.
37. Ibid., p.96.
38. Takehiko Yoshihashi, *Conspiracy at Mukden* (New Haven: Yale University Press, 1963), p.183.
39. Robert J.C. Butow, *Japan's Decision to Surrender* (Stanford: Stanford University Press, 1954), p.141.
40. John Toland, *The Rising Sun* (London: Cassell, 1971), p.850.
41. Butow, *Japan's Decision to Surrender*, p.vi.
42. J.J. Spae, *Japanese Religiosity* (Tokyo: Oriens Institute, 1971), p.96.
43. Tsunoda, de Bary, and Keene, *Sources of Japanese Tradition*, vol.2, p.280.
44. Ibid.
45. Joseph C. Grew, *Report from Tokyo* (Sydney: Angus and Robertson, 1943), p.35.
46. Edwin O. Reischauer, *Japan: The Story of a Nation* (London: Duckworth, 1970), p.35.
47. Tsunoda, de Bary, and Keene, *Sources of Japanese Tradition*, vol.2, p.194.
48. H. Paul Varley with Ivan and Nobuko Morris, *The Samurai* (London: Weidenfeld and Nicolson, 1970), p.22.
49. Ibid., pp.32–33.
50. Tsunoda, de Bary, and Keene, *Sources of Japanese Tradition*, vol.2, p.199.
51. Ibid., pp.199–200.

52. Tadayoshi Sakurai, *Human Bullets*, 6th ed. (Tokyo: Tibi, 1909), p.222.
53. Storry, *History of Modern Japan*, p.140.
54. Chitoshi Yanaga, *Japanese People and Politics* (New York: Wiley, 1956), pp.76–77.
55. Storry, *History of Modern Japan*, p.185.
56. Lory, *Japan's Military Masters*, p.122.
57. Ibid., p.123.
58. Ibid., p.124.
59. Ibid., p.126.
60. Reischauer, *Japan: Story of a Nation*, p.191.
61. Lord Russell of Liverpool, *The Knights of Bushido* (London: Cassell, 1958), p.42.
62. *Sankei Shimbun*, Special Research Team, *The Last Japanese Soldier* (London: Stacey, 1972), p.95.

4

Japanese Personality and Value Orientation

The notion that there are similarities in personality characteristics among people sharing the same culture underlies the concept of the "national character". The national character of the Japanese people has been the subject of close investigation, particularly by American and British anthropologists during World War II—Gorer, Benedict, Leighton, Kluckhohn, and others who worked for the Office of War Information in Washington and continued their investigations in peacetime. This theoretical approach, which is greatly influenced by Freudian theories, is often referred to as Culture and Personality Study.

F.C. Wallace defines *personality* as "those ways of behaviour or techniques of solving problems which have a high probability of use by the individual",[1] while Victor Barnouw suggests that "personality is a more or less enduring organization of forces within the individual, associated with a complex of fairly consistent attitudes, values and modes of perception which account, at least in part, for the individual's consistency of behaviour".[2] The study of culture and personality thus appears to be an area of research where anthropology and psychology come close together. By studying the interaction between culture ("the way of life of a group of people, the configuration of all the more or less stereotyped patterns of learned behaviour handed down from one generation to the next through the means of language and imitation")[3] and the "personality"

of the prisoners of war at Featherston and Cowra, some
further light may be thrown on the underlying reasons for
their conduct.

Barnouw lists three main determinants of personality: the
psychological and constitutional make-up, childhood training (the notion that experiences undergone in early life
significantly affect an individual's personality in adult life);
the contemporary situation in which the individual finds
himself, the roles he learns to play, the importance of his
reference groups and his interpersonal relationships; and
finally, his world view, values, attitudes, and assumptions
about life which are characteristic of the culture into which
he is born. For the purpose of this study these factors are
used selectively, in order to focus on the personality traits
of the Japanese "national character" that may have shaped
their differential responses to internment by the enemy, a
situation for which their cultural repertoire had not prepared them. Four main points are examined: (1) the
different explanations offered for the alleged "compulsive
personality" of the Japanese people (their conformity to
rules, the "planned" quality of Japanese life, and the
discontinuities inherent in their child training process); (2)
the high value accorded collaterality, and the concept of
"*amae*"; (3) the decision-making process in Japanese society; and (4) the Japanese attitude towards death.

The "Compulsive Personality" of the Japanese People

Geoffrey Gorer in his "Themes in Japanese Culture" drew
attention to the Japanese preoccupation with ritual, tidiness,
and order, comparing it with the behaviour and attitudes
attributed in the West to "compulsive individuals". Following orthodox Freudian theory, he suggested toilet training
as explanation: "In European compulsive neurotics, ex-
cessively severe early cleanliness training plays an important, indeed preponderating role in the development of
these symptoms".[4] Early and rigorous toilet training, sug-

gested Gorer, produced in the Japanese conflicts and anxieties. The hostility resulting from being forced to do something which the infant cannot fully understand and for which he is psychologically not yet ready remains, according to Gorer, a component part of the personality in adult years.

W.L. La Barre, who had been a community analyst with the War Relocation Authority at a Japanese civilian internment camp at Topaze, Utah, arrived at similar conclusions independently and interpreted the Japanese national character in a similar vein. In his study "Some Observations on Character Structure in the Orient: The Japanese", he suggested:

> The Japanese are probably the most compulsive people in the world's ethnological museum. The evidence is, I believe, conclusive that they are even more compulsive than the North Germans . . . . The analytic psychiatrist describes the individual compulsive character in a manner which is almost one-to-one correspondence with the ethnographer's description of typical Japanese character structure.[5]

La Barre goes on to list these compulsive traits: "secretiveness, hiding of emotions and attitudes; perseveration and persistency; conscientiousness; self-righteousness; a tendency to project attitudes; fanaticism; arrogance; 'touchiness', precision and perfectionism, neatness and ritualistic cleanliness; ceremoniousness; and conformity to rule".[6] In her study *The Chrysanthemum and the Sword* Ruth Benedict largely confirms Gorer's and La Barre's notions when she writes: "Everyone agrees that a baby in Japan, as in China too, is trained very early. . . . He experiences only an inescapable routine implacably insisted upon. . . . What the baby learns from the implacable training prepares him to accept in adulthood the subtler compulsions of Japanese culture."[7]

The three studies mentioned above, owing to wartime conditions, were not undertaken in Japan and thus could be called, following Mead and Metraux, "studies of Japanese culture at a distance". Neither Gorer nor Benedict had an opportunity of studying Japanese family life at close range, while La Barre had only been able to observe it in a War Relocation Centre, where, at least in the initial stages, "enforced crowding—sometimes eight people were accommodated in one room",[8] the crudeness of living quarters, and the lack of privacy may have made early and rigorous toilet training almost mandatory. Life in a relocation camp, with all its inherent tensions and strains, might foster in individuals of whatever nationality such traits as secretiveness, hiding of attitudes, and "touchiness", as well as intensify existing tendencies towards compulsive cleanliness.

However, Douglas G. Haring, who lived in Japan before the war and visited the country again on several occasions after it, agrees that some aspects of the "prewar Japanese behaviour characteristically resembled that of compulsive personalities".[9] On the other hand, he notes that he failed to observe a regular pattern of either early or inflexible toilet training. Neither the Norbecks, who studied child training in a Japanese fishing village during 1951–52, nor Brigitte Lanham in her study "Aspects of Child Care in Japan" suggests that infants who lapsed from cleanliness were either severely scolded or physically punished. "Toilet training", posits Lanham, "may not be too different from what occurs in the United States."[10]

While Gorer and La Barre were able to document their interpretation of the Japanese personality with a number of examples of Japanese behaviour which might strike Western observers as compulsive, the linkage with toilet training may be regarded as somewhat tenuous. Haring's theory, in which he develops the idea that the alleged compulsive traits of the Japanese personality could be explained by the existence of a police state in Japan, which exerted continuous and close supervision over all individuals for over three centuries, seems more in keeping with the established facts. Haring's theory is examined more closely in the following section.

Conformity

Of all the traits listed by La Barre as pertaining to the "compulsive personality", the tendency to conform scrupulously to rules is perhaps the most relevant in an analysis of the behaviour of the Japanese prisoner of war. As Benedict puts it, "Strength of character . . . is shown in conforming not in rebelling",[11] while Chie Nakane, for instance, suggests that the habit of conforming tends to be "deeply rooted in Japanese society and seems to continue as a dominant tendency even in contemporary Japanese society".[12] But Reischauer posits that the desire to conform is a relatively recent development in Japanese society and postulates that the Japanese people have been "an openly emotional and unrepressed people during much of their history, perhaps even as late as the 16th and 17th century."[13] He describes the life of the courtier periods as "an unending quest for love and beauty. . . . murder and treachery, uprisings and feudings, passionate outbursts and equally passionate devotions characterised the feudal age."[14]

Certainly neither Lady Murasaki's *Tale of Genji* nor Sei Shonagon's *Pillow Book* (both written in the tenth century) reflect a repressed or inhibited society. On the contrary, the men and women portrayed in the pages of the two great women novelists of the Heian period expressed their feelings and emotions with astonishing frankness. Enjoyment of life, of religious ceremonies, of seasonal festivals, and of travel alternated with periods of deep melancholia and introspection; alliances were short-lived, hostilities flared up suddenly, men and women tended to love and hate deeply. The desire to conform appeared largely absent. Individuality in behaviour, speech, and dress was highly valued and rewarded. For example, Sei Shonagon, a court lady of relatively modest status, became the favourite of the empress partly because of her ability to compose apt and original poems.

Conformity of behaviour developed gradually and only became a matter of survival during the Tokugawa period.

In order to enforce social order and stability after a prolonged period of internecine warfare, the Tokugawa government promulgated laws which tended to regulate every detail in the daily existence of the four social classes created by the regime. The *metsuke*, the special secret police created by the Tokugawa regime, developed a highly efficient system of espionage, to the extent that one could not even trust the members of one's own household. The maintenance and physical enforcement of order and stability devolved upon the samurai class, "who were authorised to decapitate on the spot anyone of lesser status whose conduct was other than expected".[15]

One can thus visualize a virtual reign of terror which over time must have blanketed every vestige of earlier individuality and nonconformity. The price of survival during the Tokugawa period was "constant vigilance, meticulous conformity to the numerous codes, and cultivation of a smiling face—or at least a 'deadpan'— regardless of emotions".[16] It was during this period, then, that the notion of conformity of behaviour became deeply embedded in Japanese society; and even later on, during the Meiji Restoration, when the samurai were stripped of their power to mete out arbitrary justice and to give short shrift to anyone who violated the rules of conduct, the power of the police to supervise and control the behaviour of the Japanese people tended to continue unabated.

In 1925, the Peace Preservation Law was enacted, which further curtailed the population's right to free speech and even legislated against "dangerous thoughts."[17] Any thought that questioned the position of the emperor or challenged in any way premises of the economic and political programme of the ruling élite was considered a crime against the state. The offenders, among them many professors and students of liberal or radical tendencies, were thrown into jail and made to recant their thoughts. Under such circumstances it does not appear surprising that a tendency towards a "compulsive personality" should have developed. Secretiveness, hiding of emotions, and conformity to the rules, as well as other traits listed by La Barre, tend to be natural concomitants of such close supervision of behaviour and thoughts.

If, as Haring suggests, most of the features of pre-war Japanese compulsive personality are the "logical fruits of the police state",[18] the question arises how deeply those traits are embedded in the Japanese national character and under what circumstances the Japanese people would divest themselves of the desire to conform and return to their original individualistic, unrepressed, and frankly emotional style of life. When Haring revisited Japan in 1952 he tested his theory that if police supervision were to be relaxed and perpetual espionage lifted the character of the Japanese people would change accordingly. The police state had, at least temporarily, vanished. Men and women tended to associate freely and to voice their opinions on political as well as economic issues without regard to the policies favoured by the government of the day. Haring reports a conversation with a spokesman of a group of farmers which accurately expresses the emotional climate prevailing in Japan after World War II. "When you return home, thank the Americans for taking the police off our necks," the farmer said. "It is such a relief to be free of prying supervision, to go and to come as we please, to read what we wish and to say what we think."[19]

Haring also studied the island community of Amami Oshima, which had been left relatively untouched by the Tokugawa order; off the beaten track, it had escaped "Tokugawa meticulosity" if not Satsuma greed and over-lordship. Pre-Tokugawa life-styles, such as those delineated by Reischauer, have survived almost unchanged, for in Amami Oshima contemporary culture appears to be "directly superimposed upon an archaic cultural base",[20] preserving ideas and beliefs which are no longer current on the Japanese mainland. While the marks of grinding poverty and protracted slavery suffered by the islanders under the Satsuma lords are only too apparent, the folkways of an earlier era have also survived. Haring characterized the people of Amami Oshima as affectionate, cheerful, and frank, who expressed their emotions openly.

As far as the "planned quality" of Japanese behaviour is concerned (see below), "Amamian behaviour is less cast in a rigid mould of codes of conduct";[21] class differences are not keenly felt, and social sanctions such as ridicule and shame carry less weight. The Amamians even poke fun at Japanese ceremonial suicide, a subject of conversation which is only rarely touched on in the mainland. "Why commit suicide?" they say. "Living is too much fun".[22]

To summarize the most important points raised by Haring: he suggests that the Japanese national character has been largely shaped by the oppressive laws framed by the Tokugawa regime in the sixteenth century, which were rigorously enforced by police coercion. Police supervision of the everyday life of all Japanese subjects tended to persist unabated until the end of World War II. The Japanese population has, therefore, tended at least outwardly, and particularly in "public situations",[23] to adopt a compliant pattern of behaviour, correlated with intense watchfulness and suspicion. Haring posits, however, that where the rules governing conformity of conduct are relaxed, non-compulsive, individualistic, and uninhibited, behaviour patterns that were typical of pre-Tokugawa times may again emerge. While dismissing the notion of early and rigorous toilet training as responsible for moulding the Japanese compulsive personality, Haring draws attention to the discontinuities in the training of children and the planned quality of Japanese behaviour, which may have contributed towards certain aspects of compulsiveness.

The Planned Quality of Japanese Behaviour

According to F.S. Hulse, "there seems to be widespread agreement that an intense desire to foresee coming situations, especially perhaps with respect to interpersonal relationships . . . is one of the outstanding features of Japanese culture".[24] It seems essential for the Japanese to have the correct responses for all foreseeable situations on tap. Benedict, who based her findings on the analysis of Rorschach tests given at Japanese relocation centres in California during World War II, carries this notion even further and suggests that "unforeseen situations which cannot be handled by rote" are frightening to the Japanese.[25] Reischauer suggests that the Japanese prefer to stick to a "narrow prescribed course . . . and deprived of their familiar situational guideposts, they seem to fall into panic somewhat more easily than we".[26]

Hulse attributes this trait of the Japanese personality largely to historical circumstances, inasmuch as during the Tokugawa period it appeared to be the practice to keep potential equals suspicious of each other—on the divide and rule principle—as well as dependent on the authority of a superior. Thus the danger implicit in meeting a situation that arose spontaneously was very real indeed. In order to prevent unplanned situations from occurring, the Japanese have woven a veritable web of rules embracing almost every aspect of interpersonal prescriptive relationships in an elaborate code of reciprocal obligations.

Here we shall touch on only a few of the codified norms, such as *on*, ascribed obligations and their reciprocals; *giri*, the contractual obligations, which have to be repaid "with mathematical equivalence"[27] and are subject to a time limit; and *gimu*, which includes *chu*, the duty to the emperor, *ko*, the duty to parents and ancestors, and *nimmu*, the duty to one's work, which "are limitless both in amount and in duration".[28] Yanaga suggests that the whole gamut of human obligational relationships is included in the concept *giri*, which is all-embracing in its implications. "No facet of life could exist outside it. Everybody must and does move within its orbit."[29] He goes on to state:

> *Giri* is an all pervading force in the behaviour of all classes of people and in all walks of life, the prime minister, the official, the businessman, financier, industrialist, intellectual, student, parent, the factory worker and the farmer. Although the complexities, and ambivalences of *giri* must be taken into account, it operates because of the universal need for respect-

ing and expressing "human feelings" (*ninjo*) in social life that
exists in closely knit communities. . . . the sanctions of *giri* are
to be found in society in the mores, customs and folkways,
and not in the laws.[30]

R.K. Beardsley endeavours to clarify the interrelationship
between *giri* and *ninjo*: "*Ninjo* refers to what one would
like to do as a human being and equally to what one finds
distasteful or abhorrent out of personal sentiment. *Giri*
pertains to what one must do or avoid doing because of
status and group membership."[31] Bennett, like Chitoshi
Yanaga, posits that these social norms are largely shared
by the Japanese population and represent a "cultural
model" which, although not always literally followed, is
"always available as a generalised protocol for use by the
individual"[32] to find his way through the maze of interpersonal relationships, and as a criterion for judging the
social actions of others. While Bennett suggests that during
the Tokugawa period only the samurai and the nobility
consistently adhered to the codified norms, during the
militaristic–nationalistic era of the 1930s and early 1940s,
the codified norms were given renewed emphasis as a
counter-measure against liberal trends and were widely
disseminated among the Japanese population as well as
incorporated in the school curriculum as ethical doctrine.

Since the codified norms covered every aspect of social
behaviour, spontaneous action was only seldom called for.
Emotional display such as weeping or excessive merriment
were considered incompatible with well-planned activity;
the stable individual—a man of few words—was believed
to be able to anticipate all eventualities and to be ready
to meet them. However, as Hulse points out, in Japan as
in other countries one meets "the problem of overt and
covert culture, of ideal standards versus practical
behaviour".[33] Thus when conflicts occur between obligations, or when the behaviour prescribed by the "cultural
model" does not actually fit the circumstances, individuals
in Japanese society are likely to fall back on two highly
favoured social techniques: indirection and self-dramatization.

Both patterns of behaviour are fairly common in the West, but tend to be more frequently and more skilfully employed in the Japanese social context. Self-dramatization is most often used in social situations where the culturally appropriate behaviour is unknown, often "as a· defence-mechanism".[34] Hulse suggests that self-dramatization "serves to make highly ritualistic behaviour not merely tolerable but actually a pleasure".[35] It involves a touch of arrogance, a flaunting of one's strength, even a degree of ruthlessness to oneself as well as to others, to demonstrate one's supreme confidence in the position one has taken. The Forty-seven Ronin are a classic example; they quite ruthlessly disregarded their ordinary obligations, neglected their families, debauched themselves in preparation for the final attack upon their dead master's adversary. To carry their action to its logical or extreme conclusion, the Forty-seven Ronin flaunted ordinary standards of behaviour and resorted not only to self-dramatization but to indirection.

As a technique of accomplishing one's end, "indirection has long been recognised as a characteristic feature of Japanese culture".[36] Hulse suggests that it could be called a "conventional method of circumventing convention".[37] Overt disagreement is considered rude and may prove socially disadvantageous, so that frankness is most often neither expected nor considered the socially appropriate behaviour. By careful use of apparently equivocal expressions, which can convey any number of meanings, Japanese avoid potentially dangerous social situations; by signifying acceptance of or at least partial acquiescence to the word or will of others, and in particular to the superior, they tend to simulate agreement. As shown in the final chapter, at Featherston and Cowra the techniques of self-dramatization and indirection were frequently used by individual prisoners and served to compound misunderstandings as well as to attenuate potentially dangerous situations.

Discontinuities in Child Training

Ruth Benedict contends that the discontinuities inherent in the child-raising process in pre-war Japan constitute one of the underlying reasons for the alleged inability of the Japanese to cope with unplanned situations. "The arc of life in Japan", postulates Benedict, "is plotted in opposite fashion to that in the United States. It is a great shallow U-curve with maximum freedom and indulgence allowed to babies and to the old. Restrictions are slowly increased after babyhood till having one's own way reaches a low just before and after marriage. This low line continues many years during the prime of life."[38] In the United States the curve is upside down: childhood is the time when firm discipline is exerted and only gradually relaxed as the child grows up. When a child matures and begins to support himself, he is entrusted with greater responsibility and given increasing freedom. The prime of life just before and after marriage is in the United States "the high point of freedom and initiative".[39] Restrictions tend to reappear when the man loses his strength and earning power and may become again dependent, either upon his family or the state.

Benedict suggests that both Japan and the United States have by their arrangement of "the arc of life" succeeded in mobilizing the individual's energetic participation in their culture during his prime of life. But the two countries have used different strategies: The United States by maximizing the individual's freedom of choice; Japan by maximizing the moral restraints. If we assume, then, that the majority of prisoners were in their prime of life, they appear to have been doubly handicapped to cope effectively with unforeseen eventualities. First, they had no rules in their cultural repertoire to cover circumstances such as internment by the enemy: surrender was not a "planned situation", and accordingly the members of the Japanese military forces did not have a culturally appropriate response ready. Second, according to Benedict, as the Japanese were in the prime of life their ability to improvise and to innovate or to act outside the cultural constraints governing their behaviour had been minimized by the arrangements which governed the Japanese individual's arc of life. And finally, the high value accorded to "collaterality" in Japanese society further limited the alternative behaviour patterns open to the Japanese prisoners.

The High Value of "Collaterality"

In Japan, whether in the urban or in the rural environment, it seems difficult to escape observation. The country is densely populated, houses tend to be close together, the building material used in their construction is rather flimsy, and even in one's own home there is likely to be little privacy. It therefore becomes imperative to exercise a large measure of self-control and to adapt one's conduct to the culturally accepted forms. Within the primary group, such as the family, explicit gradations of status exist between superiors and inferiors, largely determined by age and sex: "Hierarchy based on sex and generation and primogeniture are part and parcel of family life."[40] Appropriate rules of behaviour and the codified norms governing duties and obligations are rigorously inculcated in the growing child. Violations of the rules and norms are punished by ridicule and shame.

Harumi Befu points out that the sources of punishment tend, however, to rest outside of the family: Japanese parents often tend to resort to the menace of supernatural sanctions to frighten misbehaving children or to threaten that the police will come and take the children away. But the, most powerful sanction is the notion of shame: that "the neighbours or friends would ridicule or laugh".[41] To know shame is often translated as being a virtuous man, a man of honour; a failure to follow the explicit signposts of good behaviour, a failure to balance obligations or to foresee contingencies is a shame. Shame appears, in fact, to hold the same place in Japanese ethics as "a clear conscience", "being right with God" holds in Western ethics.[42]

Benedict distinguishes between cultures that rely heavily on shame and those that rely heavily on guilt to incalculate standards of morality:

> A society that inculcates absolute standards of morality and relies on men's developing a conscience is a guilt culture by definition . . . In a culture where shame is a major sanction, people are chagrined about acts which we expect people to feel guilty about. This chagrin can be very intense and it cannot be relieved, as guilt can be, by confession and atonement . . .
> True shame cultures rely on external sanctions for good behaviour, not, as true guilt cultures do, on an internalized conviction of sin.[43]

Shame then can be largely perceived as a reaction to other people's criticism and appears to be largely the product of the training in the self-sacrificing pursuit of repaying one's obligation: to the emperor, the nation, and the family. To maintain one's own good name and reputation is essential in order to retain the esteem of the group. Edwin O. Reischauer, whom Senator Mike Mansfield called the most knowledgeable envoy the United States ever sent to Japan (Mansfield himself was nominated by President Carter as ambassador to that country), observed that "The Japanese are taught to feel shame before society and to fear it. . . . to avoid shame and to win approval the Japanese must preserve 'face' and self-respect . . . a sense of shame and the need for self respect provide the Japanese with much the same individual driving force that we derive from conscience and a sense of guilt."[44]

In the West a sense of guilt has traditionally been related to universalistic moral systems, which govern the control of aggressive impulses interrelated with the consequences of behaviour within a group such as the family or a work group, and is thus largely conceived in prescriptive familistic terms:

> The keystone towards understanding Japanese guilt is held by the nature of interpersonal relationships within the Japanese

family, particularly the relations of the children with the mother. . . . She takes the burden of responsibility for their behaviour [and] will often manifest self-reproach if her children behave themselves badly or in any way fail to meet the standards of success set for the community. If one fails to meet the expectations, he thereby hurts his mother, and he also hurts other familial members; as a result he suffers unhappiness and feelings of guilt."[45]

The Japanese are, therefore, taught from a very early age to watch the judgement of the public, to react to other people's criticism—in other words, to respect the power of the group, and as Grew observed, the Japanese youngster learns to familiarize himself with "the discomfort which awaits him if he asserts his individual desire over the collective will."[46] Western social scientists on the whole,— R.D. Laing and his followers are notable exceptions—have tended to emphasize the supportive function of the group, and the family in particular. Talcott Parsons, however, suggests that in Japanese society group solidarity tends rather to intensify the anxieties of the individual than to support and protect him.

Instead of protecting the individual member and giving him security, the tendency, according to his status, is to push him into relations outside the group where he functions as a representative of the entire group rather than as an individual. He carries responsibility for its good name in the above sense. His success reflects credit on the group and is admired by them; but if he fails he disgraces the whole group and he is blamed and punished by their disapproval or in extreme cases by ostracism.[47]

Group goals are thus a matter of the highest priority, and "to extinguish the self and serve the group"[48] is regarded as the ideal behaviour pattern. William Caudill, in his paper "Patterns of Emotion in Modern Japan", notes that "collaterality stresses the welfare of the group, and consensus among its members, as primary goals".[49] Collaterality is distinct from lineality or individualism inasmuch as it emphasizes the importance of superior and subordinate relationships, while the latter focuses on the relative autonomy of the individual. Even in post–World War II Japanese society, collaterality appears to have remained the dominant value orientation, particularly as far as the sphere of family and occupational life is concerned. The high value placed on collaterality, together with the strains brought about by group solidarity, may have contributed to the development of some of the traits attributed to the compulsive personality.

Particularly in rural communities where the majority of the members of the modern Japanese military forces originated, the tensions engendered by collaterality must have been particularly severe. Social sanctions such as ridicule, shame, and ostracism were more powerful in the village context. Ostracism in particular was the time-favoured method of dealing effectively with nonconformists. Yoshi Sugihara in her study *Sensei and His People* vividly describes the effects of ostracism: farmers not only used to depend on the help of other villagers to till their fields, but also exchanged animals and agricultural implements; the whole community depended on the nightsoil collected in the village to manure their fields. On the psychological level, ostracism was a particularly effective sanction in the past; however, owing to modern mass communications and the relative ease of transport, villagers have been able, in contemporary Japanese society, to avoid the almost total social isolation imposed by ostracism in earlier times.[50] While ostracism has been blunted as a sanction—since the end of World War II Japanese courts have declared that ostracism is illegal—its effects are still feared by the rural population for their "nuisance value". Conformity to social rules, as well as the primacy accorded to group goals, are likely to be particularly deeply ingrained in those members of the armed forces who come from a rural environment.

"Amae"

In Japanese society the dependency of children on parents is fostered even beyond the nursing period and institutionalized in the social structure. However, the desire to be loved is not always simultaneously gratified. It might thus be useful to examine at this stage Takeo Doi's concept of *amae*, which he translates as "to depend and presume on another's love, or to seek and bask in another's indulgence".[51] Doi, who is a highly regarded Japanese psychiatrist, regards *Amae* as the "key concept for the understanding of the Japanese personality structure".[52] Although not everyone would agree with this, nevertheless the desire to "*amaeru*" (the transitive verb of the noun *Amae*) has great explanatory value. *Amaeru* is an expression of what the British psychologist Michael Balint calls "passive object love",[53] a behaviour akin to "wheedling"; the object of the behaviour is not, however, to manipulate relationships, but is largely prompted by the desire to be loved.

Benedict has called attention to the discontinuities in the Japanese child-raising process, where a period of great indulgence in early childhood tends to be followed by one of increasing discipline and regimentation, when the desire of the growing child to be loved is likely to be frustrated. Doi suggests that the frustration of primary love leads to the formation of narcissism—"as though the child said to himself, if the world does not love me enough, I have to love and gratify myself".[54] The development of narcissism at a certain stage in childhood is recognized as a universal phenomenon, but it appears likely that the Japanese "somehow continue the wish to be loved, even after the formation of narcissism'".[55] They do not relinquish the desire to establish interpersonal relations based on the notion of *amae*.

This exaggerated "dependency need" creates in the cognitive processes of the Japanese, according to the Japanese philosopher Nakamura, a tendency to emphasize a particular social nexus and to stress "immediate personal relationships".[56] Doi explains this tendency in psychological terms, by postulating that "the Japanese are always prepared to identify themselves with, or introject, an outside force, to the exclusion of other ways of coping with it".[57] Benedict has also noted this particular trait, when she posits that "the Japanese have an ethic of alternatives"[58] and that Japan's motivations are situational, referring particularly to the sudden complete turnabout of Japan following the defeat of the last war.[59] Both Benedict and Doi interpret the manner in which—to everyone's surprise—the Japanese as a whole willingly submitted to the emperor's order to surrender to the Allies in 1945—presumably as motivated by a desire to "please the Emperor, even in [Japan's] defeat".[60]

The desire to *amaeru* and the emphasis on immediate personal relationships may in certain circumstances override other firmly held values and norms. In the context of events at Featherston and at Cowra, therefore, the possibility that the actions of the Japanese prisoners may have been engendered by situational factors must also be taken into account. Values such as preserving their good name and regaining the esteem of their families, the nation, and the emperor may have been of secondary importance to the desire to be loved by their fellow prisoners by acceding to their demands, or by a wish to please superiors (as in the Featherston situation) with whom they had established close interpersonal relationships.

To sum up: there is a tendency in Japanese society, which was paramount in Tokugawa times and still appears to persist in contemporary Japan, to give priority to the requirements of the group, the enhancement of its position and its aims, rather than to the furtherance of individual goals and benefits. However, when confronted with an unforeseen situation which is not clearly charted by behavioural norms, collaterality may become a less dominant value. The situational ethic of the Japanese and the emphasis on immediate personal relations, posited by

Benedict and Doi respectively, may under such conditions override all other considerations.

The Decision-Making Process in Japanese Society

The manner in which people arrive at individual and group decisions may be regarded as the epitome of a society's ideology as well as one of the most important action products of its thinking. In Japanese society, the high value accorded collaterality, social harmony,[61] conformity, and the social norms requiring the repayment of even the slightest obligation foster a trend towards unanimous decisions. According to F.N. Kerlinger, Japanese culture does not sit comfortably with the idea of split decisions. Every unit in society, whether it be a family, social, or business organization, seems to feel that it must present a solid front to the world. Conformity to the group is a major consideration and accounts, at least partially, for the passion of unanimity in group decisions.[62] Chitoshi Yanaga, a Japanese scholar, now professor of political science at Yale, postulates: "Majority decision is unknown in Japan in spirit, although it is quite evident in form. Japanese passion for harmony and unity makes resort to the unanimity rule almost inevitable for them. This is achieved through the conversion by various sorts of persuasions of the minority point of view."[63]

Thus majority decisions which have been arrived at by the process of voting are often represented to outsiders, such as the news media, as unanimous decisions. Kerlinger cites the case of the appointment of a superintendent of education in one of the prefectures of Shikol, as an example: although the superintendent was selected by the vote of four to three members of the Board of Education, the local newspapers reported the election "as the unanimous decision of the Board of Education".[64]

Individual decisions in a society which emphasizes the group—and de-emphasizes or even decries the individual,[65]

as Sansom puts it—are largely proscribed. It is considered
brash to make definite, clear-cut decisions regarding oneself
or others, and it is culturally appropriate to maintain reserve
—*enryo*—by refraining from expressing one's own opinion,
or urging its acceptance as a possible course of action. An
individual might, however, covertly indicate his opinion by
the use of indirection and circumlocution, always careful
neither to offend the sensibilities of others nor to expose
himself to ridicule and shame. When faced with the
necessity of making outright decisions, the Japanese will go
to great lengths to avoid putting themselves into a position
from which there is no retreat. If at all possible, they will
invariably pass the onus of making the decision to a group,
or at least to some other person.

Formal or informal groups in Japanese society tend to
arrive at decisions by the *"Suisen-Sansei-Igi-Nashi*
(Recommendation–Agreement–No-Objection) System"[66] in
which decisions are reached by the entire group—almost
by a process of empathy. The chairman of the group,
usually an older and experienced individual, does not
function as in most Western societies, to help the participants to express themselves freely and to guide the discussion, but "to divine the will of the group". The special
ability of the chairman to effect a decision in this manner
is called *haragei* (belly art); he then proceeds to express
the "will" of the group and states the decision reached.

J.C. Abegglen posits that this "diffuse, group-centred
decision-making apparatus"[67] should not be compared to
the reaching of a consensus in a Western context; this could
raise inappropriate connotations since direct confrontations
are avoided. Herman Kahn postulates that "a dissident
party may also be placated by granting him a concession
on some issue totally unrelated to the decision at hand—
or by conceding an obligation to make up, whenever the
opportunity occurs, any losses suffered by a generous
concession on the matter at issue".[68]

The Japanese decision-making process appears to be
analogous to "taking decisions by the sense of the

meeting",[69] the method employed by élite councils at British universities, for instance. F.G. Bailey suggests that multiplex relationships between the participants may explain, at least partly, their reluctance to involve themselves in overt confrontations.[70]

As far as the Japanese decision-making process is concerned, Kerlinger suggests that a complex of inhibiting cultural concepts prevents a Japanese from challenging the "expressed will of the group as stated by the leader".[71] This concept of hierarchical authority, as embodied—even if only temporarily—in the leader of the group, is so strongly inculcated that even an unwanted minority decision can be forced down the majority's throat without challenge. Kahn also points out that under these circumstances it is often difficult to determine who the effective decision-makers are, since the decisions are made by all the participants, each of whom, in theory at least, "has veto power".[72]

On the basis of the emphasis accorded hierarchical status positions and their relative permanence, most decisions in Japanese society should be imposed from the top down, particularly in bureaucratic structures such as the army. However, as noted earlier, there were occasions when the junior officers reached decisions and carried them out without consulting their seniors. The *gekokujo* spirit—the overwhelming of the seniors by the junior officers—which characterized the behaviour of the lower and middle echelons of the Japanese Army in the 1930s has now become institutionalized.

In contemporary Japan the *Ringi* system has been developed, whereby junior officials in a government department or in large business enterprises achieve a consensus among themselves on an issue on which they think a decision should be made. The draft decision is then circulated, first to the lower levels of the organization, whose suggestions may be sought and incorporated in the original draft, then to the higher levels, and finally to the corporate heads "who now are under rather serious pressure" to implement the decision reached by the junior officials.[73] Thus, as suggested in the final chapter, decisions regarding the action to be taken at Cowra need not necessarily have been imposed by the senior NCOs; their hand could have been forced by the junior NCOs or even the ORs.

"Enryo"

Not only the mechanisms of decision-making but also the social norms of *enryo* have changed and adapted themselves to the requirements of modern Japanese society. While the original meaning of *enryo*—behavioural reserve and hesitancy—characterized the culturally appropriate social interaction between subordinate and superior in hierarchical status relations, *enryo* has become in modern society "an escape hatch", an alternative behaviour pattern in situations where the status differences between the participants in a social encounter have not been clearly delineated.[74] Obsequiousness and compliance are the expected responses to a superior. When frustrated, the subordinate will, in accordance with *enryo*, not only check his temper or aggressive impulses but also be prepared to bide his time.

In modern industrialized society, social interactions have become far more complex and ambiguous, with the result that violations of traditional norms are even more likely to occur. Yet because the basic hierarchical, primary group character of the behavioural rules still prevails, *enryo* has remained an important adjustive behaviour pattern, manifesting reserve and non-commitment when particular situations lack clear designation of status positions, and serving as a mechanism for the concealment of ignorance and confusion.

Face saving

Toro Matsumoto suggests that the social order that prevailed in Japanese society before World War II put a premium on social prestige; in order to maintain one's place in society, face saving—the art of finding a scapegoat who may be blamed for a failure[75]—became a generalized behaviour pattern, because in Japan no one can admit failure and expect to keep his place in society. Thus, challenging the decision of the leader or chairman of a group on the premise that it does not actually represent the will of the group would reflect not only on the ability of the leader but also on the wisdom of the whole group. The special ability of the leader to reach a decision— *haragei*—may be regarded as another form of face saving, since dissension is culturally inappropriate and the fiction of harmony and unity of a group must be by all means upheld.

The relative intolerance of Japanese society towards errors and personal failures is attributed by Matsumoto to the high value attached to group cohesiveness, for "when an individual fails, he is a broken cog and the social machine is out of order".

> If a schoolboy who is being tutored fails, the boy loses face to the tutor, and the tutor loses face to the family of the boy, and the family loses face to relatives. So the father blames the tutor, the tutor blames the boy, but the boy, poor thing, has no one to blame. In a serious matter, when the one who has failed or made a mistake has been responsible for the honour and lives of others, the only way to save face is to disappear or to commit suicide.[76]

While the damage done by failure or mistake cannot be undone, society in Japan tends to forgive those who failed but were prepared to follow the rules and pay the price of their failures.

To conclude, Robert Huntington may be justified when he suggests that "the Japanese personality has weak, indistinct, permeable boundaries between self and other; is dependent as opposed to independent; group-cooperative rather than self-reliant; conforming rather than innovative; and accepting of personal rather than rational-legal authority".[77] The average Japanese appears to have a very sensitive ego, and on the whole tends not to wish to put himself into a position where he is holding a minority (or even worse, an unpopular) viewpoint. Thus, when involved in the decision-making process, individuals might display a tendency towards forgoing personally held values, while endeavouring to adapt their views to those generally held by the group, accepting, at least overtly, the decision divined by *haragei*. But while there may be a tendency towards shirking individual responsibility for decisions in Japanese society, by no means have all individuals in Japan been socialized to the same extent. Thus, as far as the responsibility for the decision to break out at Cowra was concerned, Sergeant-Major Kanazawa, the leader of B camp, may have accepted unequivocally his responsibility for the event; on the other hand, the deputy leader, Flight-Sergeant Yoshida, stated: "Since the incident was carried out with the consent of all members, the responsibility should be shared by all".[78]

The concluding section of this chapter briefly examines some aspects of the Japanese attitudes concerning death, which tend to range from an almost mythical preoccupation with death to an explicit order to seek death rather than surrender to the enemy; from romantic notions of a glorious death for the emperor and the nation on the battlefield to the pragmatic advice of the squadron leader in Shohei Ooka's autobiographical novel, *Fires in the Plains*, in which a Japanese soldier suffering from tuberculosis has been sent back from the hospital to his unit during the last stages of the campaign in the Philippines. The squadron leader, who realizes that the man is of no further use to his unit, pulls no punches, and his admonishment, as described by Ooka, is very revealing:

> We are all fighting for our lives, we have no place for anyone who can't pull his weight. . . . You've damned well got to get back to that hospital. If they won't let you in, just plant yourself by the front door and wait until they do. They will take care of you at the end. And if they still refuse, then well, you'd better put your hand grenade to good use and make an end to it all. At least you'd be carrying out your final duty to your country.[79]

The practice of killing patients in hospital rather than let them fall into the hands of the enemies is also confirmed by Lieutenant Hiro Onoda in his book, *No Surrender: My Thirty Year War*. He supplies hand grenades to the patients of a field hospital on Lubang, as he emphasizes, on their insistent demand.

Furthermore, in a personal communication dated 6 May 1977, Mr Russell Orr, who spent some time at Featherston Camp as a trainee interpreter and later took part in the Pacific campaigns, reports: "We came upon a jungle field hospital which had been hastily abandoned by the retreating Japanese. Medical personnel had hastily decamped, leaving badly wounded patients to their own devices. The skeletons of scores of men still lay in their bedcots. Some had crawled a short distance before being overtaken by death. Some had sought quick release from their agony by grenade or a bullet through the brain. All had died horribly." He contrasts this attitude with "normal" procedures instituted in Allied field hospitals in case of retreat: "This would not have happened in an Allied field hospital. In such a situation every effort would have been made to evacuate the wounded. Failing this, some doctors and medical personnel would have stayed behind to tend the wounded and go into captivity with them."

The Japanese Attitude Towards Death

If the chronicles of the eleventh century can be relied upon, the true warrior of the earlier ages held his life to be of no more value than a feather and was prepared at all times to forfeit his life in battle, convinced that his family would benefit from the reward that his sacrifice would bring. The exaggerated sense of pride and "face" of the·samurai, which apparently caused him on many occasions to act contrary to reason and good sense, is illustrated by an incident which occurred during the civil wars:

In a certain battle a youthful warrior named Kagemasa, who
was a bare sixteen years of age, was shot in the left eye. With
the arrow shaft still protruding from his face he closed with
and destroyed his adversary. One of Kagemasa's allies,
Tametsugu, attempted to aid the fallen boy by placing his
sandalled foot against Kagemasa's cheek to withdraw the
arrow. In great indignation Kagemasa leaped up and declared
that, while he was prepared as a samurai to die from an arrow
wound he would allow no man to put a foot on his face. So
saying, he even attempted in his rage to cut down the hapless
Tametsugu.[80]

Poetic exchanges between samurai antagonists—such as
that reported by Inazo Nitobe, in *Bushido, the Soul of
Japan*, which took place in the fifteenth century—indicate
that the values of ethereal bushido continued to permeate
material virtues:

> It passes current among us [Japanese] as a piece of authentic
> history, that as Ota Dokan, the great builder of the castle of
> Tokyo, was pierced through with a spear, his assassin, knowing
> the poetical predilection of his victim, accompanied his thrust
> with this couplet:

> "Ah, how in moments like these
> Our heart doth grudge the light of life";

> whereupon the expiring hero, not one whit daunted by the
> mortal wound in his side, added the lines:

> "Had not in hours of peace,
> It learned to lightly look on life."[81]

The *Hagakure*, the manual of bushido compiled in the
eighteenth century, contains the famous lines "*bushido*
means the determined will to die"[82] and stresses that by
thinking morning and evening of death and by familiar-
izing oneself with the concept, death will carry no sting.
This attitude towards mortality, which no longer expresses
either the bravado or the romanticism of the earlier ages
but rather the sobriety of Zen Buddhism, is closely linked
with the high value accorded absolute loyalty to the feudal
lord during the Tokugawa period. "The practice of the

Zen", as Takeda Shingen (1521–73), one of the great
warlords of the sixteenth century, puts it, "has no secret,
except standing on the verge of life and death."[83]

The high values of frugality and diligence are linked with
the samurai's concept of death in another manual of
bushido, the *Budo Shoshinshu*, also compiled during the
eighteenth century states:

> One who lives long in this world may develop all sorts of
> desires and his covetousness may increase so that he wants what
> belongs to others and cannot bear to part with what is his own,
> becoming in fact just like a mere tradesman. But if he is always
> looking death in the face, a man will have little attachment
> to material things and will not exhibit these grasping and
> covetous qualities, and will become, as I said before, a fine
> character.[84]

Death in the service of one's lord was considered the most
appropriate end for a samurai and had, as R.N. Bellah
suggests, "almost a 'saving' quality, in the religious sense".[85]
Yamaga Soko's writing in the seventeenth century prepared
the way for the restoration of the emperor as the subject
of total devotion and loyalty. Thus from the beginning of
the nineteenth century the notion of dying a glorious death
for the emperor on the battlefield is expressed in a
particularly telling manner by Yoshida Shoin, whose writings on the value of death exerted enormous influence not
only on his contemporaries but also on succeeding gener-
ations:

> From the beginning of the year to the end, day and night,
> morning and evening, in action and repose, in speech and in
> silence, the warrior must keep death constantly before him and
> have ever in mind that the one death [which he has to give]
> should not be suffered in vain. In other words [he must have
> perfect control over his own death] just as if he were holding
> an intemperate steed in rein. Only he who truly keeps death
> in mind this way can understand what is meant by . . .
> "preparedness".[86]

Yoshida Shoin not only revived Yamaga Soko's emphasis
on the importance of being prepared for death, but also

referred to the values of traditional bushido as expressed
in the *Hagakure*, which exalts death as an act that
transcends all human striving and stresses the high value
of a meaningful death. Addressing his admonition to
members of the armed forces in particular, Yoshida
enlarged further on the value of death in battle:

> If a general and his men fear death and are apprehensive over
> possible defeat, then they will unavoidably suffer defeat and
> death. But if they make up their minds, from the general down
> to the last footsoldier, not to think of living but only of standing
> in one place and facing death together, then, though they may
> have no other thought than meeting death, they will instead
> hold on to life and gain victory.[87]

As Bellah suggests, death in a military context can come
to symbolize supreme loyalty and devotion.[88] Yoshida
Shoin's example of preparedness for death and self-sacrifice
—he was executed in 1859 after an unsuccessful attempt
at preventing a crucial message from the shogun reaching
the emperor—exerted great influence on the morale of
members of the armed forces. Newspapers and government
propaganda further dramatized the national effort and the
aims for which the young men of Japan were dying in
actions on the Asiatic mainland in the late nineteenth and
early twentieth centuries. After the Russo–Japanese War of
1904–5, a new shrine to honour the war dead, the Yasukini
Jinja, became the focus of patriotic fervour.

Western nations, during this period, experienced a similar
revival of nationalistic and patriotic sentiments; the British,
for instance, in Victorian times were motivated to fight for
queen and country. Although death *per se*, as symbolizing
supreme loyalty, was understressed, personal valour and
bravery were highly valued and even posthumously honoured by prestigious decorations, such as the Victoria Cross.
After World War I the British had the Whitehall Cenotaph
and the French the Tomb of the Unknown Soldier beneath
the Arc de Triomphe, which became the venue of national
days and remembrance services. But although death on the
battlefield was honoured in the West, it was never regarded

as the ultimate test of loyalty for military personnel.

The mythical element in the Japanese preoccupation with death appeared to be deeply rooted in the notions of the Shinto belief system, which were revived in the nineteenth century by Yoshida Shoin and other writers. During the twentieth century *kokutai no hongi* further elaborated these beliefs, intertwining them even more closely with the emperor cult: in order to achieve a perfect identification with the "national essence", which is symbolized by the emperor, each individual subject must be prepared to face a meaningful death. The rationale for a glorious death in the service of the emperor is expressed in the belief that only by casting one's self aside and by the total acceptance of the "august Will as one's own"[89] could the desired fusing of the individual's identity with the national essence be achieved.

Kazuko Tsurumi, a contemporary Japanese sociologist, suggests that one of the main objectives of the education system in Japan before World War II was—in conjunction with the training provided by the compulsory military service— to socialize citizens for death. In her study, *Social Change and the Individual,* Tsurumi traces the methods used by the educational process to inculcate in the students a sharp sense of the limits beyond which the students must not think rationally: "A rational way of thinking was encouraged only insofar as it did not subject the Emperor system itself to critical scrutiny. . . . The application of rational thought to analysis of the Emperor system was a criminal offense punishable as *lèse majesté.* "[90]

The infallibility of the nation's head, in whose name all government policies were proclaimed, was thus firmly established in the mind of the students. One of the ramifications of the propagation of the emperor cult through the national educational system was that fear of denunciation tended to impede rational discussion of any issue which touched on the political system. Under the provisions of the Peace and Order Preservation Law of 1925, all organizations and individuals who propagated activities regarded as intending to bring about changes of the national polity were liable to arrest and prosecution. The spectrum of ideologies held by individuals or groups charged with offences under this law ranged from anarchism and communism to Christianity and democracy.

The socialization processes employed by the military authorities were designed to further reinforce the commitment of Japanese subjects to the national ideals. The continuity between the type of moral education inculcated by the education system and the army socialization process was moreover emphasized by the stress placed by both systems on rote learning. The Imperial Rescript on Education, which was recited within the school system not only in the regular classes on moral education, but on all ceremonial occasions, was replaced in the context of military training by the Imperial Rescript to Soldiers and Sailors. The language used in both moral codes was formal and ceremonial, and, as Tsurumi asserts, "the common denominator was the fetishism of words as words".[91] To train individuals to recite meticulously, word for word, either the Rescript on Education or the Rescript to Soldiers and Sailors was seemingly the objective of both the educational system as well as military training, rather than to encourage an understanding of the true meaning of these moral codes.

The technique of employing language to convey "imperfect communications" where the recipient of a message is not expected to comprehend fully the meaning of the words, "but only to grasp vaguely what they were about"[92] has of course not only been exploited by the Japanese authorities to create an aura of sanctity as far as the emperor's pronouncements were concerned. A multiplicity of religious beliefs and ideologies have made use of similar strategies. One-way systems of communications, where the subject of the socialization process is expected to absorb the messages of the socializing agency, and internalize them, even if their meaning is not entirely clear, are as old as history. The utterances of the oracle of Delphi, the injunctions of some of the minor prophets, the sayings of Buddha, and papal encyclicals, as well as the exhortations of Orwell's Big Brother, are some instances where imperfect communications were used in the context of the socialization process.

The Japanese authorities, however, according to Tsurumi, used imperfect communications as a method of indoctrinating soldiers in the ideology of death. In contrast with perfect communications, which in theory at least clearly define the duties and obligations of the socializee—in this case the Japanese serviceman—imperfect communications tend to create an ambience of ambiguity, expanding "the range of duties and obligations that can be demanded of the socializee almost without limits, at the discretion of the socializer".[93] When therefore the Rescript solemnly admonishes soldiers and sailors to bear in mind that duty is weightier than a mountain, while death is lighter than a feather, this glorification of death could be interpreted as providing an incentive for seeking death to advance the national cause and thus the cause of the emperor.

Positive incentives were also provided to socialize Japanese servicemen for death, in the form of prestige. Not only were they told that they would become "gods of the fatherland" and venerated in the Yasukini Shrine, but popular beliefs were fostered such as that any dead member of a family who succumbed to a glorious death in battle would become a god and be able to protect the members of his family. As Tsurumi puts it:

> Whereas a family god protects just his own family, a Yasukuni god protects the entire fatherland. This mark of distinction ennobles not only the individual soldier but his whole family, since his family name is listed among the gods. According to the Confucian doctrine . . . the achievement of fame for one's family name is the ultimate stage of filial piety. Thus, in the act of dying for the Emperor, the unity of loyalty and filial piety was held to be fully realized. In contrast, to fail to die like a soldier and to allow oneself to be captured by the enemy was to disgrace not only oneself but one's family and village community.[94]

Filial piety, loyalty to the group, and absolute obedience
to the emperor demanded that a soldier sought death on
the battlefield; any other course of action would bring
dishonour not only upon the individual but his family.
Tsurumi, however, notes that, broadly speaking, those who
had only received compulsory elementary education tended
to accept unquestioningly that they had to die for the glory
of the emperor, in much the same spirit that they accepted
their life-long obligation to support their parents. Excerpts
published by Tsurumi from diaries and letters of men who
had attended secondary schools and universities give the
impression that at least some of the members of the better
educated sector of the Japanese population only grudgingly
submitted to the rigorous socialization process of the
military authorities, and were reluctant to accept that it
was indeed their sacred duty to lay down their lives for
the emperor.

But even the doubts of this sector of the population about
the methods used by the military in the training of recruits,
as well as the injunction to die for the emperor, were often
allayed by the strong patriotic attitudes engendered by
nationalism, which had been deeply inculcated in every
Japanese. While patriotic notions such as the sacred obligation of laying down one's life in the service of king and
country had been hotly debated in the West, and often de-
emphasized by the more educated sector of the population,
such sentiments, fanned by the flames of militarism and
ultranationalism, had continued to flourish in the Japan of
the 1930s. The lines—

> My friend, you would not tell with such high zest
> To children ardent for some desperate glory,
> The old lie *Dulce et decorum est*
> *Pro patria mori.*[95]

had made a great impact on the undergraduates of British
universities, while the popularity of Hemingway's novel *A
Farewell to Arms* and Remarque's *All Quiet on the
Western Front* indicate that the disenchantment with war

and dying for one's country was an international phenomenon.

In Japan, however, sentiments of patriotism and self-sacrifice, which are deeply rooted in cultural traditions, continued to flourish. Yukio Mishima, for instance, in his short story "Patriotism" vividly describes the conflicting loyalties and emotions of a young officer, Lieutenant Takeyama, during the heady days of the February 1936 army mutiny. The hero is profoundly disturbed by the knowledge that many of his fellow officers, some of whom are his close friends, are on the side of the mutineers, whose aim it is to destroy the evil men who monopolized access to the throne[96] and to restore imperial rule. But the large majority of the imperial forces had refrained from joining the dissident elements, and rather than become involved in a confrontation between the opposing forces, Lieutenant Takeyama chooses to commit *seppuku*, together with his wife, reaffirming in a suicide note his dual loyalty to the emperor and the imperial forces.

Mishima, one of the most gifted of the contemporary Japanese novelists, himself committed *seppuku* in November 1970. The officers and soldiers, whom he addressed from a balcony at Itchigaya, refused to listen to his harangue, enjoining them to uphold the great Japanese traditions of the past and to refute the blandishments of Western materialism, "Are you not going to listen to a samurai who is ready to die for your cause?" This final appeal to his audience appeared to have no effect and, in a dramatic gesture, Mishima disembowelled himself in the traditional ceremonial manner. His last words, before one of his followers cut off his head with a sword, were "Long live the Emperor!"[97]

In a farewell message to his American translator, Donald Keene, Mishima outlined his motives for his final action: by commiting *seppuku*, he hoped to free his spirit from degradation and, referring to the theme of his novel *The Sailor Who Fell from Grace with the Sea*, implied that he could only atone by a blood sacrifice for the moral

degeneration of his nation. Not unlike General Nogi, who
in 1912 also committed *seppuku*, Mishima hoped to draw
attention to the "cultural emasculation and moral degeneration" of post-war Japan and thereby inspire a revival of
samurai virtues.[98]
There is, however, yet another aspect of Mishima's
dramatic gesture which may be relevant to our understanding of the behaviour of the Cowra prisoners, who faced
almost certain death when attempting to escape from the
well-guarded camp: Mishima, following the dictum of the
well-known fifteenth century philosopher Wang Yang-ming
that "to know and not to act is the same as not knowing
at all", believed that being aware of the decadence of
contemporary Japan, it was morally incumbent upon a man
of strong convictions, like himself, to take action. *Yomei*,
Wang Yang-ming's neo-Confucian philosophy, had been an
important, if intermittent, influence on Japanese scholars
since the fifteenth century, and had been revived in the
nineteenth century by Oshio Heihachiro, whose ideas may
have largely determined Mishima's final action. Thus in a
communication addressed to Ivan Morris shortly before his
death, Mishima wrote: "You may be one of the few people
who can understand my conclusion. Influenced by *Yomei*
(Wang Yang-ming) philosophy, I have believed that knowing without acting is not sufficient and that action itself does
not require any effectiveness. . . . "[99]
In the context of the Cowra situation, it would therefore
be possible to surmise that at least some of the prisoners,
following in cultural traditions established and perpetuated
since the fifteenth century, may have believed that the
inherent value of a sincere self-sacrificial act—such as
seeking to escape from the well-defended camp when the
outcome was an almost foregone conclusion—had a value
which transcended its actual effectiveness. The glorification
of failure, in the true Japanese heroic tradition, appears to
be deeply rooted in her culture. In his study *The Nobility
of Failure*, Morris provides a number of telling examples,
including the dismal fate of Oshio Heihachiro (the reviver

of *Yomei* philosophy), and notes that the certainty of failure may have added to the intrinsic value of Mishima's act, for as Morris puts it "it is the journey and not the arrival that matters".[100]

However, it is not only firmly entrenched philosophical and moral convictions about the value of a meaningful death that may offer explanations for the behaviour of the Japanese captives; features of the Japanese psychology, such as the concept of *amae* as expounded by Takeo Doi, should also be carefully examined. To Western society, individual freedom is a cherished article of faith, although Doi notes that some Western philosophers have cast doubt on the universal validity of this fundamental concept. In particular, he refers here to Marx's concept of alienation, Nietzsche's interpretation of Christianity as the morality of slaves, and Freud's emphasis on the control of the spiritual life by the unconscious as antithetical to individual freedom. In contrast with Western society the Japanese have long ago—certainly since the end of the Heian period—held that the freedom of the individual is a psychological impossibility. This may be another instance of Japan's impressive cultural continuity on the psychological level; as Doi suggests, "For the Japanese, freedom in practice existed only in death, which is why praise of death and incitement towards death could occur so often. This occurred because the Japanese were living according to the *amae* psychology."[101]

It is therefore not surprising that praise of and incitement towards death should appear so frequently in the Japanese Military Field Code of 1941. Under the heading of "Unity", for example, the code admonishes: "It is essential that each man, high and low dutifully observing his place, should be determined always to sacrifice himself for the whole, in accordance with the intentions of the commander, by reposing every confidence in his comrades, and without the slightest thought to personal interest and to life and death."[102]

The official view of life and death, perhaps, expresses

Doi's notion of the Japanese acceptance of the loss and suppression of individual freedom most succinctly: "The lofty spirit of self-sacrificing service to the state must prevail in life or death. . . . calmly face death rejoicing in the hope of living in the eternal cause for which you serve."[103] While death on the metaphysical level appears to symbolize the fusion with the essence of Japan, on the psychological level it may be the only means of becoming truly free—free from the all-prevailing ties of dependency inherent in the concepts of *ninjo* and *giri*, for example.

Whether one wishes to suggest that compliance with Japanese codes of ethics is one of the explanations for the behaviour of Japanese prisoners of war, or whether one accepts that the concept of *amae* may have played a pivotal role, three important points have to be considered at this stage, all of them closely related to the cultural consistency that characterizes values and norms in Japanese society.

First, adherence to ethical codes appears to be deeply rooted in Japan's historical tradition. Outward manifestations of the codes may change over time—*bushido*, for instance, has developed from ethereal bushido to militant bushido, and some of its tenets are incorporated in *Kokutai no hongi* and the Military Field Code of 1941—but certain concepts, such as loyalty, obedience, and filial piety have remained an important part of the infrastructure of social life.

Second, the notion of *amae*, which according to Doi plays such an important part in the psychological make up of the Japanese personality, may also provide a motivation for the behaviour of Japanese prisoners of war, particularly of those involved in the Cowra incident.

Third, the value of an action in Japanese society may not necessarily be directly related to its successful outcome: if the philosophical notions of *Yomei*, as expounded by Mishima, were indeed widely held, the Featherston as well as the Cowra prisoners of war may have felt it necessary to act, to indicate they knew that they had transgressed against the code of ethics rather than considered whether the outcome of their action would have any chance of succeeding.

It is therefore indeed possible that the notion of seeking death "when the time came", as Asada suggests in *The Night of a Thousand Suicides*, permeated the thoughts of the Cowra prisoners and that the break-out was not an incident brought about by the initiative of a few fanatics, but represented a 'unanimous' decision by the prisoners held in B camp. As Asada puts it, it "was intended to create a place in which to die; in other words, mass suicide. Why Japanese prisoners should desire to do this could only be understood by Japanese, because the cause lies in ethnical beliefs rather than in reason."[104]

However, it is important to keep in mind that all sectors of the Japanese population (including, of course, the members of the armed forces) were differentially inculcated with the values and norms of *Kokutai no hongi*, and those inherent in the Military Field Code of 1941. Furthermore one cannot assume that the personality structure of the prisoners of war was identical. Their response to the crises that arose at Featherston and at Cowra was unlikely to be characterized by conformity. It seems that the key to the events at Cowra and Featherston must be sought in the impressive cultural continuity which appeared to permeate the value orientation of Japanese society to such a high degree.

Notes

1. A.F.C. Wallace, *Culture and Personality* (New York: Random House, 1966), p.6.
2. Victor Barnouw, *Culture and Personality* (Homewood, Ill.: Dorsey Press, 1963), p.8.
3. Ibid., p.26.
4. Geoffrey Gorer, "Themes in Japanese Culture", in *Personal Character and Cultural Milieu*, ed. D.G. Haring (Syracuse: Syracuse University Press, 1949), p.285.

5. W.L. La Barre, "Some Observations on Character Structure in the Orient: The Japanese", *Psychiatry* 8, no.3 (1945): 326.
6. Ibid.
7. Ruth Benedict, *The Crysanthemum and the Sword* (London: Routledge, 1967), p.181.
8. A.H. Leighton, *The Governing of Men* (Princeton: Princeton University Press, 1946), p.92.
9. D.G. Haring, "Japanese National Character: Cultural Anthropology, Psychoanalysis and History" in *Personal Character and Cultural Milieu*, ed. D.G. Haring, 3rd rev. ed. (Syracuse: Syracuse University Press, 1964), p.428.
10. Brigitte Lanham, "Aspects of Child Care in Japan", in *Personal Character and Cultural Milieu*, ed. D.G. Haring, 3rd rev. ed. (Syracuse: Syracuse University Press, 1964), p.581.
11. Benedict, *The Crysanthemum and the Sword*, p.146.
12. Chie Nakane, *Japanese Society* (London: Weidenfeld and Nicolson, 1970), p.150.
13. Edwin O. Reischauer, *The United States and Japan*, 3rd ed. (Cambridge, Mass.: Harvard University Press, 1965), p.134.
14. Ibid.
15. Haring, "Japanese National Character", p.430.
16. Ibid.
17. Edwin O. Reischauer, *Japan Past and Present* (London: Duckworth, 1964), p.199.
18. Haring, "Japanese National Character", p.432.
19. Ibid., p.433.
20. Ibid., p.435.
21. Ibid., p.436.
22. Ibid.
23. J.W. Bennett, H. Passin, and R.K. McKnight, *In Search of Identity* (Minneapolis: University of Minnesota Press, 1958), p.228.
24. F.S. Hulse, "Convention and Reality in Japanese Culture", *Southwestern Journal of Anthropology* 4, no.4 (1948): 345.
25. Benedict, *The Crysanthemum and the Sword*, p.292.
26. Reischauer, *United States and Japan*, p.141.
27. Benedict, *The Crysanthemum and the Sword*, p.82.
28. Ibid., p.81.
29. Chitoshi Yanaga, *Japanese People and Politics* (New York, Wiley, 1956), p.59.
30. Ibid., p.60.
31. J.W. Hall and R.K. Beardsley, eds., *Twelve Doors to Japan* (New York: McGraw-Hill, 1965), p.95.
32. Bennett, Passin, and McKnight, *In Search of Identity*, p.227.
33. Hulse, "Convention and Reality", p.347.
34. Ibid., p.350.
35. Ibid.

36. Ibid., p.351.
37. Ibid.
38. Benedict, *The Crysanthemum and the Sword*, p.177.
39. Ibid., p.178.
40. Ibid., p.34.
41. Harumi Befu, *Japan, an Anthropological Introduction* (San Francisco: Chandler, 1971), p.158.
42. Benedict, *The Crysanthemum and the Sword*, p.157.
43. Ibid., pp.156–57.
44. Reischauer, *United States and Japan*, pp.143–44.
45. Edward Norbeck and George de Vos, "Japan", in *Psychological Anthropology*, ed. Francis L.K. Hsu (Homewood, Ill.: Dorsey Press, 1961), p.27.
46. Joseph C. Grew, *Report from Tokyo* (Sydney: Angus and Robertson, 1943), p.35.
47. Talcott Parsons, "Population and Social Structure", in *Japan's Prospects*, ed. Douglas G. Haring (Cambridge, Mass.: Harvard University Press, 1946), p.100.
48. D.W. Plath, *The After Hours: Modern Japan and the Search for Enjoyment* (Berkeley: University of California Press, 1969), p.78.
49. William Caudill, "Patterns of Emotion in Modern Japan", in *Japanese Culture*, ed. R.J. Smith and R.K. Beardsley (London: Methuen, 1963), p.115.
50. Yoshie Sugihara and D.W. Plath, *Sensei and His People* (Berkeley: University of California Press, 1967), p.327.
51. Takeo Doi, "Giro and Ninjo: An Interpretation", in *Aspects of Social Change in Modern Japan*, ed. R.P. Dore (Princeton: Princeton University Press, 1967), p.327.
52. Takeo Doi, "Amae: A Key Concept for the Understanding of the Japanese Personality Structure" in Smith and Beardsley, *Japanese Culture*, p.132.
53. Michael Balint, *Primary Love and Psychoanalytic Technique* (London: Hogarth, 1952), p.69.
54. Doi, "Amae", p.135.
55. Ibid.
56. Ibid., p.137.
57. Ibid.
58. Benedict, *The Crysanthemum and the Sword*, p.214.
59. Doi, "Amae", p.137.
60. Ibid.
61. T.L. Blackmore in "Post-War Developments in Japanese Law" (*University of Wisconsin Law Review*, July 1947, p.649) calls attention to "the amazing lack of litigation in Japan". This attitude correlates with the attitudes observed by Yanaga, "that differences in social relations should be settled without resort to legal means and something is wrong with individuals who cannot compose

differences and live harmoniously" (Yanaga, *Japanese People and Politics* p.362.)

62. F.N. Kerlinger, "Decision-Making in Japan", *Social Forces* 30, no.1 (1951–52): 37.
63. Chitoshi Yanaga, "Japanese Tradition and Democracy", *Far Eastern Survey* 17 (1948): 69.
64. Kerlinger, 'Decision-Making in Japan", p.38.
65. G.B. Sansom, *Japan: A Short Cultural History*, rev. ed. (London: Cresset, 1962), p.vi.
66. Kerlinger, "Decision-Making in Japan", p.38.
67. Herman Kahn, *The Emerging Japanese Superstate* (Englewood Cliffs, N.J.: Prentice Hall, 1970), p.40.
68. Ibid., p.41.
69. F.G. Bailey, "Decisions by Consensus in Councils and Committees", in *Political Systems and Distribution of Power*, ed. M. Banton, ASA Monograph no.2 (London: Tavistock, 1965), p.11.
70. In primitive societies where an individual's behaviour is restrained by considerations of mutual self-interest and reciprocity and where a close network of interlocking rights and obligations upholds the social order, decisions are arrived at in a similar manner. A good example are the Garia, of the Madang district, a cognatic society of 2,500 people, studied by Peter Lawrence, "The Garia of the Madang District" in *Politics in New Guinea*, ed. R.M. Berndt and Peter Lawrence (Nedlands, W.A.: University of Western Australia Press, 1971).
71. Kerlinger, "Decision-Making in Japan", p.38.
72. Kahn, *The Emerging Japanese Superstate*, p.41.
73. Ibid., p.44.
74. Bennett, Passin, and McKnight, *In Search of Identity*, p.231.
75. Toro Matsumoto, "Japanese are Human", *Asia*, January 1946, p.10.
76. Ibid., p.11.
77. Robert Huntington, "Comparison of Western and Japanese Cultures", *Monumenta Nipponica*, vol.23, no.3–4 (1962), p.477.
78. Australian War Memorial, Canberra, CRS A2663, item 780/3/3.
79. Shohei Ooka, *Fires in the Plain* (London: Secker and Warburg, 1957), p.8.
80. H. Paul Varley with Ivan and Nobuko Morris, *The Samurai* (London: Weidenfeld and Nicolson, 1970), p.24.
81. Inazo Nitobe, *Bushido, the Soul of Japan* (New York: Putnam, 1905), p.33.
82. Robert N. Bellah, *Tokugawa Religion* (Glencoe, Ill.: Free Press, 1957), p.91.
83. Ibid., p.92.
84. Ibid.
85. Ibid., p.93.
86. Ryusaku Tsunoda, Wm. Theodore de Bary and Donald Keene,

comps., *Sources of Japanese Tradition* (New York: Columbia University Press, 1964), vol. 2, pp.113–14.
87. Ibid., p.114.
88. Bellah, *Tokugawa Religion*, p.97.
89. Tsunoda, de Bary, and Keene, *Sources of Japanese Tradition*, vol.2, p.280.
90. Kazuko Tsurumi, *Social Change and the Individual* (Princeton: Princeton University Press, 1970), p.111.
91. Ibid., p.120.
92. Ibid., p.121.
93. Ibid.
94. Ibid., p.125.
95. Wilfred Owen, *Collected Poems* (London: Chatto and Windus, 1964), p.55.
96. M. Ichiyo, "Mishima and the Transition from Post-War Democracy to Democratic Fascism", *Liberation*, January 1972, p.7.
97. Ibid.
98. Ibid., p.10.
99. Ivan Morris, *The Nobility of Failure* (London: Secker and Warburg, 1975), p.183.
100. Ibid..
101. Takeo Doi. *The Anatomy of Dependence* (Tokyo: Kodansha, 1973), p.95.
102. Tokyo Gazette Publishing House, *Field Service Code* (Tokyo: Kakehi, 1941), p.17.
103. Ibid., pp.12–13.
104. Teruhiko Asada, *The Night of a Thousand Suicides* (Sydney: Angus and Robertson, 1970), p.107.

5
External Influences and Possible Explanations

By July 1944 the Allied forces had regained the initiative in the Pacific against daunting Japanese opposition. Even in defeat the Japanese left an indelible impression on Allied field commanders. Focusing on the campaign around Buna in Papua in 1943, where Tamagawa and Suzuki, the Cowra survivors interviewed by Clarke and Yamashita, were taken prisoner, Lieutenant-General George C. Kenney reported to General H.H. Arnold, the chief of Allied air forces in the south-west Pacific, that "those back home, including the War Department, had no conception of the problems".

> The Jap is still being underrated . . . Let us look at Buna. There are hundreds of Bunas ahead for us . . . The Jap has been outnumbered heavily throughout the show. His garrison has been whittled down to a handful by bombing and strafing. He has had no air support, and his own Navy has not been able to get past our air blockade to help him . . . The Emperor told them to hold, and, believe me, they have held!"[1]

The Japanese forces which suffered a crushing defeat at Buna in January 1943 had landed there in July 1942, fresh from their easy victories at Rabaul. Their objective was to attack Port Moresby: they had fought their way through the forbidding mountains and jungles of the Owen Stanley Ranges to within fifty-two kilometres of that town. Encamped on the Ioribaiwa Ridge and poised for the final assault, General Horii, who commanded these forces, received the order to withdraw to some point in the Owen

Stanley Ranges. Owing to the escalation of the campaign at Guadalcanal, the forces originally allocated to reinforce Horii could not be spared, and since "nearly eighty per cent of his original force had been killed, wounded in action or disabled by illness",[2] a strategic retreat was, the only alternative. Furthermore, food and ammunition were short and the supply lines through Buna had been constantly harassed by Allied aircraft and submarines.

The hopelessness of their position dawned slowly on the withdrawing Japanese forces which fought desperate rearguard actions as they retreated through the winding, climbing, and falling jungle tracks to Buna, most of the time under attack from Australian and American troops. By November, when tropical rain had converted the whole area into "one vast evil-smelling swamp",[3] Japanese resistance had shrunk to a small semicircular perimeter around Buna, Gona, and Sanananda. As General Kenney reported, the Japanese, exhausted from the rigours of the retreat, racked by tropical illness, and weakened by lack of food, defended their position with fierce determination. After the fall of Buna, some Japanese fled into the jungle, where both Suzuki and Tamagawa were captured, completely exhausted and unable to defend themselves. Both had asked their captors to kill them at once, and Tamagawa, who spent fifteen months in hospital, repeatedly attempted to kill himself.

This then was the calibre of fighting men—courageous, tough, and disciplined—who first arrived as prisoners of war at the Graythorne Transit Camp, near Brisbane, and were later interned at Cowra. According to Yamashita's book *Nihonjin Koko Ni Nemuru* (Here Lie the Japanese), nearly a half of the men killed on 5 August 1944 at Cowra had been captured around the Buna area.[4] These men were aware of the severe reverses the Japanese forces had suffered since their capture at Buna, not only having access to Australian newspapers, but also having witnessed the arrival of an ever increasing number of prisoners at Cowra.

Saipan, in the Mariana Islands, "the main bastion protecting Japan's homeland", had been seized on 9 July 1944. The lowlands of southern Saipan offered the Allies the first site from which massive bombing raids could be launched against Japanese cities. But formidable resistance was encountered. "Of the 71,000 Americans who had landed on Saipan, 14,111 were killed, wounded or missing in action". On the other hand, almost the whole Japanese garrison—"at least 30,000"—and 22,000 civilians had lost their lives in the campaign.[5]

Bad news can act as a stimulus for morale. Gregory Bateson, in his study "Morale and National Character", suggests that Dunkirk served as such for the British in 1941. He distinguishes between complementary and symmetrical patterns of relationships engendered by bipolar characteristics such as dominance–submission, succouring-dependence, and exhibitionism–spectatorship. Where complementary strivings tend to characterize national behaviour—i.e., in Japanese society—the weakness of the enemy would stimulate greater efforts and higher morale, while the superior strength of the enemy would tend to depress morale and eventually force Japan to submit. In the case of Britain, however, Bateson speculates, it is the vision of the greater power of the enemy which evokes the greater effort and higher morale, while he demonstrates, drawing his examples from recent wars, that if the enemy is perceived as relatively weak, the British are likely to relax their efforts. Yet while Churchill's promise in 1940 of nothing but "blood, toil, tears and sweat" acted as a stimulus to morale among Anglo-Saxon nations, the Germans or the Japanese might not have reacted in the same manner had they been told that their armed forces were threatened by disaster and that only extraordinary feats of self-denial and heroism by the population as a whole could avert a national catastrophe.

Bateson did not test his correlation between national character and morale in wartime in the Japanese context, but following his argument it would be possible to assume that a steady flow of disastrous war news might tend to depress the morale of the Japanese civilian population as well as that of her armed forces. Thus "news of the last-ditch stand and defeat at Saipan", as Asada put it, "came as a tremendous shock" to the prison community at Cowra.[6] While no one was willing to admit defeat, the. fact that Japan's long string of reverses would soon have to end was openly discussed. But it was generally felt that the enemy had now repeated the mistake made by Japan and overextended his lines of communications, and that the tide of battle would soon turn again in favour of Japan. Speculation was rife among the prisoners whether the "kid-glove treatment" they were now accorded would continue,[7] or whether it would cease once Japan's defeat was certain, since many of the prisoners were convinced that the behaviour of the officers and men of the garrison was motivated by secret fear of the might of Japan and "a desire to placate" the prisoners.[8]

The anxieties and tensions experienced by the prisoners about their future were exacerbated by rumours that the list of prisoners' names forwarded by the Australian authorities to the Japanese government by the International Committee of the Red Cross had been dismissed by the Japanese government with the rejoinder that "there were no Japanese prisoners".[9] Even after the Cowra outbreak the Japanese government did not wish to acknowledge the existence of Japanese prisoners of war. The following broadcast, which was monitored on 10 September 1944 and which came from Japanese-occupied Batavia, tends to confirm the official attitude:

What is the true story of the Australian prison camp murder? Bursting with indignation at the cold-blooded murder of Japanese civilian internees, the Nippon people demand to know the true story of the midnight murder of more than 200 innocent Japanese which Prime Minister Curtin belatedly reported one month after the incident occurred [Here followed the Australian prime minister's statement quoted in full]. It is perfectly clear to the Japanese people that these unfortunate Japanese who were murdered in the prison camp *cannot have been prisoners of war* for it is a well-known and accepted fact that the Japanese soldier never permits himself to be taken prisoner. His military creed is that death by his own hand is preferable to the dishonour and humiliation of capture by the enemy. Curtin may not care to admit it, but the fact then is perfectly obvious that the unfortunate victims of the midnight mass murder were internees who had lived in Australia for long years before the war.[10]

While it appears that the prisoners had cut themselves off from their families and country, first by only rarely volunteering their true name and even sometimes concealing their military rank,[11] and secondly by not availing themselves of the opportunities offered to correspond with their families, these rumours could only have deepened their despair and hopelessness. In a newspaper article published in 1970, a former guard at Cowra during this period suggested that "no Australian of any rank in Cowra really understood how deep the anguish of spirit was which these men suffered day and night, as they contemplated on return home being hated and despised—even by those dearest to them—wives and children, fathers and mothers".[12]

The prisoners were thus unable to envisage a happy reunion with their loved ones, nor did they consider that they had any future in Japan. On the other hand, freed from the constant and rigorous police supervision, to which D.G. Haring attributes the overt desire of the Japanese population to conform to the rules, at least some of the prisoners may have responded positively to their circumstances. For instance, in March 1944 Australian Intelligence reported that for the first time a Japanese prisoner called Chiya wrote a letter to his family. He requested, however, that this fact should be kept quiet, as he feared that he would be victimized if it became general knowledge.

While the level of interaction between individual prisoners had been very low in the initial stages of internment, each prisoner tending to keep himself to himself (Goffman describes this behaviour as "attempting to conceal from others what he takes to be the new fundamental facts about

himself"[13]—in this case that he has been disloyal to his
family, the emperor, and the nation), the prisoners had
established, over time, new and close social bonds among
themselves. These tended to overshadow all former social
ties and, in keeping with Japanese cultural conditioning,
involved rights and obligations which apparently were
rigorously adhered to. The dependency needs of the
prisoners could well have been heightened under the
conditions of imprisonment, and together with the tendency
towards a "situational ethic", as postulated by Benedict and
others, the immediate social nexus became all-important.

It may thus be argued that the Japanese prisoners, cut
off from their former ties and aware of the reverses suffered
by their own forces, took stock of their situation and
discussed the alternative courses of action open to them.
At first, possibly only among a few individuals who had
established close relationships between themselves and later
among ever widening factions sharing a common point of
view, there was a progressive increase of group cohesion.
Asada notes that several shades of opinions prevailed among
the prisoners. In his novel the diehards were a number of
navy pilots, centred on Flight-Sergeant Tobé, who had been
taken prisoner during the early phase of the war and neither
had first-hand experience of battle nor envisaged the
possibility of defeat. They believed firmly in the invincibili-
ty of the imperial forces and could not conceive of an Allied
victory. Furthermore, these men were among the oldest
inmates of the camp, and had in the process of inculcating
their rules and regulations to newly arrived prisoners
appropriated the position and power of leaders. The
diehards were, according to Asada, firmly convinced that
only suicide or a suicidal attack on the enemy would clear
their name and re-establish their honour. The other two
main factions among the prisoners were the moderates, who
saw no merit in violence, but wished to serve their country
in a meaningful way; and a large group of neutrals whose
minds were easily swayed either way by arguments advanced by the opposing sides and who were, therefore,

largely undecided as to what the best course of action would be.

The increasing number of prisoners who continued to arrive at Cowra as a result of the reverses suffered by the Japanese forces also created a problem. Having been warned by Matsumoto, a prisoner of Korean descent, in June 1944 that a plan was afoot to overpower the garrison and break out, Group Headquarters in Sydney had been advised that it was imperative not only to reinforce the camp but also to reduce the numbers of Japanese prisoners held within the camp. But not until 4 August 1944 were measures announced to reduce the numbers by moving the Japanese ORs and NCOs to Hay and Murchison camps three days later. In the meantime, however, more Japanese prisoners continued to arrive at Cowra.

The Australian authorities' attitude towards the Japanese prisoners of war had not been altered by the news of the reverses suffered by the enemy. They endeavoured at all times to administer the camp in keeping with the terms of the Geneva Convention of 1929, and there is no indication that the prisoners were subjected to any brutal treatment at this stage. Not only is it unlikely that Dr Morel of the Red Cross would have suppressed unpalatable facts in describing the conditions he found on his visits to the camp, but testimonies from Japanese survivors of the Cowra incident leave us in little doubt that nothing untoward took place at No. 12 Prisoner of War Group.

Thus Suzuki and Tamagawa, whom Clarke and Yamashita interviewed in Japan, volunteered the information that even then they were still using the shaving brushes issued to them when they had been prisoners of war at Cowra (Takeo Yamashita was good enough to send me a photograph of the shaving brushes). "These things", they said . . ., "are a gentle reminder of the many kindnesses and humane treatment which, on the whole, we received from the Australians."[14]

Particularly telling are some of the excerpts from the diary of Matsuoka, another prisoner of war at Cowra, which

Shaving brushes used by Tamagawa and Suzuki at Cowra. (Photo: Takeo Yamashita)

are included in Yamashita's book. Major Ramsay, the commander of B camp, whose attitude of tolerance and understanding probably set an example to the rest of the men under his command, is characterized by Matsuoka as "full of good will" towards the prisoners, and he notes in his diary: "Had we been roughly or cruelly treated, we would have at once chosen to seek death rather than wait for it."[15]

"Orloff", the White Russian interpreter and perceptive observer who plays an important part in Mackenzie's novel *Dead Men Rising*, confirms Matsuoka's estimate of the camp commander, "Major Shawe", the novel's commandant of B camp, is described as "a kindly, middle-aged man" who "discouraged unkindness in his guards, and strictly forbade anything approaching brutality, no matter how insolent or refractory the prisoner. . . . The major, ruddy and happy and a good man, saw nothing but sensible, friendly, obedient prisoners for whose well-being he was always pleased to exert himself."[16]

The humane treatment accorded to the prisoners, then, may at least partially explain why they did not avail themselves earlier of the opportunity to commit suicide. Some of course may have been influenced by the message contained in the leaflets which they were handed at Graythorne Transit Camp, encouraging them to accept the Western interpretation of the status of prisoner of war and desist from committing suicide, but to continue to live in order to serve their country again in peace time. Others again may have only paid lip service to the principles propounded in *kokutai* and incorporated in the Military Field Code, and may have responded to the situation in an individualistic manner, hoping perhaps to start a new life upon returning home.

While the behaviour of the Australians towards the prisoners had seemingly not been influenced by the string of Japanese reverses, the garrison became aware that the conduct of the prisoners had gradually altered. Where they had been at least outwardly docile in the earlier stages of their internment, as their strength and health improved and their numbers increased they tended to manifest greater hostility as well as a certain degree of arrogance. Major Timms suggests that the strict adherence to the terms of the Geneva Convention "merely amused them and further convinced them of our moral and spiritual weakness".[17]

Timms's assessment of the attitude of the Japanese prisoner is further corroborated by Orloff, the interpreter in *Dead Men Rising*, who alone understood both sides of the wire. Born and educated in Tokyo, he warns that the prisoners do not comprehend "the foolish considerateness of your people towards war prisoners".[18] He takes the view that the Japanese had expected to be treated in an arbitrary fashion and with contempt, and to be severely punished for even minor insubordination. Orloff cites the case of a newly arrived prisoner who after attacking a guard is not summarily executed as "he had always been taught to expect" but tried by a court martial and sentenced to a term of imprisonment.[19] Orloff is convinced that such incidents only served to compound the conviction of the Japanese that the Australians lacked moral fibre and were afraid of the might of Japan.

The Australian authorities noted that discipline within the ranks of the prisoners had tightened considerably; while earlier they had been lackadaisical about keeping their huts tidy or looking after their clothes and equipment, their hut leaders now seemed to be able to excercise greater control. Furthermore, the prisoners tended their gardens with renewed zeal and also spent many hours in physical training and playing vigorous games of baseball.

To summarize: the tensions and strains experienced by the Japanese prisoners of war, who felt that neither their families nor their country had any further use for them, were aggravated by anxieties about their future treatment at the hands of the Australian authorities. The prisoners had established close social bonds between themselves and developed factions with divergent views about the course of action likely to resolve their dilemma. Meanwhile, the

Australian authorities at Cowra were also under increasing stress, for although the garrison had been reinforced with modern automatic weapons and new alarm orders drafted, which included support from the nearby Recruit Training Centre in case of emergencies, they were fully aware that violence could break out at any time. But as Yamashita suggests, the Australian authorities may have failed to take full account of the strength of the bonds formed between prisoners; they did not realize that the order to transfer the ORs to Hay and Murchison would create a unity (albeit temporary) of purpose among them. Had this been understood, the garrison would have been on full alert on the night of 4–5 August and the authorities might have taken earlier steps to distribute the prisoners among different camps at an earlier stage.

Possible Explanations

Three alternative explanations for the incident at Cowra are offered below. Some elements of one explanation may well be part of others, and it is possible that further facts may yet be revealed to modify or substantiate any one of the following hypotheses.

Mass Suicide

Here it may be useful to define the function of suicide in Japanese society. Suicide is not only regarded as an extreme form of retreat from role performance, caused by either excessive integration of an individual into a group or isolation from the group, as Emil Durkheim postulated,[20] but is also a "legal and ceremonial" institution.[21] Nitobe suggests that during the Tokugawa period suicide was a means whereby warriors could expiate their crimes, apologize for errors of judgement, escape from disgrace, admonish their lords, redeem their friends, and prove their sincerity. The notion of *seppuku* was an integral element of the ethos of ethereal bushido and according to Nitobe an end befitting a warrior.[22] Where suicide was imposed as a legal punishment, as in the case of the Forty-seven Ronin in the early eighteenth century, it was carried out with "the utmost coolness of temper and composure of demeanour".[23] Ernest Satow and A.B. Mitford (later Lord Redesdale) when attached to the British Embassy in Tokyo in 1868 were invited to witness an act of legal *seppuku* which had been imposed as a penalty on Taki Zenzaburo, "for ordering his soldiers to fire on foreigners".[24] Satow describes the elaborate ritual and the calm deliberation with which Taki, who declared that he alone was responsible for the attack on the foreigners at Kobe, proceeded to disembowel himself. Satow reported: "The countrymen of this Bizen man told us that they considered the sentence a just and beneficial one."[25]

While Nitobe suggests that, after the promulgation of the Criminal Code by the Meiji government, there was theoretically no further need for legal ceremonial suicide, he writes: "We still hear of it [*seppuku*] from time to time, and shall continue to hear, I am afraid, as long as the past is remembered."[26] The ceremonial suicides of General Nogi and his wife in 1912, of General Anami, the War Minister on the eve of Japan's surrender to the Allies, in August 1945, and of Yukio Mishima in 1970 are reminders that even in the twentieth century *seppuku* is still considered a means to atone for errors of judgement, or, as in Mishima's case, to voice a protest.

It is beyond the scope of this study to examine in great detail the causes for the mass suicides among civilians on Saipan in July 1944, and later on Okinawa and Iwo Jima in 1945. While there appears no historical precedents for these events, their sources might be found in the notions enunciated in *kokutai*, such as that the emperor and subjects are one, and that the disgrace of defeat and surrender could be wiped out by choosing a glorious death, which would fuse an individual's identity with the spirit of Japan. On the other hand, as Reischauer and other writers have postulated, Japanese when confronted with unplanned, unknown situations tend to panic more easily and are likely to react violently. J.C. Moloney notes that "identification with the authoritarian" is a psychological mechanism that develops to escape anxiety stemming from the presence of a threatening authority.[27] Thus committing suicide may have been a means of identifying with the emperor, as well as atoning for disloyalty.

But the civilians' action cannot be equated with *seppuku* —ceremonial suicide—which after all was largely a component of the samurai ethic, an individualistic refinement of purposive self-destruction. Nor is it likely that the Cowra prisoners, who, like the rest of Japan's modern army, no longer came from samurai backgrounds, would have chosen to disembowel themselves as a means of resolving their problems.

The Military Field Code refrains from advocating ceremonial suicide, commanding merely that members of the armed forces use their last grenade to kill themselves or charge the enemy in a last suicidal assault rather than surrender. But this order refers only to the battlefield, and since internment by the enemy is not foreseen, there are no culturally appropriate rules of behaviour which apply. The prisoners thus had to draw upon their cultural repertoire to structure their behaviour.

The testimony of both Sergeant-Major Kanazawa and Flight-Sergeant Yoshida dwells on their wish to die, since "the shame of being a Japanese prisoner of war was beyond endurance".[28] Yoshida states, "I could not kill myself and had been waiting for some force [to kill me]".[29] The prisoners, then, were culturally disoriented—being treated in a humane manner according to the provisions of the Geneva Convention—and faced with an unplanned situation, with which, according to Benedict, at their particular stage of life they were least able to cope. Thus unable to innovate and to act effectively outside the cultural constraints that governed their behaviour, they were fatalistically waiting for an external force to determine their fate.

The order for the separation of the ORs and the NCOs

might have been the means to galvanize the various factions in the camp into action. The diehards, most likely a vocal minority group, may have succeeded in imposing their decision on the majority: for there was an opportunity to die a glorious death, the opportunity they had failed to grasp on the battlefield. By forcing a confrontation with the well-armed garrison they could redeem their honour and clear their name of shame. Both Yamashita and Asada stress in their accounts that none of the prisoners could bear to be thought a coward by their comrades, and that fact, together with the high value accorded harmony and unity in the decision-making process, may well have inhibited individual prisoners from expressing an unpopular opinion. Even those who, like the deputy camp leader, Sergeant Kojima, held moderate views may have finally thrown their lot in with the diehards, or at least tacitly consented to the outbreak.

Those who were rash or brave enough to voice objections to the plan could have been either forcibly persuaded to participate or murdered. The identities of the twelve charred bodies in the burnt-down huts, as well as the manner of their death, will probably never be known. It is, however, a fact that 138 prisoners never left their huts and did not participate in the outbreak.[30]

A Planned Escape

Another possiblity is that the prisoners had formulated a plan to rush the fences, overpower the guards, and with the weapons thus obtained, attack the nearby Recruit Training Centre. The objective could have been to escape into the bush, live off the land and carry out a series of guerilla-type operations against Australian forces. A passage in Asada's novel refers to the hopes and aspirations of the Cowra prisoners:

All dreamed of the day when Japanese forces would land on the Australian mainland. Now the days were passed in inactivity but then they were resolved to rise up, break the barricades, attack the Australian barracks, capture weapons, and fight. They would establish contact with the invading Japanese forces and fight a guerilla action behind the lines to cause confusion. They felt that there would be little hope of really succeeding—that, most likely, all would be killed. But that was, after all, what they wished, every single one of them.[31]

The cache of stones collected as far back as 1943 and the growing fervour with which physical exercises were performed in the months before the outbreak are also evidence to support this hypothesis. But perhaps the most convincing evidence is contained in the warning of Matsumoto, the prisoner who informed the authorities in June 1944 of a carefully planned project for an outbreak.

A Spontaneous Response to the Transfer Order

The decision to stage a break-out could also have been a response to the unexpected announcement that the ORs and NCOs were to be separated and transferred to Hay and Murchison respectively. The prisoners may well have interpreted this transfer as (a) an attempt to weaken their group solidarity, and (b), as Yamashita suggests, a means of bolstering the "depleted Australian work force".[32] The prisoners believed that the Australian authorities had decided that the Japanese OR prisoners would work better if left on their own and not influenced by their NCOs, who discouraged them from co-operating.

The intimation of leaving fellow prisoners with whom intense inter-relationships had been established, of facing yet another unplanned situation, might have evoked a violent response. Furthermore, in situations where the culturally appropriate response is unknown, as we have already observed in the case of Lieutenant Adachi at Featherston Camp, a tendency towards self-dramatization is likely to manifest itself. The high value accorded to collaterality could also have been crucial: since the welfare and the existence of the whole group was at stake, individual concerns may have been sublimated and the notion of escaping or of dying together may have overridden all other considerations.

The Merits of the Alternative Explanations

Whether one supports any of the hypotheses offered above, or whether one considers that they all contribute to a plausible explanation of the events at Cowra, it is important to realize that the tendencies towards self-dramatization and indirection, inherent in the Japanese personality, played a crucial role in each one of them. As pointed out earlier, self-dramatization and indirection are the two favoured social techniques which Japanese are likely to resort to when confronted with an unplanned situation. Clearly at a loss as to what the expected conduct in the internment situation should be, their predicament was made worse by the news of defeats suffered by their own forces, which increased their anxieties with regard to their future.

To confront a well-armed garrison with home-made weapons—whether the aim was to seek death or to escape —seems just the sort of dramatic, if foolhardy, gesture (the spectacular act of bravery advocated by Yoshida Shoin) to which the prisoners might have resorted. The major elements of self-dramatization discerned by Hulse were present: the touch of arrogance, the flaunting of superior strength as well as the ruthlessness to oneself as towards others, and the manifestation of supreme confidence in the ability of Japanese spiritual power to overcome Western material strength. The memorandum presented by the Japanese officers to the Australian authorities following the outbreak, demanding the immediate death penalty for themselves, although they had not been involved in the actual outbreak, is perhaps the epitome of self-dramatization.

In order that any action might eventuate, a decision had to be arrived at; and in terms of Japanese cultural precepts, such a decision had to be represented as a unanimous one. The tendency towards indirection, towards signifying acceptance in order not to be regarded as the odd man out or suffer ridicule and ostracism, may well have induced a large proportion of the prison community to give lip service to whatever plan was finally agreed upon. Since frankness is not encouraged and overt disagreement culturally inappropriate, many of the prisoners may have chosen to keep their own counsel, thus upholding the fiction of a unanimous decision.

Furthermore, once again the inclination towards *gekoku-jo*—the overpowering of senior officers by juniors—manifested itself, for both the accounts of Asada and Yamashita stress that the camp leader as well as his deputy were prudent men unlikely to favour violent action. Asada traces the process whereby the conviction of a few fanatic NCOs and ORs that the only alternative left is to court death by attacking their well-armed captors permeates the entire prison community. He describes how a consensus was reached on the night of 4 August that a suicidal charge was the only way to atone for the disgrace brought upon themselves and their families by surrendering to the enemy. Asada, like Clarke and Yamashita, suggests that the prisoners' determination to die together, to commit mass suicide, was the underlying cause for the outbreak.

Several arguments, however, can be marshalled against this hypothesis. First, eyewitnesses do not describe a wild, disorganized, lemming-like rush towards the machine-gun emplacements. From all accounts, the action of the prisoners was a well-mounted military operation by disciplined soldiers. The prisoners formed themselves into four groups of approximately two hundred each and fanned out in the best tradition of military tactics, endeavouring to scale the barbed-wire fence at the least defended points of the perimeter.

Secondly, it seems unlikely that if death by pitting themselves against machine-gun fire was their sole objective, the Japanese would have taken the precautions of protecting their hands with baseball gloves and their bodies with protective clothing, such as wearing several pairs of pants, winding toilet paper around their arms and legs, and carrying blankets and towels to help them scale the barbed wire. Thirdly, the increasing emphasis on discipline, together with the stress on physical fitness and training in the weeks preceding the outbreak could be interpreted rather as preparation for future guerilla activities than for mass suicide. Finally, one must call attention to the absence of suicide notes: General Nogi, General Anami, and Yukio Mishima all left brief formal notes explaining their actions, but none were found after the Cowra outbreak. Yamashita published some of the poems found on the dead prisoners, which express their sense of hopelessness and their longing for their loved ones:

> What sweet sorrow it is when my innocent child appears
>   before me in dreams,
> And how bitter the heart throbs every time I awake at
>   this sorrow.

> In the twilight, a bird calls out "Okachan" [mother]!
> Memories come to life.
> The bird in its cage returns to its homeland in its dreams.

> Forgetting myself,
> every day, every night,
> I think of my father, I think of my mother.
> How are they now, I wonder?

> Far from my native land of hope,
> Though I suffer tedium,
> There is no longer anywhere to return,
> The wind blows coldly down my miserable body.

> Awake in the cold night
> I push away the thoughts of home.
> At the distant flute of the blind man
> I drench my pillow and lament for the world.[33]

These poems, however, do not resemble the formal suicide notes left, for instance, by General Anami; they are expressions of real feelings, very much in tune with those prompted by ethereal bushido in the tenth century.

As to the second hypothesis—a planned escape—both the tactical skill with which the operation was carried out and the precautions taken to protect hands and bodies against injuries suggest that escaping in order to regroup and create confusion among the enemy may well have been the ultimate objective. Matsumoto's warning also tends to support this hypothesis. More obliquely, perhaps, the clandestine note written on toilet paper to Sergeant Kanazawa, the former camp leader, by the five officers who, like him, were detained in the prison block, tends to sustain the argument that escape was uppermost in the minds of the prisoners (see appendix B).

The officers, who were not actively implicated in the planning of the action or in the outbreak, advised Sergeant Kanazawa, in the note which was intercepted by the Australian authorities, what he should say at the court of inquiry: that he should stress the spontaneous nature of the action and emphasize that the projected separation of the ORs from the NCOs was its immediate reason. Had this been its real cause, Kanazawa would surely have needed no prompting from the officers; the fact that he was secretly instructed to volunteer such an explanation leads one to suspect that there may have been another motive. But, while some of the escapees repeatedly alleged they had been told by their superiors that the Japanese Army had landed in Sydney and was advancing west, and that they had broken out in order to join it, there is no concrete evidence that the Japanese prisoners either collectively or individually had formulated detailed plans for further action once they had scaled the barbed wire.

If the outbreak was in fact a carefully preconceived plan, the decision of the Australian authorities to move the ORs and NCOs to Hay and Murchison on 7 August may have spoiled the timetable of the Japanese prisoners. Suddenly confronted with the unexpected, they may have been forced to make a quick decision: the separation of the ORs from the NCOs might have been construed as the first move towards instituting the harsher treatment which the prisoners expected to follow the news of Japanese reverses. Alternatively, the ringleaders could have felt that the news of the transfer might effect a change of attitude among the members of the neutral and moderate factions; these men might then feel that the chance of effecting an escape would never offer itself again and that they might as well join in the outbreak.

Turning to the third hypothesis, as mentioned earlier many of the Japanese prisoners perceived themselves as abandoned by their families and government and had cut themselves off from their former lives. Nevertheless, during their internment they had established new social bonds whose importance for their moral and social well-being cannot be underestimated. The dependency needs of the Japanese, subsumed by the concept of *amae*, focus on immediate and tangible interpersonal relationships. There is, therefore, a real possibility that the threat of being separated from individuals with whom they had established a mutually satisfying relationship may have triggered off a spontaneous and violent response. The notion of *amae* may well have operated also on a different level: individuals who tended towards neutral or moderate views might have changed their attitudes in order to please their comrades who had either chosen to escape or to seek death.

The role played by the Japanese officers at Cowra deserves close scrutiny. From all accounts they tended to keep very much to themselves and sought neither to establish close relationships with the enlisted men nor to assert their authority. They refused to avail themselves of the services of batmen and looked after their own needs. The fact that the officers were paid a military salary by the Australian authorities and thus could buy necessities or luxury items such as cigarettes at the canteen while the enlisted men received no remuneration may have contributed to the rigidly upheld separation of the officers from the enlisted men.[34]

On the night of the outbreak, about fifty enlisted men forced their way into the officers' compound—either to seek refuge or to enlist the participation of the officers in their venture. The enlisted men, whatever their aim, must have shared their plans with the officers, who realizing that nothing could be gained at that stage by their joining the rioters, decided to remain in their huts and apparently persuaded the enlisted men to follow their example. Only Sub-Lieutenant Oikawa ventured outside and was wounded by a shot in the leg. His testimony as to his intentions is rather ambiguous. On the one hand, his signature heads those on the memorandum presented by twelve Japanese officers to the Australian authorities on 5 August implicating themselves in the outbreak and requesting "death by shooting of all of us officers".[35] On the other hand, when the court of inquiry adjourned on 14 August to visit the camp hospital to record the statements of the five Japanese prisoners who had expressed a desire to give evidence, Oikawa volunteered the following information: "I had *nothing* to do with the incident, but I would like to know why I was shot while sitting in the hut. I have nothing more to say" (emphasis added).[36] This statement conflicts with the one he signed, which implicated himself together with the Japanese officers in the incident, and demanded the death penalty for them all.

The testimony of Captain Nishio and Sergeant-Major Kanazawa, who were also isolated from the rest of the prisoners by confinement to the Group Detention Barracks, is also not quite in tune with the purported unanimity of the prisoners' decision and purpose. Nishio stated: "I am the leader of the Officers Camp and am at the moment kept in the Detention Barracks. I heard that as a result of the outbreak on the 5th August, 1944, my assistant camp leader [Oikawa] was injured and an officer killed. I know something about it, but from what I can gather the bullets did not come from the officers camp but from B camp. I should like to inquire into the question of the firing."[37]

Since as far as it is known none of the garrison troops were actually in B camp during the incident, Nishio seems to imply that one of the prisoners in B camp or several of them had weapons. In the confusion created by the incident, the NCOs and ORs might have taken the opportunity to settle scores with one or more of the officers. Nishio went even further and implied that several shots passed over the Detention Barracks. "There is no reason to aim at that hut where I was and I conclude that there was some mistake on the part of firing."[38]

The testimony of Sergeant-Major Kanazawa, who had accepted full responsibility for the outbreak, tends to support the spontaneous response hypothesis; referring to the abrupt manner in which the order for the transfer of the NCOs and ORs was issued, he said: "If the order had been explained to us probably there would have been some solution to it, but since the order was given without any words of explanation it resulted in the action which caused this incident. For the sake of maintenance of peace I desire that if they have to be separated again a full explanation should accompany the order."[39] Perhaps had the response of Japanese to sudden unstructured changes been known, the order could have been framed in a different way. But if definite plans had been made to escape, or to commit mass suicide, the form in which the order was transmitted would not have influenced the course of events.

Conclusions

Cultural continuity in Japanese society is indeed striking; throughout its history the strands woven into the ethos of bushido, the moral code, have adapted to social and political changes, showing a certain degree of variation in emphasis, but never veering too far away from its precepts. Japan's belief system, Shinto, while absorbing elements of Buddhism, Confucianism, and Neo-Confucianism, has provided a stable framework for Japanese culture. While the actual power of the emperors waxed and waned during the centuries, the fact that the roots of the imperial dynasty were deeply embedded in Shinto mythology ensured that the imperial house remained the focal point for the spiritual unity of Japan.

The great homogeneity of Japanese society is largely due to geographical and historical circumstances, for, as Professor J. Roggendorf put it in a radio talk, for over two thousand years the Japanese, in their small, mountainous four islands have huddled together in the few plains around their few river deltas to fish and cultivate their rice.[40] The Japanese population has been isolated from the outside world during long periods of their history and thus has achieved a high degree of sameness in physical character- istics such as stature, colour and texture of hair, the shape of the head, and their eyes, as well as in speech and behaviour.

The behaviour of the Japanese people is regulated by a great many rules and a rigid system of duties and obliga- tions, which provide a strict pattern of conduct for all foreseen social situations. However, Japanese soldiers were trained to regard capture as an impossible alternative, and confronted by an unexpected situation for which their cultural conditioning had not prepared them they "had no universal ethic to fall back on to give consistency to their behaviour".[41] The notion of seeking death rather than surrender to the enemy, however, had been deeply in- culcated into the Japanese armed forces, and the fact that they had failed to observe the command of the Military Field Code never to surrender to the enemy appeared to weigh heavily upon the conscience of the prisoners at Featherston as well as at Cowra.

In this context it may be important to mention that even at the time of writing there may exist Japanese servicemen on lonely Pacific islands who still adhere to the policy of no surrender. Despite the fact that World War II ended on 15 August 1945, "some 3570 Japanese World War II veterans are still unaccounted for",[42] among whom a number are believed to be still alive. Two who did not surrender until many years after the war were Sergeant Shoichi Yokoi and Lieutenant Hiro Onoda. When the Americans landed in the closing months of the war on Guam, Yokoi, together with ten companions, headed for the dense forests of the Telofofo district. Although the last two of his comrades died mysteriously in 1964—perhaps

from malnutrition or from food poisoning—Yokoi stubborn-
ly held on in the belief that surrender would mean
intolerable shame. When finally captured in February 1971
he stated that he had kept his determination alive by
thinking: "I am living for the Emperor and the spirit of
Japan."[43] It is worth noting that Yokoi was not a soldier
of the regular army, nor did he belong to the samurai class;
he was a tailor's apprentice who had been conscripted to
the Japanese forces in 1941.

Lieutenant Hiro Onoda, on the other hand, came from
a middle-class family background; his father was a newspaper editor, and his mother was far better educated than
most Japanese women of her generation. Onoda, a bright
and tough youngster, proved his independence of spirit by
not attending university after completion of his secondary
education, but instead joined a commercial firm in China.
During this period he showed little of the grim dedication
to duty which was to sustain him through the thirty years
of solitary struggle for survival on Lubang. He enjoyed
parties and the good life in Shanghai but in 1944 was
drafted into the army and after attending the regular
officers training school was transferred to the military
intelligence school at Futamata. The purpose of this establishment was to train experts in guerilla warfare, to teach
sabotage and partisan tactics, and to prepare the young
officers for the eventuality of fighting indefinitely behind
enemy lines. Contrary to the provisions of the Military Field
Code, the trainee officers of this school were told that "they
were absolutely forbidden to die by their own hand. . . .
under no circumstances were they permitted to give up
their lives voluntarily."[44] Whatever happened, the Japanese
would return, and in the meantime the task of these
specially trained officers was to lead their men and to harass
the enemy.

Armed with these instructions, Onoda was landed on
Lubang in early 1945, to prevent the Americans from
taking over its small airstrip. He found a very war-weary
garrison whose members were reluctant to become guerilla

fighters. Initially Onoda's group numbered several hundreds, but the Americans managed to persuade a large number to give up the unequal struggle, while others were killed in guerilla operations. Finally, only Onoda and three companions fought on. Onoda writes revealingly how he felt that he had disgraced himself, allowing the Americans to take the airstrip; forgetting all he had learned at Futamata, he reverted to the suicidal tactics he had been taught in officers training school. But he was not killed in an abortive last-ditch effort to dislodge the Americans and changed back again to guerilla tactics, after receiving orders from his commanding officer, Major Taniguchi, to hold out and wait for the return of the imperial army.

Days, months, and years slipped by, and although all his companions had been killed, Onoda fought on. He had seen the leaflets announcing the surrender of Japan; he had read copies of newspapers and magazines dropped for him; he had heard his brother's voice (and that of other friends and comrades) who had asked him on the loud hailer to abandon his mission and come out of the jungle. But he believed these were all enemy tricks to entice him to surrender, and he refused to do so. To strengthen his resolution, he repeated to himself passages from the Military Field Code, like a ceremony of rededication. The Japanese government, now under public pressure to dislodge all military stragglers, sent mission after mission to Lubang. Onoda's former comrades were convinced, however, that he would continue his fight alone, and Sergeant Yokoi stated his belief that even if he himself went into the jungle and found Onoda, the effort would prove to be a fruitless one: after all the imperial army had instructed its members never to surrender.

It was a young adventurer and university drop-out, Norio Suzuki, who finally succeeded where official initiative had so dismally failed. He surmised that loneliness pressed more heavily on Onoda after the death of his last companion and that he might crave companionship much more than was generally believed. He therefore pitched his tent close to

where Onoda had last been reported and waited patiently
for the defiant recluse to approach him. Suzuki's strategy
proved successful. In long conversations he persuaded
Onoda that the war had indeed ended and that it would
be quite in keeping with traditional military ethics to
surrender. Suzuki's value orientation, a mixture of traditional beliefs (he carried the samurai's classical code of
behaviour among his belongings), together with his radical
political ideas advocating, *inter alia*, increased popular
participation in politics, may have struck a sympathetic
chord with Onoda's views. Onoda agreed that he would
surrender, but only if he received explicit orders to do so
from his commanding officer. Suzuki therefore returned to
Japan and brought Major Taniguchi, who had retired from
the army and was now a bookseller in Kyoto, back with
him to Lubang. After Taniguchi had read the emperor's
1945 proclamation to him, Onoda surrendered. Later, in
a formal ceremony he presented his cherished sword to
President Marcos of the Philippines.

Onoda's account of his thirty-year war is indeed revealing; his training at the Intelligence School at Futamata had
led him to regard all attempts to lure him out of the jungle
with the deepest suspicion. He firmly believed that the
Americans would indeed go so far as to drop specially
prepared newspaper accounts to deceive him, and he was
certain that all the radio broadcasts he heard were doctored.
He admitted that he almost succumbed to the pleas of his
brother (who was brought out to Lubang by the Japanese
government). However, when his brother's voice cracked
with emotion at the end of the message, he became again
suspicious, and feared he was dealing with an impostor.

On his return to Japan, Onoda received a hero's welcome.
His courage and adherence to the imperial precepts demanding absolute obedience to orders inspired the admiration
of those who still cherished the old traditions and values.
Conservative Japanese saw in Onoda's actions all that was
good and noble in the past, and a right-wing member of
parliament declared that Onoda made him proud to be

Japanese. There were, of course, other reactions condemning the old system of education and military training which suppressed individual, critical thought and defined morality and ethical beliefs only in terms of the good of the nation and the emperor.

Whether Onoda was particularly stubborn and single-minded, or whether a number of special circumstances conspired to make him one of the last and most impressive stragglers to emerge from the jungle after fighting the non-existent enemy for thirty years, there seems little doubt that he is representative of many others who had internalized the injunctions of the Military Field Code and acted accordingly. Sergeant Yokoi and Lieutenant Onoda came from very different social and educational backgrounds, and neither was a member of the regular imperial army; one could speculate that their level of indoctrination was therefore not the most extreme. But if their actions are indicative of the effect of the "socialization for death", which draftees as well as regular military personnel underwent before and during World War II, it seems more than probable that the conduct of the prisoners of war at Featherston and Cowra was determined by their adherence to the principles laid down by the Military Field Code.

If, then, these cases are any indication of the scope of the cultural conditioning of Japanese servicemen, the conduct of a large proportion of the prisoners at Cowra, regardless of their social background, was undoubtedly determined by the tenets of the Military Field Code, which incorporated many facets of militant bushido and *kokutai*. But adherence to the no-surrender code does not offer a completely satisfactory explanation of the events at Cowra. Until such time as it is possible to resolve some of the ambiguities in the testimony volunteered by the Japanese prisoners at the proceedings of the court of inquiry, and to interview other survivors of the incident, the most plausible explanation appears to be that the action of the prisoners combined elements of all three hypotheses offered: an attempt to seek death, which derived largely from the cultural conditioning of the prisoners; a planned escape, which would be in keeping with the behaviour expected from prisoners of war, regardless of their nationality; and a spontaneous response to the order of transfer, which might have been engendered by facets of the Japanese personality structure and value orientation.

Notes

1. John Toland, *The Rising Sun* (London: Cassell, 1971), p.427. The emperor took a lively personal interest in military operations. On 9 January 1943 "His Majesty told Sugiyama, 'the fall of Buna is regrettable, but the officers and men fought well' " (p.426n).
2. Hugh Clarke, *Break-Out!* (Sydney: Horwitz, 1965), p.17.
3. Ibid., p.24.
4. Takeo Yamashita, *Nihonjin Koko Ni Nemuru* (privately printed, 1969), p.54.
5. Toland, *The Rising Sun*, p.519.
6. Teruhiko Asada, *The Night of a Thousand Suicides* (Sydney: Angus and Robertson, 1970), p.57.
7. Ibid., p.58.
8. E.V. Timms, "The Blood Bath at Cowra" in *As You Were!* (Canberra: Australian War Memorial 1946), p.177.
9. Yamashita, *Nihonjin Koko Ni Nemuru*, p.75.
10. Commonwealth Archives Office, Canberra, CRS A989, item 44/925/1/140, pp.140–62.
11. Asada in *The Night of a Thousand Suicides* suggests that most of the prisoners were using assumed names: "Among them were some which were obviously borrowed from famous characters in history —Oishi Yoshio, Kikuchi Kan, Takayama Kikukuro and so on" (p.50). As far as not volunteering their correct rank is concerned, Professor Henderson, in a private communication (23 August 1973) notes that "giving false names was commoner among officers but that in general, people did not give incorrect ranks, since this might have been noticed and resented within the Japanese groups". In a mimeographed account, "The Path from Guadalcanal", a former prisoner of war, Michiharu Shinya, a Japanese naval officer who had been captured in the waters around Guadalcanal, admits that he only disclosed his true rank when he arrived in Featherston: "Since Guadalcanal I had concealed from the enemy the fact that I was an officer, but after arriving in this compound I undertook procedures to be united with the officers' group, and this was immediate-

ly put into effect" (chapter 5, p.7). This fact may well account for the discrepancy in the number of officers reported by Dr Léon Bossard, the ICRC delegate, and the New Zealand authorities, mentioned earlier.

12. *Sydney Morning Herald*, 8 August 1970, p.22.
13. Erving Goffman, *Asylums* (Harmondsworth, Mddx.: Penguin, 1970), p.123.
14. Clarke, *Break-Out!*, p.124.
15. Yamashita, *Nihonjin Koko Ni Nemuru*, p.136.
16. Kenneth Seaforth Mackenzie, *Dead Men Rising* (Sydney: Pacific Books, 1969), pp.86–87.
17. Timms, "Blood Bath at Cowra", p.177.
18. Mackenzie, *Dead Men Rising*, p.148. There were several White Russian interpreters employed at Cowra, so that Orloff may well be a composite portrait. Sergeant Oleg Eugene Negerevich, interpreter, in his testimony at the court of inquiry about signs of conspiracy or of a plan to break out said: "Only that some of the camp leaders tried to dodge me and would not talk to me when I wanted to ask them something—before that they would always be friendly to me." (Australian Archives Office, Canberra, AA1973/254, p.119).
19. Ibid.
20. Durkheim in his study *Le Suicide* (Paris: Alcan, 1897) posited that the degree to which an individual was integrated into group life determined whether he could be motivated to commit suicide. He distinguished between altruistic, egoistic, and anomic suicide; anomic and egiostic suicide both spring from low social integration, while altruistic suicide may be a manifestation of over-involvement in a group. The kamikaze pilots of World War II are often cited as an example of altruistic suicide.
21. Inazo Nitobe, *Bushido, the Soul of Japan* (New York: Putnam, 1905), p.116.
22. Ibid.
23. Ibid.
24. Ernest Satow, *A Diplomat in Japan* (London: Seeley, 1921), p.344.
25. Ibid., p.347.
26. Nitobe, *Bushido, the Soul of Japan*, p.129.
27. J.C. Moloney, *Understanding the Japanese Mind* (Rutland, Vermont: Tuttle, 1954), p.116.
28. Commonwealth Archives Office, Canberra, AA1973/254, exhibit X.
29. Ibid., exhibit Y.
30. Ibid., p.120.
31. Asada, *Night of a Thousand Suicides*, pp.58–59.
32. Yamashita, *Nihonjin Koko Ni Nemuru*, p.86.
33. Ibid., pp.76–79.
34. On the occasion of his last visit to Cowra, 22–24 March 1944, Dr

Morel notes that the financial situation of the enlisted men in B camp is "précaire, car ils ne recoivent point de solde militaire"; commenting on the financial situation of the Japanese officers he stated: "La situation des officiers japonais de ce camp est satisfaisante, sauf celle de l'ingénieur chef qui appartient à la marine marchande. Les officiers touchent les soldes militaires mensuel les suivantes: General, £30.14.10½; Lieut. General, £34.18.6½; Major General, £30.2.2; Colonel, £22. 8. 0½; Lieut. Colonel, £15.18. 0½; Major, £12. 5. 1; Captain, £8.17. 1; Lieutenant, £6. 2. 9; 2nd Lieut., £5. 2. 5." (Australia, Department of External Affairs, Correspondence Files, CAO, CRS A989, item 44/925/1/140, pp.22–26).

35. Commonwealth Archives Office, Canberra, AA1973/254, exhibit BB.
36. Ibid., p.129.
37. Ibid., p.131.
38. Ibid., p.132.
39. Ibid.
40. J. Roggendorf, ABC Guest of Honour Broadcast, 6 May 1973, mimeographed, p.2.
41. Kazuo Kawai, *Japan's American Interlude* (Chicago: University of Chicago Press, 1960), p.5.
42. "World War II: Voices in the Wilderness", *Newsweek*, 30 October 1972, p.62.
43. "The Last Blossom", *Newsweek*, 7 February 1972, p.30.
44. Hiro Onoda, *No Surrender: My Thirty Years War* (London: Deutsch, 1975), p.54.

Postscript

What actually happened to the repatriated Japanese prisoners of war from Featherston and Cowra on their return to Japan? Did they suffer the stigma of having violated the Field Service Code? Were their fears that they might be court-martialled, discriminated against, and not welcomed back into their family circle justified? I have recently had the opportunity to examine a few accounts—as yet not published in English—as well as receive some personal communications from ex-Featherston captives, which throw some light on these relevant issues.

Here I must thank Mr Russell Orr, who acted as trainee interpreter at Featherston and who provided some of the photographs of the camp and its inmates, Mr E.H. Thompson, who served as an interpreter with the New Zealand forces in the Pacific and spent the closing months of World War II at Featherston, as well as Mr Keith Robertson, who was the interpreter at Featherston from 1942 until the end of hostilities, accompanying the Japanese prisoners of war on their return voyage to Japan in 1946, for their invaluable assistance. I was thus able to examine Mr Thompson's translation of Michiaru Shinya's account of his internment at Featherston. *Shi no Umi Yori Seidan* (The Path from Guadalcanal) and of Seihachiro Saito's article "Gimei Senshi No Haka" (The Graves of the Incognito Warriors"), which was published in *Bungei Shunju* in March 1963 and which relates the experiences of Lieutenant Oikawa, the only

Toshio Adachi, photographed with his wife in 1975. (Photo: Mr T. Adachi)

Michiharu Shinya in 1973 (Photo: Mr. M. Shinya)

officer who was wounded in the Cowra incident, and gives Lieutenant Adachi's account of the Featherston riot.

The fundamental differences between the two events which I stressed in chapter 2 are further highlighted by these accounts, as well as by the personal communications I received. As Clarke and Yamashita put it:

Suzuki and Tamagawa returned to their home towns in Japan in April 1946, and to their families and friends it was as though they had returned from the grave. They had both been reported killed in eastern New Guinea on 2nd January 1943, and their families had built their tombstones.

On arrival in Japan the prisoners repatriated from Cowra introduced themselves afresh under their real names and, then and there, their former comradeship ceased.

Since that time none of them has mentioned the incident at Cowra and even after the passage of twenty years the lips of most of them will remain sealed.[1]

Saito relates that when interviewing Lieutenant Akira Oikawa at the Repatriation Assistance Office set up by the Japanese government at Uraga to deal with the "special returnees" (as those who had been taken prisoner during the war were designated),[2] he suspected that this was not his informant's real name. Oikawa was very reluctant to talk about the events at Cowra, but eventually volunteered the information that the majority of the captives "did not reveal their true identities to each other. Also it was tabu to enquire about anybody's background. They had either assumed the names of war comrades already dead, or were using completely false names".[3]

Oikawa, who had not actually participated in the outbreak, suggested that the aim "was to overthrow the security of the enemy troops at the prison camp and, further, to subject their lives to sacrifice".[4]

This was to be a final suicidal battle. Disregarding the rights and wrongs of the affair, I thought their solidarity most admirable. And so it was all the more tragic that, as men who had become prisoners of war even if they had been able to make an ignominious return home, all that awaited them

Reunion held in Tokyo in 1974 of former prisoners of war at Featherston. (Photo: Russell Orr)

would have been a court martial. . . . such must have been
their despairing state of mind. No one ever said anything about
it. But they all agreed on it.[5]

Lieutenant Oikawa, like Suzuki and Tamagawa, the other
Cowra survivors, "faded away". Not so the Featherston
survivors—they formed themselves into the Association of
Survivors of Featherston on their return to Japan, and those
who had served on the warship *Furutaka* (which was sunk
at Guadalcanal) meet annually in Nagoya at a memorial
service.

According to Michiharu Shinya, the Featherston prisoners
of war were as apprehensive with regard to their future
as the Cowra internees. "Now it is also true" he wrote in
a personal communication dated 10 June 1977, "that most
of the men were very worried what their reception would
be once they returned. This is because . . . in the Imperial
Forces there existed a strict principle that anyone who
became a prisoner of war had to receive the death penalty.
Many of us thought that we could never go back home
again". Toshio Adachi in a letter dated 8 August 1977,
further elaborates on this theme: "We had become dishonourable prisoners and did not want to return to Japan.
If we had been able to remain in New Zealand, most of
us would have stayed there. They forced us to return to
Japan."

Léon Bossard, the delegate of the International Committee of the Red Cross, who like the interpreter Keith
Robertson had gained the confidence and the respect of the
Japanese prisoners of war, reported that the men were very
apprehensive about the fate which awaited them on their
return to Japan. However, as Adachi wrote, in his letter:
"When we came back to Japan, all Japanese were just like
prisoners because of their defeat in the war. So all of them
welcomed me joyfully."

Another ex-Featherston prisoner of war, who was badly
wounded in the incident, but who requested that his name
should not be mentioned, also suggested that he had never
expected to be able to return home. However, as he put

it: "Unfortunately or fortunately our country had an unconditional surrender unprecedentedly in history. I heard that all Japan were under occupation, and all Japanese were captured now, so we made up our minds to come home inevitably" (personal communication, 30 July 1977)

The Featherston survivors had rationalized their situation, believing as Michiharu Shinya stated in his letter: "The unconditional surrender of Japan and the fall down of old Empire had for the first time broken down that traditional principle towards a prisoner of war completely". One could thus suggest that the "situational ethic", which Benedict and Doi attribute to the Japanese personality structure, permitted the repatriates to assimilate once again with the Japanese population and to resume their former associations. The relative homogeneity of the Featherston prisoners of war, the majority of whom were naval ratings and naval officers, may well have contributed to their adjustment.[6] Their bonds, unlike those of the Cowra prisoners of war, have not been broken; Keith Robertson on a trip to Japan in 1977 was welcomed at the airport by a very large group of ex-Featherston captives. He was the guest in the homes of a number of them:[7] and one does not get the impression that the men had kept their "lips sealed" about their experiences, as Clarke and Yamashita suggested was the case as far as the ex-Cowra captives were concerned.

It may be relevant to add another note with regard to the cultural conditioning of the prisoners of war. I inquired about their social class and family backgrounds, and found out that like Yokoi and Onoda, the men came from very different social milieus. Adachi's family, for instance, were farmers, and he suggested in his letter that he was "taught the Samurai spirit at the Naval Academy". But perhaps Michiharu Shinya's reply is the most significant; he indicated that family or social class did not really matter. "Every Japanese soldier", he wrote, "was so educated to behave on old samurai virtues."

Notes

1. Hugh Clarke, *Break-Out!* (Sydney: Horwitz, 1965), p.124.
2. Seihachiro Saito, "Gimei Senshi No Haka" (trans. by E.H. Thompson, "The Graves of the Unknown Warriors), in *Bungei Shunju* 31, no. 3 (March 1963): 4.
3. Ibid., p.6.
4. Ibid., p.8.
5. Ibid., p.9.
6. The Japanese naval forces were first trained by French naval officers, and later by British, in contrast to the Japanese army who was drilled by German officers. The discipline among naval forces was therefore deemed to be less rigid and the naval ratings and officers interned in Featherston may have felt the disgrace of having become a prisoner of war not as intensely as members of the army.
7. In his letter of 18 August 1977, Adachi wrote: "When Mr Robertson came to Japan the other day he stayed with my family for one night. We had a million things to talk about that night. It was a time of memories and I was happy to meet him again . . . We could welcome him beyond love and hate." Another ex-Featherston prisoner of war refers to Robertson, who stayed in his home, as "my friend Mr Robertson" (personal communication, 30 July 1977).

Appendix A

Letter to the editor of the Dominion, *Wellington, 31 March 1973*

Featherston Parallel

Sir—I note that in your issue of March 21 you feature an advertisement from a group calling itself the New Zealand–South Africa Forum. The advertisement deals in some detail with the shooting of Japanese prisoners of war at Featherston in 1943. Unfortunately the interpretation of the event is quite incorrect.

The officer who fired two pistol shots at the prisoners was panicked after a shower of missiles, and had forgotten that two pistol shots was a signal to open fire.

The Japanese did not rush the guards, they were fleeing from their officer who was firing wildly at them with a pistol.

When you're surrounded you can only run towards the guard. The guards, whose nerves were badly frayed, opened fire, and the only person who kept his head was the sergeant in charge who ordered a cease-fire.

It should also be recalled that the prisoners had refused to provide a work party only after there had been sadistic beatings by some guards over some months, and after a reasonable request for an interview with the camp commandant had been refused.

There are indeed parallels between what happened at Featherston and what happened at Sharpeville but I don't think they were the parallels those placing the advertisement were seeking.

Tony Simpson

Mt. Victoria

Appendix B

TRANSLATION OF Message to Sergeant Major Kanazawa Written on a Strip of Sanitary Paper. (Found in the Detention Barracks on 14 August, 1944)

I have understood the true meaning of the incident. We all sympathise with your feelings. Please however remain calm. A lot remains for you to do. Naturally I believe that you wished to die with the rest; however, personally I believe that because you are alive the incident is more significant. You are to go ahead with the settlement of the incident with the utmost vigour and let the enemy know clearly what are the spirits of the Japanese soldiers. This will prove that although our bodies are imprisoned our spirits are free, and will be the supreme service we can offer under the circumstances.

We five officers got together and are forming the policy in regard to the incident so use this as a reference:

(1) The basic policy in regard to settlement is absolute opposition to the segregation of NCO's and OR's. In the Japanese Army the relation between NCO's and OR's is that of brothers or parents or children who sleep and eat together in a family and [are] therefore inseparable. In spite of this, the order of the Australian Army is to segregate us. We cannot comply with this, even at the cost of our lives. This is the reason of the incident. Should the enemy ask, "Why did you not consult us in this respect", the reply is that the Australian Military Authorities have handled Japanese P.W. for more than a year and that therefore they should know thoroughly the characteristics of the Japanese soldiers, particularly the Camp Commandant of "B" Camp who understands things very well. In spite of this they decided to submit such an unreasonable problem that further discussion was considered fruitless and so we opposed at the cost of our lives.

(2) The reason for breaking through the fence. The effect is insignificant if only a minority have died. In order that a majority might die simultaneously it has been realised that there is no better method than to go across the fence.

(3) Reason for escape. If we are to die it was thought best to create confusion in the rear of the Australian forces (for instance setting fire) would be most effective if this point would be stated clearly.

(4) The reason for burning huts. This is in order to let all Australian forces know that there was a riot in "B" Camp by simultaneously setting fire to the huts. Unless we go as far as this, because the Commander of "B" Camp is an able man the fire will be put out and we will probably have to face another difficult problem. If you attend interrogations and subsequent Military Court Martial with this thought in mind I believe that the significance of the riot will go deeper. What do you think about this? Please select and incorporate these ideas as you think best in conformity with your own determination.

The reason for suggesting the above is to create the maximum effect (of the incident) and as a result the punishment which may be imposed on you as one of the responsible parties may be extended from one year to two years or from two years to three years, however, I believe that those 200 men who died will be pleased. It will be in order to say that you led; however, due to the fact that the incident is of such grave importance it would be better if you said the idea was spontaneous and that everybody responded and went into action (therefore there was no preconceived plan).

Remarks

1. I believe that it is advisable to bear in mind that the present incident was caused through the question of segregating NCO's from OR's and that it was not a preconceived plan.
2. If this policy agrees with your policy for settlement, please let me know in a few words that you will proceed

with it. I shall arrange through Matsuoka with the camp to follow this policy. Of course if this policy coincides with that of the camp, well and good.

3. As for Mr. Matsushima because there is some rumour about him try not to involve him in this incident. Under no circumstances tell him that such direction came from an officer.

4. Because the enemy fears very much the liaison between Officers and you three, let us limit the communications to the minimum.

5. When interrogated, if you are asked about a question which might be to your disadvantage, pretend that you do not understand what the interpreter says, take time, think it over calmly and then reply. Do not always behave like an honest Sergeant Major Kanazawa.

6. Do as much as you can because this is a great diplomatic campaign in which two hundred men sacrificed their lives.

7. Try and talk as much as possible at the Court because by excess talk the punishment will not thereby be worse. The more you talk the more advantageous it will be for you.

P.S.

1. There was in the newspaper that recently Japanese P.W. in New Zealand rioted and eighty died.

2. As regards the Officers incident, we have practically won the case. There only remains the sentence for us three.

3. Destroy the note immediately. There is only a wall between us but conversation is impossible. You have carried out this incident splendidly. I do not think there will be a better event than this. I think from now on you will live a prison life for one or two years. Keep your chin up.

Special Note

Because every word you say in connection with this incident will be relayed to the Japanese Government verbatim, speak with caution and confidence.

P.P.S. This note should be disposed of immediately.
(Australian Department of the Army, AA1973/254, exhibit Z)

Bibliography

Abegglen, J.C. "Subordination and Autonomy Attitudes of Japanese Workers". *American Journal of Sociology* 63: 181–89.

Aida, Yuji. *Prisoner of the British*. Translated by Louis Allen. London: Cresset, 1966.

Asada, Teruhiko. *The Night of a Thousand Suicides*. Sydney: Angus and Robertson, 1970.

Asahi, Shimbun. *Twenty-Eight Years in the Guam Jungle*. Tokyo: Japan Publications, 1972.

Balint, Michael. *Primary Love and Psycho-analytic Technique*. London: Hogarth Press, 1962.

Barnouw, Victor. *Culture and Personality*. Homewood, Ill.: Dorsey Press, 1963.

Bateson, Charles. *The War with Japan*. Sydney: Ure Smith, 1968.

Bateson, Gregory. "Morale and National Character". In *Civilian Morale*, edited by G. Watson. New York: Houghton Mifflin, 1942.

Befu, Harumi. *Japan, An Anthropological Introduction*. San Francisco: Chandler, 1971.

Bellah, Robert N. *Tokugawa Religion*. Glencoe, Ill.: Free Press, 1957.

Benedict, Ruth. *The Crysanthemum and the Sword*. London: Routledge and Kegan Paul, 1967.

Bennett, J.W., and Nagai, M. "The Japanese Critique of the Methodology of Benedict's 'Crysanthemum and the Sword'". *American Anthropologist* 55 (1952): 404–11.

Bennett, J.W.; Passin, H.; and McKnight, R.K. *In Search of Identity*. Minneapolis: University of Minnesota Press, 1958.

Bergamini, D. *Japan's Imperial Conspiracy*. London: Heinemann, 1971.

Boxer, C.R. *The Christian Century in Japan, 1549-1650*. Berkeley: University of California Press, 1951.

Braddon, Russell. *The Naked Island*. London: Laurie, 1952.

Brickhill, Paul. *The Great Escape*. London: Faber, 1951.

Brooks, Lester. *Behind Japan's Surrender*. New York: McGraw-Hill, 1968.

Browne, Courtney. *Tojo: the Last Banzai*. Sydney: Angus and Robertson, 1967.

Butow, Robert J.C. *Japan's Decision to Surrender*. Stanford: Stanford University Press, 1954.

Caudill, William. "Patterns of Emotion in Modern Japan". In *Japanese Culture*, edited by R.J. Smith and R.K. Beardsley. London: Methuen, 1963.

———. "Japanese Value Orientation and Culture Change". *Ethnology* 1 (1962): 59–91.

Clarke, Hugh. *Break-Out!*. Sydney: Horwitz, 1965.

Clarke, Hugh V., with Yamashita, Takeo. *To Sydney by Stealth*. Sydney: Horwitz, 1966.

Doi, Takeo. "Amae, a Key Concept for the Understanding of the Japanese Personality Structure". In *Japanese Culture*, edited by R.J. Smith and R.K. Breadsley. London: Methuen, 1963.

———. "Giri and Ninjo: an Interpretation". In *Aspects of Social Change in Modern Japan*, edited by R.P. Dore. Princeton: Princeton University Press, 1967.

———. *The Anatomy of Dependence*. Tokyo: Kodansha, 1973.

Dore, R.P. *City Life in Japan*. London: Routledge, 1958.

Durkheim, Emil. *Le Suicide*. Paris: Alcan, 1897.

Embree, John F. *Suye Mura, a Japanese Village*. Chicago: University of Chicago Press, 1939.

———. *The Japanese*. War Background Studies, no.7. Washington: Smithsonian Institution, 1943.

Freedman, M. *Chinese Lineage and Society*. London: Athlone, 1966.

Fukutake, Tadashi. *Man and Society in Japan*. Tokyo: University of Tokyo Press, 1962.

Gibney, Frank. *Five Gentlemen of Japan*. New York: Farrar and Strauss, 1953.

Goffman, Erving. "The Nature of Deference and Demeanour". *American Anthropologist* 59 (1956): 473–502.

———. *Asylums*. Harmondsworth, Mddx.: Penguin, 1970.

Gorer, Geoffrey. "Themes in Japanese Culture". In *Personal Character and Cultural Milieu*, edited by D.G. Haring. Rev. ed. Syracuse: Syracuse University Press, 1949.

Grew, Joseph C. *Report from Tokyo*. Sydney: Angus and Robertson 1943.

Guillain, R. *The Japanese Challenge*. London: Hamish Hamilton, 1970.

Hall, John W. *Japan: from Pre-History to Modern Times*. London: Weidenfeld and Nicolson, 1970.

Hall, John W., and Beardsley, R.D., eds. *Twelve Doors to Japan*. New York: McGraw-Hill, 1965.

Hall, R.K., *Kokutai No Hongi: Cardinal Principles of the National Entity of Japan*. Cambridge, Mass.: Harvard University Press 1949.

Hancock, K.R. *New Zealand at War*. Wellington, NZ: Reed, 1946.

Haring, Douglas G., ed. *Japan's Prospects*. Cambridge, Mass.: Harvard
University Press, 1946.
———. *Personal Character and Cultural Milieu*. Syracuse: Syracuse
University Press, 1949 (rev. ed.) and 1964 (3rd rev. ed.).
Hetherington, L. "Kenneth Mackenzie: Poet Novelist". MA thesis,
University of Sydney, 1972.
Hudson, Manley O. *International Legislation: a Collection of the Texts
of Multipartite International Instruments of General Interest*.
Vol.5. Washington, DC: Carnegie Endowment for International
Peace, 1936.
Hulse, F.S. "A Sketch of Japanese Society". *Journal of American
Oriental Society* 66 (1946): 219–29.
———. "Some Effects of the War upon Japanese Society". *Far Eastern·
Quarterly* 8, no.1 (1947): 22–42.
———. "Convention and Reality in Japanese Culture". *Southwestern
Journal of Anthropology* 4, no.4 (1948): 345–55.
Ichiyo, Muto. "Mishima and the Transition from Post-War Democracy
to Democratic Fascism". *Liberation* 16, no.8 (1972): 6–19.
Ike, N. *Japan's Decision for War*. Stanford: Stanford University Press,
1967.
Inukai, Michiko. "Agreeing to Differ". *Japan Quarterly* 13, no.2 (1966):
181–87.
Jeanmougin, G. "Les Composantes ethnopsychologiques du caractère
japonais". *Revue de Psychologie des Peuples*, June 1969,
pp.138–56.
Kahn, Herman. *The Emerging Japanese Superstate*. Englewood Cliffs,
NJ: Prentice Hall, 1970.
Kawabata, Yasunari. *Snow Country*. London: Secker and Warburg, 1957.
Kawai, Kazuo. *Japan's American Interlude*. Chicago: University of
Chicago Press, 1960.
Keene, Donald, trans. *Chushingura* (The Treasury of the Loyal Re-
tainer). New York: Columbia University Press, 1970.
Kerlinger, F.N. "Decision-making in Japan". *Social Forces* 30, no.1
(1951–52): 36–41.
———. "Behaviour and Personality in Japan: A Critique of Three Studies
in Japanese Personality". *Social Forces* 31 (1953): 250–58.
Kluckhohn, F., and Strodtbeck, F.L. *Variations in Value Orientations*
Evanstown, Ill.: Row, Peterson, 1961.
Lanham, Brigitte. "Aspects of Child Care in Japan". In Personal
Character and Cultural.Milieu, edited by D.G. Haring, 3rd rev.
ed.. Syracuse: Syracuse University Press, 1964.
Lau, D.C. *Mencius*. Harmondsworth, Mddx.: Penguin, 1970.
Lawrence, Peter. *Road Belong Cargo*. Manchester: Manchester Univer-
sity Press, 1964.
———. "The Garia of the Madang District". In *Politics in New Guinea*,

edited by R.M. Berndt and P. Lawrence. Nedlands, WA: University of Western Australia Press, 1971.
Leighton, A.H. *The Governing of Men.* Princeton: Princeton University Press, 1946.
Long, Gavin, *The Final Campaigns. Australia in the War of 1939-1945: The Army,* vol.8. Canberra, Australian War Memorial, 1946.
Lory, Hillis. *Japan's Military Masters.* New York: Viking, 1943.
Mackenzie, Kenneth Seaforth. *Dead Men Rising.* Sydney: Pacific Books, 1969.
McKie, Ronald. *The Heroes.* Sydney: Angus and Robertson, 1960.
Maki, J. *Japanese Militarism.* New York: Knopf, 1945.
Maraini, Fosco. *Meeting with Japan.* London: Hutchinson, 1962.
Martin, Christopher. *The Russo-Japanese War.* London: Abelard, 1967.
Maruyama, Masao. *Thought and Behaviour in Modern Japanese Politics.* London: Oxford University Press, 1963.
Mason, W.W. *Official New Zealand War History, 1939-1945: Prisoners of War.* Wellington: Government Printer, 1954.
Matsumoto, Toru, and Lerrigo, M. *A Brother Is a Stranger.* London: Gollancz, 1947.
Mead, Margaret, and Metraux, R. *The Study of Culture at a Distance.* Chicago: University of Chicago Press, 1966.
Meo, L.D. *Japan's Radio War on Australia, 1941-45.* Melbourne: Melbourne University Press, 1968.
Mishima, Yukio. *The Sound of the Waves.* London: Secker and Warburg, 1957.
———. *Death in Midsummer and Other Stories.* Harmondsworth, Mddx.: Penguin, 1967.
———. *The Sailor Who Fell from Grace with the Sea.* Harmondsworth, Mddx.: Penguin, 1970.
Moloney, J.C. *Understanding the Japanese Mind.* Rutland, Vermont: Tuttle, 1954.
Monigatti, C.R.I. *New Zealand Headlines.* Wellington, NZ: Reed, 1963.
Morris, Ivan. *The World of the Shining Prince.* Harmondsworth, Mddx.: Penguin, 1969.
———. *The Nobility of Failure.* London: Secker and Warburg, 1975.
Morris, John. *Traveller from Tokyo.* Harmondsworth, Mddx.: Penguin, 1969.
Murasaki, Shikibu. *The Tale of Genjii.* Translated by Arthur Waley. London: Allen and Unwin, 1965.
Nakane, Chie. *Japanese Society.* London: Weidenfeld and Nicolson, 1970.
Newsweek. "The Last Blossom". 7 February 1972, p.30.
———. "World War II: Voices in the Wilderness". 30 October 1972, p.62.
———. "World War II: Where It Is Still 1945". 6 November 1972 p.58.
Nitobe, Inazo. *Bushido, the Soul of Japan.* New York, Putnam, 1905.

Norbeck, Edward. *Changing Japan*. New York: Holt, Rinehart, and Winston, 1965.

Norbeck, Edward, and de Vos, George. "Japan". In *Psychological Anthropology*, edited by Francis L.K. Hsu. Homewood, Ill.: Dorsey Press, 1961.

Onoda, Hiro. *No Surrender: My Thirty Year War*. London: Deutsch, 1975.

Ooka, Shohei. *Fires in the Plain*. London: Secker and Warburg, 1957.

Owen, Wilfred. *Collected Poems*. London: Chatto and Windus, 1964.

Pacific War Research Society, comp. *Japan's Longest Day*. London: Corgi, 1969.

Parsons, Talcott. "Population and Social Structure". In *Japan's Prospects*, edited by D.G. Haring. Cambridge, Mass.: Harvard University Press, 1946.

Passin, H. "Japanese Society". In *Encyclopedia of Social Sciences*, 1954, pp.236–49.

Plath, D.W. *The After Hours*. Berkeley: University of California Press, 1964.

——. "Japan and the Ethic of Fatalism". *Anthropological Quarterly* 33 (1966): 161–70.

Reischauer, Edwin O. *Japan Past and Present*. 3rd ed. London: Duckworth, 1964.

——. *The United States and Japan*. 3rd ed. Cambridge, Mass.: Harvard University Press, 1965.

——. *Japan: The Story of a Nation*. London: Duckworth, 1970.

Riesman, David, and Riesman, E.T. *Conversations in Japan*. London: Lane, 1967.

Red Cross International Committee. *Inter Arma Caritas: the Work of the International Committee of the Red Cross during World War II*. Geneva, 1947.

——. *Prisonniers de guerre japonais en Nelle Zélande, 1942–1945*. Unpublished abstracts from reports by the delegate of the ICRC in New Zealand, Léon Bossard. Abstracted by G. Douvernoz. Geneva, 4 January, 1977.

Roggendorf, J. ABC Guest of Honour Broadcast, 5 June 1975.

Royal Institute for International Affairs. *Japan in Defeat*. London: Oxford University Press, 1945.

Russell of Liverpool, Lord. *The Knights of Bushido*. London: Cassell, 1958.

Saito, Seihachiro. "Gimei Senshi No Haka" (The Graves of the Unknown Warriors). *Bungei Shunju* 31, no.3 (March 1963; transl. June 1977), pp.230–40.

Sakurai, Tadayoshi. *Human Bullets*. 6th ed. Tokyo: Tibi, 1909.

Sankei Shimbun. Special Research Team. *The Last Japanese Soldier*. London: Stacey, 1972.

Sansom, G.B. *Japan: A Short Cultural History.* Rev. ed. London: Cresset, 1962.

Satow, Ernest. *A Diplomat in Japan.* London: Seeley, 1921.

Shinya, Michiharu. *Shi No Umi Yori Seidan.* Tokyo, 1975.

————. "The Path from Guadalcanal". Translated by E.H. Thompsom. Manuscript, 1977. Alexander Turnbull Library, Wellington, NZ.

Shonagon, Sei. *The Pillow Book of Sei Shonagon.* Harmondsworth, Mddx.: Penguin, 1970.

Smith, R.J., and Beardsley, R.K. eds. *Japanese Culture.* London: Methuen, 1963.

Sofue, Takeo. "Japanese Studies by American Anthropologists: Review and Revaluation". *American Anthropologist* 62 (1960): 306–17.

Spae, J.J. *Japanese Religiosity.* Tokyo: Oriens Institute for Religious Research, 1971.

Stoetzel, J. *Without the Crysanthemum and the Sword.* New York: Columbia University Press, 1955.

Storry, Richard. *A History of Modern Japan* . Harmondsworth, Mddx.: Penguin, 1960.

Sugihara, Yoshie, and Plath, D.W. *Sensei and His People.* Berkeley: University of California Press, 1969.

Timms, E.V. "The Blood Bath at Cowra". In *As You Were!: A Cavalcade of Events with the Australian Services from 1788-1946.* Canberra: Australian War Memorial, 1946.

Tokyo Gazette Publishing House. *Field Service Code,* adopted by the War Department on 8 January 1941. Tokyo: Kakehi, 1941.

Toland, John. *The Rising Sun.* London: Cassell, 1971.

Tsunoda, Ryusaku; de Bary, Wm. Theodore; and Keene, Donald, comps. *Sources of Japanese Tradition.* 2 vols. New York: Columbia University Press, 1964.

Tsurumi, Kazuko. *Social Change and the Individual.* Princeton: Princeton University Press, 1970.

Varley, H. Paul, with Ivan and Nobuko Morris. *The Samurai.* London: Weidenfeld and Nicolson, 1970.

Wallace, A.F.C. *Culture and Personality.* New York: Random House, 1966.

Yamashita, Takeo. *Nihonjin Koko Ni Nemuru* (Here Lie the Japanese). Privately printed, 1969.

Yanaga, Chitoshi. "Japanese Tradition and Democracy". *Far Eastern Survey.* 17 (1948): 68–71.

————. Japanese People and Politics. New York: Wiley, 1956.

————. *Big Business in Japanese Politics.* New Haven, Conn.: Yale University Press, 1968.

Yoshihashi, Takehiko. *Conspiracy at Mukden.* New Haven, Conn.: Yale University Press, 1963.

Official Documents

Australian Archives Office, Canberra

AA1973/254. Department of the Army, Proceedings and Findings of Court of Inquiry into Outbreak from Cowra POW Camp, 1944. 2 vols.

CP337/1. Attorney-General's Department, Court Martial Proceedings, Prisoner of War Trials. Item POW 36: Military Court (Trial) PWJA 145648 Flt. Sgt. Yoshida Hiroshi. Item POW 39: Military Court (Trial) PWJA 145535 Sgt. Maj. Kanazawa Akira.

CRS A461. Prime Minister's Department, Correspondence Files, Multi-number Series (third system), 1939–50. Item G337/1/1: Prisoners of War. General. 1939–45.

CRS A989. External Affairs, Correspondence Files, Multiple-number Series, 1943–44. Item 44/925/1/140: Prisoners of War—Escape of Japanese POW from Cowra. Item 43/925/1/16: Prisoners of War—Reports on Japanese Camps, 1954–44. Item 43/925/1/30: pt. 1, Treaties, Red Cross, Reports on POW Camps in Australia, including reports by Australian Delegate (Dr Morel), 21.8.1942–10.7.1943; pt. 2, 18.12.1943–20.1.44; pt. 3, 22.6.1944–21.12.1944. Item 43/925/1/37: Treaties, Red Cross, POW, regarding treatment immediately after capture, 1943. Item 43–44/925/1/69: Treaties, Red Cross, POW Policy, 1944. Item 43/925/1/97: Treaties, Red Cross, Intelligence Reports on POW and Internee Camps in Australia, 1943. Item 44/925/1/134: Treaties, Red Cross, Establishment of POW Camps, 1944. Item 44/925/1/150: Treaties, Red Cross, Treatment of POWs, General 19.9.1944–23.11.1944.

CRS A1608. Prime Minister's Department, Correspondence Files, Secret and Confidential War Series (fourth system), 1939–45. Item AK 20/1/1: Prisoners of War, Disturbance at Featherston Camp, New Zealand, 1943. Item AX 20/1/1: Mutiny of Japanese Prisoners of War at Cowra Camp, 1944. Item AY 20/1/1: Political Warfare, Japanese Prisoners of War, 1944.

Australian War Memorial, Canberra

CRS A2663. Written Records/Files, War of 1939–45, Multiple-numbers System, 1939. Item 780/3/3: Japanese Prisoners of War, Trial by Military Court of PWJA Kanazawa Akira and PWJA Yoshida Hiroshi—Disturbance at Prisoner of War Camp Cowra, 1944. Item 780/10/1: Prisoner of War and Internment Camps, Security and Escapes, 1942. Item 780/10/2: Correspondence, Signals, and Miscellaneous Documents re Meeting P.W. Cowra, 5 Aug. 1944. Item 780/10/3: Findings of a Court of Inquiry on Mass Escape of Japanese Prisoners of War, Cowra, NSW, 5 Aug. 1944, including Nominal Roll of Deceased Japanese Prisoners of War. Item 780/12/2: NSW L. of C. Administration, Transfer of Japanese Prisoners of War to Hay, NSW, and Murchison, Victoria, from Cowra, 1944. Item 780/3/2: Notes from POW Camps, 1942–45. Item 780/7/1: POWs and Internees—Commonwealth Surveys. War Diaries, 1939–1945 War, 1/1/14 Adjutant-General—Prisoners of War.

National Archives, Wellington, New Zealand

New Zealand Military Forces, Proceedings of a Court of Inquiry on Mutiny at Prisoner of War Camp Featherston, 25 February 1943.

Index

Abegglen, J.C., 147
Adachi, Sub-Lt. T., 43, 48, 50–55, 66, 80–81, 183, 200–204
Adowa, xiii
Aida, Y., 4, 17, 19
Akihito, Crown Prince, 13, 14
Allen, Prof. Louis, 19
Amami Oshima, 134, 135
Amaterasu (Sun Goddess), 86–88, 101, 116
Anami, Gen., 180, 186
Andersonville POW camp, 8
Anglo–Boer War, ix
Aoyama, 62
Arnold, Gen. H.H., 169
Asada, T., 4, 24, 56, 59–64, 164, 172, 182, 185
Asano, 98, 99
Ashton, Capt., 44
Association of Survivors of Featherston, 203
Australian Archives, 5
Australian Intelligence, 63, 65, 77, 173
Axis Powers, 111

Bailey, F.G., 148
Bakufu, 92, 94, 96
Balint, M., 144
Batavia, 172
Bateson, G., 171
Beardsley, R.K., 137

Befu, H., 140
Bellah, R.N., 154, 155
Bellevue Hill, 15
Benedict, Ruth, xii, 25–26, 30–31, 128, 130–32, 136, 139, 141, 145–46, 174, 181, 204
Bennett, J.W., 137
Bergamiri, L., 110
Billington, J., 13
Black Dragon Society, 106
Bossard, Dr. L., 6, 18, 19, 22, 38, 41, 42, 44, 203
Brainwashing (in Korea), 8
Brickhill, Paul, 17
Bridge on the River Kwai, ix, x
Brisbane, 62, 63, 170
Britain's Asian colonies, 109
Broadway, 59, 60, 70, 73
Brooks, L., 110
Brussels Conference (1937), 8, 109
Buddha, 158
Buddhism, 88, 89
Budo Shoshinshu, 154
Buna (Papua), 169, 170
Bungei Shunju, 199
Burma, 26, 111
Burma Railway, 4, 56
Bushido, 85, 92, 98, 102, 113–17, 124, 153, 163, 195
Butow, R., 112

California, 136

Cambodian Royal Dynasty, 88
Canton, 108
"Captain Kaji", 59, 61–63, 77–78
Carter, President, 141
Caudill, W., 142
Changi, 3
Charter Oath (1868), 105
Chie Nakane, 132
China, 27, 90, 107–108, 110, 192
    characters, 91; cosmology, 88;
    culture, 86, 91; railways, 108
Chiya, 173
Chomage (topknot), 95
Choshu clan, 103–104, 117–18, 120
Christianity, 157
Churchill, Sir Winston, 171
Clarke, H., 3, 56, 66, 175, 185, 201,
    204
Comparison of events at Cowra
    and Featherston, 17, 79–81
Communism, 157
Confucius
    ethics, 85, 190; classics, 91
Coral Sea, battle of, 111
Cowra
    links with Japan, 12, 15; munici-
    pal council, 15; new ceme-
    tery, 12; Rotary Club, 13

Daimyo (feudal lords), 93, 95, 98,
    104
Dan, Baron, 122
de Gaulle, Gen., 120
Dillon, J.V., 10
Doi, T., 144–46, 162–63, 204
Dominion, 55, 206
Donaldson, Lt-Col., 52
Doncaster, Lt. H., 74
Dore, R., xi
Donvernoz, G., 6
Dunkirk, 171
Durkheim, E., 179

Eastern army, 105
Edo, 103, 115

Events at Cowra, 56–79
    aftermath, 73; increasing unrest,
    64–68; outbreak, 69–73; siting
    of camp, 59–60
Events at Featherston, 38–56
    immediate causes of outbreak,
    48–51
Evolution of Japanese culture,
    85–125
    civil wars, 92–93; early cultural
    influences, 89–91; evolution of
    bushido, 113–16; Fujiwara
    family, 90; fusion of Bud-
    dhism with Shinto, 88–89;
    growth of bushido, 96–97;
    Heian period, 91–92; isola-
    tion, 89–90; Meiji era, 103–12;
    modern armed forces, 117–25;
    myths of Japan's origin,
    86–88; Tokugawa period,
    94–103
Explanations of outbreak at Cow-
    ra, 179–96
    conclusions, 190–96; evolution of
    explanations, 184–90; mass su-
    icide, 179–82; planned escape,
    182–83; spontaneous reaction,
    183
External influences on POW's at
    Cowra, 169–79
    changes in behaviour, 177–79;
    despair of prisoners, 172–74;
    Japanese resistance and mor-
    ale, 169–72; treatment of
    POW's, 175–77

Ferguson, G., 56
"Flight-Sgt. Toké", 77, 174
Formosans, 64
Forty-Seven Ronin, 98
Franco–Prussian War, xiii
French Indo-China, 108–109
Freud, 128–29, 162
    Freudian theory and Japanese
    psychology, 128–29

Fundamentals of Our National Polity, 116
Furntaka, 203
Futamata, 192–94

Gallipoli, ix
Geneva Convention, 7–12, 22, 28–31, 35, 41, 51–54, 64, 69, 175, 178, 181
  Article 34, 51; Article 42, 28; Japan's non-ratification, 29
Genovese, E., xi
Genro advisors, 106
German colonies, 106
German POW's 60–61
Gilbert and Marshall Islands, 111
Goffman, E., 32–34, 173
Gorer, G., 128–31
Graythorne Transit Camp, 63, 170, 177
Greater East Asia Co-Prosperity Sphere (new order in Asia), 109
Grew, J.C., 27, 117, 142
Group Detention Barracks, Cowra, 189, 190
Group H.Q., Sydney, 175
Guadalcanal, 38, 53, 80, 111, 170, 203
Guam, 191

Hagakure, 114, 118, 153, 155
Hague Conferences (1899 and 1907), 8
Hankow, 108
Haring, D.G., 131, 134–35, 173
Hay POW camp, 60, 69, 175, 179, 183, 187
Hayashi, 97, 99
Heian period, 91, 113, 162
Heihachiro, O., 161
Hemingway, E., 159
Henderson, Prof. G., 31
Hideyoshi, 94
Hirohito, Emperor, 109, 110, 112
Hiroshima, 112
Hizen, 103

Homewood, 73
Hong Kong, 111
Horii, Gen., 169–70
Hulse, F.S., 135–38
Huntington, R., 150

Imperial Conference (1941), 110
Imperial Military Orders, 123
Imperial Palace, 103
Imperial Rescript on Education, 157
Imperial Rescript to Soldiers and Sailors (1882), 118–19, 122, 124, 157–58
Imperial Work Force, 38, 44, 52
Inada, Princess, 87
India, 111
Indonesia, 4, 111
Inonye, Finance Minister, 122
Inter Arma Caritas, 35
International Committee of the Red Cross, 5, 6, 11, 19, 29, 32, 35, 38, 42, 172, 203
  in Australia, 64
Inukai, Prime Minister, 122
Italian POW's, 60, 61
Itchigaya, 160
Ito Hirobumi, 102, 103
Iwo Jima, 180
Izanagi and Izanami, 86
Izumo, 7

Japan and China, 108, 109
Japanese and Western behaviour in wartime, 25–36
Japanese aristocratic families
  Fujiwara, 90, 92; Minamoto, 90, 92; Tachibana, 90; Taira, 90, 92
Japanese General Staff and War Ministry, 107
Japanese mandates, 106
Japanese modern army, 106, 117–25
Japanese Military and Naval Dis-

ciplinary Codes, 29
Japanese military families
   Ashikaga, 93, Hojo, 93
Japanese Military Field Code
   (Field Service Code or
   Battlefield Commandments),
   25, 30, 41–42, 53, 56, 64, 67, 80,
   122–23, 162, 164, 177, 181,
   191–95
Japanese POW's
   arrival at Cowra, 61; of Korean
   descent, 41; repatriation, 43
Japanese Repatriation Assistance
   Office (Uraga), 201
Junshi, 119

Kabuki theatre, 98
Kahn, H., 147, 148
Kamakura, 92, 114, 115
Kamikaze, 90
   pilots, 113
Kana (phonetic syllabary), 91
Kanaya, Gen., 110
Kanazawa, Sgt.-Major, 69, 78, 151,
   181, 187, 189, 190, 207, 209
Keene, D., 160
Keiki, 103
Kellogg–Briand Pact, 121
Kenney, Lt.-Gen. G.C., 169, 170
Kerlinger, F.N., 146, 148
Kido Koin, 102–104
Kira, 98
Kobe, 180
Kojiki, 86
Kojima, Sgt., 69, 182
Kokutai no Hongi, 85, 163. See
   also National Polity
*Kokutai no Hongi: Cardinal Prin-
   ciples of the National Entity of
   Japan* (Hall), 108
Komei, Emporer, 103
Kondratenko, Gen., 32
Korea, 64, 90
Kyoto, 90, 92–93, 103, 114, 194
Kydo University, 17

Kynshu, 56
Kwantung Army, 107

La Barre, W.L., 130–32
Laing, R.D., 142
Lanham, B., 131
League of Nations, 106–107, 109
   racial equality clause, 106
Lees, Capt., 64
Lévi–Strauss, C., 87
"Lieutenant Kimura", 64
"Lieutenant Takeyama", 160
London Naval Conference (1930),
   121–22
Lord Russell, 26, 29, 30, 122
Lubang, 152, 192–94
Lytton Commission, 107

MacArthur, Gen., xii
Mackenzie, K., 24, 56, 60, 177
"Major Shawl", 177
Malaya, 111
Malcolm, Lt., 48, 55
"Manchukuo", 107
Manchuria, 107, 108, 112, 122
Manchurian Incident, 27, 109, 110
Mansfield, Senator M., 141
Marcos, President, 194
Marianas, 111, 171
Martin, C., 32
Maruyama, M., 29
Marx, K., 162
"Massacre of Nanking", 122
Matsumoto, T., 67, 149, 150, 175,
   183, 187
Matsuoka, 175, 177
Matsushima, 74, 77
Mayor Oliver, 12, 13
Meiji, Emperor, 103, 105–106, 109,
   119
Meiji regime, xi, 102, 104, 108,
   117, 123
   constitution, 106; criminal code,
   180; restoration, xi, 106, 116,
   133

Mencius, 102
Metsuke (secret police), 95, 133
Midway, battle of, 111
Minami, Gen., 110
Minami, Sgt.-Pilot, 69
Minamoto Yoritomo, 103
Mishiko, Princess, 13
Mishima, Yukio, xii, 160–63, 180, 186
Mito school, 101
Mitsui Industries, 122
Molière, 100
Mongols, 90, 93
Moore, B., x
Morel, Dr. G., 6, 18, 19, 23, 64, 65, 175
Morris, I., 161–62
Mount Fuji, 88
Mujaki, 91
Mukden Incident, 107
Murasaki, Lady, 91, 132
Murchison POW camp, 175, 179, 183, 187
Murashino, 13

Nagasaki, 99, 112
Nagoya, 203
Naka, Lt., 66
Nakamura, 144
Nanking, 108, 122
Nara, 90
National polity, 29, 80, 85, 108, 114–17, 124, 156, 164, 177, 180, 195, 199. See also *Kokutai no Hongi.*
Neo-Confucianism, 89, 114, 161–63, 190
Netherlands colonies, 109
New Guinea campaign, 61, 111
Nietzsche, 162
Nihongi, 86
Nishimura, Lt., 50, 52
Nishio, Capt., 59, 65, 77, 78, 189
Nitobe, I., 113, 153, 179, 180
Nobunaga, 94

Nogi, Gen., 119, 120, 122, 161, 180, 186

Office of War Information, Washington, 128
Oikawa, Sub.-Lt., 73, 79, 189, 199, 201, 203
Okinawa, 180
Onoda, Lt. H., 152, 191–95, 204
Ooka, S., 151
"Orloff", 177–78
Orr, R., 152, 199, 202
Osaka, 99
Owen Stanley Ranges, 169

Papua, 169
Parsons, T., xii, 142
Peace Preservation Law (1925), 108, 133, 156
Pearl Harbour, 21, 110, 111
Personality of Japanese, 127–64
  "amae" (dependence), 144–46;
  "arc of life", 139–40; "collaterality" and shame, 140–43; compulsiveness, 129–31; conformity, 132; decision-making process, 146–49; "enryo", 149; face saving, 149–51; indirection and self-dramatization, 137–38; influence of oppression, 132–35; its planned quality, 133–35; preoccupation with death, 151–64
Philippines, 21, 111, 151, 194
Pictet, J., 8
Port Arthur, 32, 105, 119, 120
Port Moresby, 169
Potsdam Declaration, 111
Prince of Wales, 21
Proceedings of a Court of Inquiry on Mutiny at Prisoner of War Camp, 25 February 1943, 5

Rabaul, 169

224   *Index*

Ramsay, Major R., 66, 69, 177
Razan, H., 96, 114
Recruit Training Centre, 68
Reischauer, E.O., 112, 117, 136, 141, 180
Remarque, Erich Maria, 11, 159
Repulse, 21
Robertson, K., 199, 203, 204
Roggendorf, Prof. J., 191
Ronin (masterless warriors), 98, 138
Rorschach tests, 136
Russian declaration of war (1945), 112
Russo–Japanese War, 119, 155

Saigo, 104, 119
Saipan, 31, 81, 111, 171–72, 180
Saito, S., 199
Sakai, 99
Sakeida, 66
Sakhalin, 121
Sakurai, T., 119
Samurai, xi, 92, 94–95, 104, 115, 117–18, 204
Sanananda, Papua, 170
Sansom, G.B., 100, 147
Satow, E., 180
Satsuma clan, 103–104
Seikei Upper Secondary School, 13
Sei Shonagon, 91, 132
Seppuku (ceremonial suicide), 98, 160–61, 179–81
Shanghai, 108, 192
Shibaoka, Mrs., 15
Shimazikazi, T., 123
Shimoyama, Sgt.-Major Y., 74
Shingen, T., 154
Shinto mythology, 85, 88–89, 114–15, 156, 190
Shinya, Lt. M., 43, 199, 200, 203, 204
Shogun, 92, 98, 115, 155
Siberia, 121
Simpson, A., 55, 206

Singapore, 3, 21, 111
16th Australian Garrison Battalion, 60
Social Origins of Dictatorship and Democracy, x
Solomon Islands, 21
Spae, J.J., 114
Stalag Luft, 3, 17
Sugihara, Y., 143
Susano-o (Storm god), 86–87
Suzuki, Prime Minister, 112
Suzuki, Norio, 193–94
Suzuki (prisoner), 169–70, 175–76, 203
Switzerland, 28
Sydney, 187

Taisho, Emperor, 105
Tamagawa, 66, 169, 170, 175, 176
Tanaka, K., 29
Taniguchi, Major, 193–94
Telefofo district, Guam, 191
Thompson, E.H., 199
Timms, Major E.V., 60, 68–69, 73, 178
Tobruk, ix
Tojo, 30
Topaze internment camp, Utah, 130
Tokugawa period, 89, 94–103, 100–101, 136–37, 145, 153, 179, 203
castle, 103; regime, 103–104, 108, 114–16, 132–35; religion, x
Tokyo, 103, 107, 124, 178, 180
bombing, 111
Tosa clan, 103
Treaties between U.S.A. and Prussia, 8
Tsukuhara, Capt., 64, 65
Tsurumi, K., 156–59
Tufts University, 31
22nd Australian Garrison Battalion, 60

Uraga, 201
U.S.A., 102, 109, 139
  embargo against Japan, 109
U.S.–Japanese Commercial Agreement, 109
U.S. marines, 31

Versailles Peace Conference, 106
Vichy Government, 109
Victoria Barracks, Sydney, 67
Vietnam, ix
Volunteers Act (1927), 20

Wairarapa Plains, 38, 46
Wallace, F.C., 128
Wang Yang-ming, 161
War Crimes Trials, 3
War Memorial Museum, 5
War Relocation Authority and Centre, 130–31
Wars of the Samurai, 96
Washington Peace Conference (1921–22), 121
Weir, Mrs W., 74
Wellington, 21
Western clans, 103
Western industrial influence on Japan, 105
Whitehall Cenotaph, 155

World War I, 8–10, 38, 105, 106, 120, 121, 155
World War II, 9–12, 16, 18, 28, 29, 35, 56, 59, 88, 107, 111, 116, 122, 128, 134, 135, 143, 149, 156, 191, 195

Yamaga Sritomo, 102
Yamaga Soko, 96–99, 102, 114, 154
Yamagata, 106, 118, 119, 120
Yamashita, T., 3, 56, 59, 170, 175–77, 179, 182, 185, 186, 201, 204
Yanaga, C., 136, 146
Yangtze, 108
Yedo (Tokyo), 94, 95
Yokoi, Sgt. S., 191–93, 195, 204
Yomei. See Neo-Confucianism
Yoritomo Minamoto, 92, 93
Yoshida, Flight-Sgt., 69, 151, 181
Yoshida Shoin, 101, 102, 115, 154–56, 184
Yoshihashi, T., 110
Yasukini Jinja (war shrine), 155, 158

Zaibatsu (pressure groups), 106
Zen Buddhism, 89, 153
Zenzaburo, T., 180